Telling Lives

Both interest in and understanding of narrative analysis have developed rapidly in recent years and it is now a mainstream element of research across many disciplines. In the groundbreaking *Telling Lives: exploring dimensions of narratives*, the author illustrates as many facets as possible of the stories people tell about their lives. She demonstrates the interconnectedness between engagements in narrative research and shows that the theoretical understanding of the nature of narrative is bound up with the methods for biographical narrative research.

Through a combination of three independent, connected narrative dimensions, an embodied, a cognitive, and a sociocultural narrative, the author focuses on life story narratives as symbolic expressions where cultural constructions allow for interpersonal interaction. This book also outlines the influence that cultural and social environments have upon our own unique narrative memories, coupled with our own physical movements in space. The author concludes that the telling and exchanging of human narratives is the primary way of making sense and creating meaning of our own being.

This book brings together neurophysiology, philosophical perspectives, and research data and methodology to formulate a new understanding of narrative analysis. It will also help you to produce and analyze your own narrative interviews and perform biographical research. Innovative and thought-provoking, this book will cut across disciplines and be of interest to all students at advanced undergraduate and postgraduate level and researchers in education, social sciences, and humanities.

Marianne Horsdal is Professor in Educational Research at the University of Southern Denmark. She is seen as a key international specialist in the study of narratives.

Telling Lives

Exploring dimensions of narratives

Marianne Horsdal

Routledge
Taylor & Francis Group

LONDON AND NEW YORK

First published 2012
by Routledge
2 Park Square, Milton Park, Abingdon, Oxon OX14 4RN

Simultaneously published in the USA and Canada
by Routledge
711 Third Avenue, New York, NY 10017

*Routledge is an imprint of the Taylor & Francis Group, an informa
business*

British Library Cataloguing in Publication Data
A catalogue record for this book is available from the British Library

Library of Congress Cataloging in Publication Data
Horsdal, Marianne, 1946–
    Telling lives: exploring dimensions of narratives/by Marianne
    Horsdal.
    p. cm.
    Includes bibliographical references and index.
    1. Discourse analysis, Narrative. 2. Storytelling—Psychological
    aspects. 3. Autobiography—Psychological aspects. 4. Narrative
    inquiry (Research method) 5. Self. 6. Experience. 7. Identity
    (Psychology) I. Title.
    P302.7.H67 2012
    808—dc22
    2011008094

ISBN 978–0–415–68023–3 (hbk)
ISBN 978–0–415–68024–0 (pbk)
ISBN 978–0–203–80504–6 (ebk)

Typeset in Galliard
by Book Now Ltd, London

MIX
Paper from
responsible sources
FSC
www.fsc.org   FSC® C004839

Printed and bound in Great Britain by
TJ International Ltd, Padstow, Cornwall

Contents

Acknowledgements

I wish to express my gratitude to all the narrators whose life stories I had the privilege to listen to or read. Each story invites us to follow a different path in time and space. Every single story is a gift that widens our horizons.

I would also like to thank my head of department, Anne Jensen, who permitted me to have some free time to write this book. The basis for this book is the thesis (*disputats*) which I submitted for defense of the Danish academic title Doctor of Philosophy. I want to thank the assessment committee and reviewers, Professor Ph.D. Agnieszka Bron, Stockholm University, Dr Professor Linden West, Canterbury Christ Church University, Professor Ph.D. Marianne Børch, University of Southern Denmark for their fine work.

Writing a book in English was a challenge. Allow me to warmly thank Helen Reynolds and Professor Emeritus Jacob Mey for valuable comments and suggestions. I have learnt a lot from our discussions.

Thank you to Rasmus Tvergaard for scanning and saving a "lost" chapter. I am indebted to Marianne Lysholt for technical support, and I am so grateful for the encouragement I have received throughout the process from colleagues and friends, not least for the enthusiasm with which my publisher, Philip Mudd, greeted my work.

Marianne Horsdal
February 2011

Introduction

My parents' house had a big attic, full of trunks and boxes containing fragments of past lives, things left behind, somewhere in between treasures and trash. To me, as a child, they were mostly treasures. I loved to nose about and rummage in the attic exploring and imagining the stories behind the items. "Now, what are you doing up there?" my mother would call out. "I hope you are not making a mess!"

Thirty years later, after my mother died, I had to empty my parents' house, including that attic. One last time I visited the remnants of lives long gone, the half-perished stories hidden in things no longer used. I sorted out all the boxes and trunks, keeping a few valuable fragments, my mother's wedding bouquet from 1935, a silk dress from her stay in London during the 1920s, and a few old school books, but discarding most of it into a trash dumpster.

Later that year, 1989, I began collecting and writing life stories. Life stories and narrative theory have been my central field of research ever since.

Emptying the house where one's family has lived for a very long time can mark the crossing of a strict dividing line. Reminiscences are triggered, entirely new bits of information are discovered but there is no longer anybody to complete the fragmented stories and, in the time to come, the family's life can only be shared through narratives based on memory.

Experiences like these make us realize the importance of narrative coherence for making meaning. They make us aware of how much is needed in order to make sense of temporality, both through narrative and through a cultural space between teller and listener. How may I know where to go, if I do not know where I am? And how do I know where I am, if I do not know how I got there? And how can we share the paths we traveled on our own, if we cannot narrate our experiences to each other?

Before I started collecting life stories I was well acquainted with narrative theory, having an academic background in the Department of Literature. I taught textual analysis for several years, but moved into an outlying district when I wrote a thesis on psycho-sexual development and identity (Horsdal, 1982). Narrative was predominantly a subject of interest in literary studies when I was a student, but this was about to change in the years to come. The increasing interest in narrative during the 1980s significantly expanded the field. Mitchell's anthology *On narrative*, first published in 1980, was one of the first very influential books and many fine studies were to follow (for example, works of Sarbin, 1986; Bruner, 1986; Ricoeur, 1984; McAdams, 1985; Polkinghorne, 1988). Soon narrative became a focus in the fields of psychology, sociology, organizational studies, cultural studies, history, and in education, and the interest has since spread much further. No wonder, actually. As Elinor Ochs wrote in 1998:

> Imagine a world without narrative. Going through life not telling others what happened to you or someone else, and not recounting what you read in a book or saw in a film. Not being able to hear or see dramas crafted by others. No access to conversations, printed texts, pictures, or films that are about events framed as actual or fictional. Imagine not even composing interior narratives, to and for yourself. No. Such a universe is unimaginable, for it would mean a world without history, myths or drama; and lives without reminiscence, revelation, and interpretive revision.
>
> (1998: 185)

At first, I did not collect stories for research but in order to produce material for teaching foreigners Danish, for a textbook that contained a cultural history and, at the same time, enabled some degree of identification through the individual life story narratives. Then I moved on to the Department of Cultural Studies and continued working with life stories and narrative, and soon became involved in biographical research. The field of research was adult education, and I have been employed in the Educational Department for the past decade.

I have a bilateral engagement and commitment in this field of research. On the one hand, I have tried to develop a method for doing biographical narrative research both in terms of collecting the life stories as narrative interviews, and in relation to the analysis of the collected material. On the other hand, I have continuously tried to expand my theoretical knowledge of the nature of narrative. I have approached this field from various theoretical points of view, from various disciplines, in order to look for answers to the numerous questions which arose as I learned more about narrative. My trajectory between different departments in the university was enriching in this respect as I became acquainted with theoretical literature from different fields and accustomed to applying an interdisciplinary approach. During my theoretical research and the applied narrative research on life stories, I became acutely aware of the significance of narrative competence. There are fabulous storytellers around, as well as people who are hardly able to recount or make sense of what happened. This led me to explore the acquisition of narrative competence. How do small children learn to tell stories and to talk about the past and about the future? And what is the interconnection between the development of memory and the capability for storytelling? The focus on learning – in infancy and in a lifelong perspective – and on identity prevailed in all aspects of my research.

My objective in this book, *Telling lives: Exploring dimensions of narratives*, is thoroughly to illustrate as many facets as possible of the stories people tell about their lives. My intention is to demonstrate the interconnectedness between my bilateral engagements in narrative research. The theoretical understanding of the nature of narrative should be bound up with the methods for biographical narrative research, and it is my ambition to contribute to both sides with this work. Furthermore, I want to argue for the significance of supporting the development of narrative competence in educational settings as the need to integrate and make sense of experience increases in a rapidly changing world.

My proposal for a theory of narrative involves a combination of three interdependent and intertwined narrative dimensions: I wish to combine an embodied, a cognitive emotional, and a social, cultural approach to the study of narrative, and in this account to keep a special focus on life story narratives. It is my intention to connect the embodied experience (the phenomenological perspective), cognitive psychology (including the contributions from emotional and social neuroscience), and the social and cultural constructions between participants in interpersonal interaction. *I want to link the bodies, the minds, and the stories in interaction. And I want to give these perspectives a temporal and historical dimension through the focus on the life story narratives.* I regard narratives as symbolic expressions, and narrative competence as gradually acquired during childhood in the cultural space of interpersonal interaction and, as such, depending on existing cultural forms of interaction and on the development of memory and language. Though the cultural forms of interaction differ from place to place, there are no cultures without extensive use of narratives. I further suggest that life story narratives are influenced by memory traces of our physical journey from place to place in a social and cultural environment. The path we travel in time and space is unique to each individual. Also, because of neural plasticity, the brain structure is probably unique to each individual, dependent on the experiential history of interaction. At the same time, we are always already entangled in a social net of intersubjectivity and interdependence, which affects our experience and emotions. Our individuality is founded on, and intertwined with, personal relationships. We exist by virtue of others, and we did not give birth to ourselves.

We experience life as both continuity and change. In the interaction with the environment new things emerge, things disappear or reappear, we recognize the same, the similar and the different, both in ourselves and in the environment we encounter, interact with, and respond to. We are in a state of becoming, continuously in a process in which we try to make sense of and create meaning from what happens. Telling stories and exchanging stories is the primary human means of accomplishing this.

Inspired by and indebted to philosophers, Paul Ricoeur (1992, 2004), Calvin O. Schrag (1997), and Charles Taylor (1989), I try to take up a position equally critical of relativism and universalism; and given the priority of the significance of the interaction with the environment, I strongly resist a subject–object dichotomy. I do, however, feel free to involve and draw inspiration from the points of view of researchers of different convictions, not least social constructivists who look at the individual person as a social construction, although I do not completely share their views.

In Chapter 1, Time and plot, I seek to identify the basic features of narrative; beginnings and endings, duration and temporality. I describe a narrative as a bounded temporal sequence and discuss the narrative time space from a cognitive and an experiential perspective, mainly drawing on Lakoff and Johnson, Wheeler, Stuss, and Tulving, Aristotle, Augustine, Kermode, and Ricoeur. I suggest that our conceptualization and experience of the narrative time space are based on physical movement in space. Furthermore, our mental capability as human beings to expand and go beyond the immediate present and travel backward and forward in time is closely connected to the nature of narrative. We need and use narratives to make sense of what happens and to negotiate the meaning of temporal courses of events. A linear organization of happenings is rarely sufficient to make sense of what happens. Emplotment is a central feature of narrative in order to accomplish the construction of meaning and transcend a simple list or succession of happenings and events. Narrative sense making is situated and tentative; why the configuration of meaning represents an interpretation of existence, a narrative causation which is singular and only adaptable by analogy in future situations. In the final part of the chapter, the special feature of the life story narrative, as a configuration of our experiences of participation and affiliation to different communities, is briefly discussed.

Not only are we able to go beyond the present, to remember what happened, imagine what is going to happen and tell a story about it, we are also able to identify with the experience of other people through their stories. In Chapter 2, I discuss how narratives give us access to vicarious experience as *mimesis*. Narratives represent interactions and emotions. I argue that social and emotional neuroscience may inform our understanding of how this is possible and I discuss the theories of the mirror-neuron system with reference to Rizzolatti, Craighero, Gallese, Johnson, and Carr. According to these theories, vicarious experience is mediated by a simulation of actions and emotions, which we witness, imagine or listen to. Our intersubjectivity and shared feelings are probably grounded in pre-motor representations of actions. I further discuss the theory of the social brain (Cozolino) and "the social synapsis" with the focus on what happens between people and how this interaction and interdependence shape our brains. The theory of mirror-neurons and the social brain links the bodies, the minds, and the stories, as vicarious experience narratives make cultural transmission possible across time and space. The theory of mirror-neurons has implications for the methodology relating to narrative interviews which will be discussed later in Chapter 8.

Telling stories is a practice and a performance, and this aspect is the focus of Chapter 3. In the first part of the chapter I look at the narrative dimensions in interlocution following Bruner, Ochs and Capps, and Nair. Then I discuss the conditions of voice and tellability. Who is allowed to tell what kind of story to whom? Who is allowed to listen? And when and where is the right situation. What version is acceptable and when is an account accepted as plausible? Power relations, cultural conventions, secondary goals and intentions, as well as the issue of reliability, matter. Narrative practice takes place in a cultural space between teller and listener. But not all interactional spaces are equally responsive and attentive. Narratives may become rhetorical justifications instead of shared experience.

While the first three chapters deal with narrative features and dimensions, in the following chapters I adopt a developmental perspective, directed towards the acquisition of narrative; the first two treating significant cognitive and social development as a basis for and support of narrative skills. In Chapter 4, The body, the brain, and experience, I discuss consciousness, emotions, and the development of the extended autobiographical self following Damasio's theory of consciousness with its starting point in the encounters and interaction with the environment. I refer to neuropsychological contributions to cognitive development based mainly on the writing of Siegel and Cozolino, who emphasize how the development of our brains depends on the character of social interactions and relationships. Representation of events is treated with reference to Katherine Nelson. I also refer to the discussions of Trevarthen, Schore, and Tomasello on the decisive parent–infant communication. I argue for the significance of preverbal and non-verbal communication and "phatic" collaboration, and for the importance of the character of the environment in which children grow up.

The subject of Chapter 5 is memory. We cannot tell about our lives if we have no memory of our experiences. In the chapter, I go through the different kinds of memory: implicit and explicit forms of memory and discuss how they work together. In my examination, I build mainly on writings by Tulving, Milner, Squire, Kandel, and Siegel. I argue that autobiographical memory has a narrative structure. Next, I focus on the acts of remembering and forgetting, and explain how our memories are influenced by the present.

In Chapter 6, I focus on the early interactions between infants and caregivers, which support the acquisition of narrative skills in a transitional and cultural space: the development of symbolization, expanding the attention beyond the present, the almost magical entry into cultural communication, different kinds of memory talk, and the use of fictional narratives. I emphasize the influence of the cultural environment on the shaping of the development of memory and narrative. Examples of refigurations and retelling are mentioned in the last part of the chapter. In this chapter I refer to a number of researchers, among others Winnicott, Aukrust, Wolf, Fivush, Reese, K. Nelson, and P. Miller.

Chapter 7 is an inquiry into narrative competence and its impact. A list of 16 features of narrative competence is a result of many years of applied narrative biographical research combined with theoretical inspiration, mainly from Siegel and Bruner. I discuss the features and functions one by one and argue for an integration of narrative in the school and pre-school curriculum in order to enhance children's possibility for sense making, regulation of emotion and integration of experience. Rich narrative practices also promote tolerance towards difference, reflexive and analytic abilities, community building and help people navigate between order and chaos in a changing world. Next, I refer to some narrative practices in education and I emphasize the importance of the narrative environment in the homes and institutions where children grow up. Finally, I discuss the breakdown of narrative competence and of the ability to tell a coherent life story due to traumatic experiences or overwhelming transformations. Also here, an empathic environment is crucial for narrative integration.

From the acquisition of narrative competence we now turn to the application of narrative in biographical research. The following two chapters, with their focus on methodology are central. In Chapter 8, after a brief overview of applied research, I explain the method I have developed for the collection of narrative interviews in accordance with the theories discussed in the previous chapters. The life stories are written by hand by the interviewer as they are told, so the interviewer follows the path of the narrator through vicarious experience in order to capture how the narrator makes sense of her life. The configuration of the narration is not interrupted by questions during the telling of the life story. The theory of the mirror-neuron system and the social synapsis suggests an explanation of what is going on during the interview as the interviewer mirrors the representation of actions and their emotional impact. The ethical implications for this method and the creation of a safe space for the narrative performance are emphasized. Subsequently, a fair copy of the interview is returned to the narrator for proof-reading and amendment before it is, hopefully, approved and used. Several variations of the method are discussed and, finally, the theoretical implications of the situated interview are set out.

Chapter 9 deals with the interpretation and analysis of life story narratives. I find that the development of analytic methods and tools is badly needed in biographical research. The methodological framework presented here, developed during a decade of biographical research in education, is primarily hermeneutic as the main purpose of the analysis is to understand how people make sense of their lives. First, the role of the researcher and her situation and its impact are considered. Time and space in the narrative interview can be analyzed applying insights from literary analysis using Genette's (1972) concepts: "order," "duration," and "frequency." Next, participation in, and affiliations to, the various communities of practice and the impact of this on identity construction in the narrative and on biographical learning provide the focus, with reference to Lave and Wenger. Also, the different voices should be analyzed, differentiating between the narrator "I" and protagonist "I." The construction of "I," "we," and "the other" is significant. Thematic analysis and the relationship between change and stability in the narrative are discussed and, finally, an analysis of the metaphors used is suggested. Analysis of samples is mentioned, and at the end of the chapter I argue against a reduction or fragmentizing of the narrated lives in the analysis.

Against the backdrop of more than 100 life story narratives, cultural identity is discussed in Chapter 10. From the polyphony of samples of life story narratives, common cultural narratives emerge. Patterns of interpretations of self and existence stand out from the multiple voices in biographical research. I analyze these interpretations of self and existence, which people more or less consciously take for granted, and the cultural narratives in which the interpretations are embedded, and I describe how they change over time. Three generations are distinguished to set out the transformations. The change may be summarized as a transformation from a representation of life as a common destiny due to given circumstances to a matter of individual choice and responsibility. Increased mobility plays a significant role. At the end of the chapter I touch upon the conditions and possibilities for negotiations of narrative cultural identity and open the discussion of the relationship to the other which is further developed in the following chapter.

In Chapter 11, I explore the issue of personal identity. The issue of "self" involves co-construction of narratives in a cultural space, but there is more to personal identity than a co-construction of stories. The point of departure for my inquiry is the philosophical writings of Schrag and Ricoeur. For both, there is a shift of focus on self from *what* to *who*. Both are inspired by Levinas, and both of them oppose relativism as well as ahistoric universalism. Schrag discusses *The self after postmodernity* in discursive contexts, contexts of action, ritual contexts and transcendental contexts. Ricoeur, in *Oneself as another*, makes ten studies of self and identity, exploring who is speaking, who is acting, who is recounting and who is the moral subject of imputation. The response to the question, "It is me," illustrates how the otherness is primary. We did not give birth to ourselves and we are always entangled in a net of intersubjectivity. The self in the accusative, not the Cartesian I, is the starting point for personal identity. There is no self without the other who calls for a response and responsibility. The priority given to responsiveness delimits the notion of self both against a lack of, and against a rigid form of constancy. Ricoeur argues that we, in our interactions and relationship to each other, are interchangeable and reciprocal and, at the same time, equal and irreplaceable. Later, I refer to Ricoeur's work on history and memory from 2004. In the final part of the chapter, I discuss the experiential dimension of the existential fact of continuity and change, the I–me relationship, and I argue for an emphasis on the self as becoming. Sense making is always provisional.

Besides the significant issue of identity, citizenship and learning are the focus of the analyses of the life story narratives. Chapter 12 is about active citizenship and biographical learning. First, I discuss briefly the development of democratic citizenship and present some of the challenges in a rapidly changing society. I criticize universalist ideas of individual autonomy and emphasize our interconnectedness, and I argue in favor of educational initiatives which help people to cope with change and diversity. I refer to the Education for Democratic Citizenship project from the Council of Europe and my own research on competencies for active citizenship. The latter confirmed the significance of participation and affiliations in various contexts, and of the need to be of use. A rich poly-contextual formation seems to be significant. The scope and quality of biographical learning plays a key role in broadening the life-world. I suggest an affinity between the development of narrative competencies and competencies for active democratic participation. Furthermore, life stories may be a short cut to combat the ignorance of the other who is different.

Finally, educational perspectives are considered in Chapter 13. The educational consequences of Immordino-Yang and Damasio's (2007) statement that: "[m]odern biology reveals humans to be fundamentally emotional and social creatures" is discussed. A problem concerns possibly contradictory emotional and social feedback in different learning contexts and communities which may create ambivalence or fear; further research is needed in this field. Some educational perspectives with regard to the application of narratives are considered and viewed against the backdrop of the current biographical research with reference to a volume on neuroscience and adult education (Johnson & Taylor, 2006) in which the emotional and social dimensions of learning are emphasized. The significance of narratives in education should, however, not neglect the acknowledgement of the life story as a freely given gift which you receive. I conclude by suggesting that, in order to promote rich biographical learning, a wide range of educational opportunities and wide access to lifelong learning is necessary, along with pedagogic initiatives and the creation of better learning environments.

Chapter 1

Time and plot

Demarcations and pauses

> "Read them," said the King.
> The White Rabbit put on his spectacles. "Where shall I begin, please your Majesty?" he asked.
> "Begin at the beginning," the King said, very gravely, "and go on till you come to the end: then stop."
>
> (Carroll, *Alice's Adventures in Wonderland* ([1865] 1982: 109)

Punctuation is necessary if we are to make sense of a written text. The commas and periods mirror the pauses of oral language. Paragraphs and parts mirror more extensive pauses, and the blank sheets before the beginning and after the end of a book signify the demarcation of the story. In spite of the contemporary praise of flow, we cannot do without pauses, breaks, and limits if we are to make sense, and create meaning and coherence. This is obvious in a temporal sequence, such as a story, written or told. In the same way, music without pauses is as incomprehensible as pictures without frames; although the frames and other demarcations may be challenged in various ways, as we know from works of art and fiction such as the novels and plays by Samuel Beckett. The violation of demarcations and frames in works of art is, however, played out against their truism.

But how can we understand the beginnings and endings, so crucial for meaning and narrative? In the introduction to *Philosophy in the flesh* (1999: 3) Lakoff and Johnson express their basic understanding of cognitive science in the following three statements: "The mind is inherently embodied." "Thought is mostly unconscious." "Abstract concepts are largely metaphorical." I fully accede to these assumptions and find that, although Lakoff and Johnson do not focus on narrative, their description of conceptual schemas and conceptual metaphors based on embodied (sensorimotor) experience may deepen our understanding of narrative in significant ways. To Lakoff and Johnson, spatial-relations concepts are "at the heart of our conceptual system" (p. 30). They consider the container schema fundamental for cognitive categorization. We conceive of things and happenings to be either inside or outside or on the edge or border of the container as a matter of course, in a way similar to Aristotle's definitions of beginnings and ends of stories and dramas,[1] that is, if we want to focus on them as a whole – a meaningful entity. The container category may include not only objects but spaces, periods, and mental states. We can be in or out of a room, of a decade, of a depression, and we can consciously focus our attention on something specific leaving other possible impressions or occupations out of account for the time being.

From a phenomenological perspective we are always visually framed by the horizon; and, although the horizon slightly changes as we move, we experience some degree of wholeness and sameness in spite of our movements in space.[2] We can move about *in* a larger space (container) without crossing the border.

But when we are moving we can also focus on the changes. We can move from one room to another, walk round the points of the coastline to discover what lies behind, see a destination approach, or a place disappear. On board a train or a plane we may attend to the flux of the changing landscape, but our journey has a beginning and an end.

The continuous appearance and emergence and disappearance and vanishing is a crucial part of our experience of life, together with the reappearances and redundancies which make our world seem familiar. Changes as well as recognitions are basic and indispensable aspects of experience.

In the flow of time of appearance and disappearance we can perceive movements in organized periods. When we listen to a piece of music or to a story, the single tones or words form an organized coherence, in anticipation of what is coming, in extension to what went before.

In the opening paragraph of his fine book, *The sense of an ending*, Kermode says:

> It is not expected of critics as it is of poets that they should help us to make sense of our lives; they are bound only to attempt the lesser feat of making sense of the ways we try to make sense of our lives.
>
> (1966: 3)

One of our ways of doing this lies in our ability to exchange the chronological conception of time as mere succession[3] to kairetic time by organizing and humanizing the perception of time into a duration between a beginning and an end, "*kairos* is the season, a point in time filled with significance, charged with a meaning derived from its relation to the end" (1966: 47). The kairetic span may be vast, from the first beginning to the end of time, or tiny. According to Kermode, we are able to reproduce the duration from tick to tock of the clock but not the empty space between tock and tick. Kermode suggests that we borrow this organized perception of time from fiction that enables us to make sense of and create meaning out of lived experience. It may be so; at any rate, the cognitive category of a bounded space has some very coherent and formally organized expressions in works of fiction, while this is not always the case in human lives. We are in the middle in our experience of life, as Ricoeur stated in 1984;[4] we may witness other people's birth and death, but not our own. According to Albright (1994), our beginnings and endings vanish into oblivion and nothingness; he speaks about "the Alzheimer of infancy" (infantile amnesia) as well as the impoverished memory of the old. It is exactly this perspective of being in the middle – from the individual point of view – that illustrates our need of others in order to make sense of and find coherence in a life course. We cannot establish our own beginnings and ends on our own. We owe our life to others and give life to others. Neither is the act of meaning making an individual achievement.

Movement in space and temporality

A narrative can be defined as a course of events with a beginning and an end, as a bounded temporal sequence. A narrative unfolds in a time span from its beginning to the end. As the container category is at work in the demarcations of the story, the temporal course of events implies the cognitive schemata of a path from a point of departure to a destination.

Lakoff and Johnson mention the "source-path-goal" schema as a cognitive topological schema with an internal spatial "logic" (1999: 33).[5] This schema is applied when you imagine a trajectory traversing a route from a point of departure to a destination.

A narrative structure can be described as a cognitive blending of the two schemas through which we infer spatial relations, the container schema – a bounded region in space – and the source-path-goal schema through which we may infer a temporal course of actions and events.

In spite of their focus on concepts for philosophical reasoning, rather than on narrative, Lakoff and Johnson's discussion of our conceptualization of concepts such as "states," "changes," and "events" may shed light on our understanding of the embodied experience behind the narrative structure. "States are conceptualized as containers, as bounded regions in space. Changes are conceptualized as movements from location to location" (1999: 176). In the description of the Location Event-Structure metaphor they write:

> [The Location Event-Structure metaphor] is a single, complex mapping with a number of submappings. The source domain is the domain of motion – in space. The target domain is the domain of events. This mapping provides our most common and extensive understanding of the internal structure of events, and it uses our everyday knowledge of motion in space that comes from our movements and from the movements of others that we perceive.

> Some movements are movements to desired locations (called destinations). Some movements begin in one bounded region of space and end in

another. Some movements are forced, others are not. The force of a forced movement may be internal or external. If someone moves to a desired location, that person must follow a path. There are various kinds of impediments that can keep someone from moving to a desired location, for example blockages or features of the terrain. What this mapping does is to allow us to conceptualize events and all aspects of them – action, causes, changes, states, purposes, and so forth – in terms of our extensive experience with, and knowledge about, motion in space.

(1999: 179)

Lakoff and Johnson could well have added that this mapping allows us to conceptualize a narrative time span. I am suggesting that our physical experience of motion in space is the source of our conceptualization of a temporal sequence. The temporality of narrative, the time span from the beginning to the end, is thus more than an arbitrary form of a certain literary or discursive genre, it is rather a conceptualization of lived time based on our experience of the spatial relations of our moving bodies.

Our physical and perceived experiences of movements in space, and our experiences of moving from one place to another, from a point of departure to a destination (with the inferred "logic" of a relation between the temporal and the physical extent, as a longer distance takes more time to cover than a shorter) makes up the embodied foundation for our cognitive understanding of the temporal space of time and, thus, of the format of a narrative. The form of a narrative, a course in a space of time, beginning in one place and ending in another, builds on our experience of physical movements in space. By definition, a narrative covers a time space.

The experience of demarcations between spaces, and between time spaces where we call the limits beginnings and endings, may be regarded as a very commonplace, or "natural" part of life based on innumerable experiences of bodily interactions accompanied by cognitive-emotional processes. This is far from being a new thought. Through my reading of Ricoeur (2004) I became aware of the fact that Aristotle in *De memoria et reminiscentia* connects intervals to movements and assumes that simultaneity and succession characterized the relation between remembered events.[6] Ricoeur quotes Aristotle:

> This primitive character of a sense of intervals results from the relationship time maintains with movement. If time "has something to do with movement," a soul is required, in order to distinguish two instants, to relate them to each other as before and after, and to evaluate their difference (*heteron*) and to measure the intervals (*to metaxu*), operations thanks to which time can be defined as the "number of motion in respect to 'before' and 'after'" (*Physica* 4.219b).
>
> (Ricoeur, 2004: 154)

From a developmental perspective, infants experience the movements of others who approach or disappear even prior to their own ability to crawl or walk. Infants are carried around or transported in prams or other vehicles. But soon they begin their self-propelled movements from place to place. Physically, each human being travels a path in time and space from infancy to the end of life. Apart from Siamese twins, no two single individuals traverse the same path in time and space. As individual mobile bodies, our journeys throughout life are truly individual.

Cognitively we are able to focus on a specific part of this journey that we travel in time and space. We can focus on a certain period, a certain distance, or a certain place. And we can imagine new routes and destinations, new paths to follow.

Autonoesis

Not only are we moving creatures in space, able to travel in various environments and contexts, but we are also able to go beyond the current moment, we are not limited to the experience of here and now; in our minds we are able to go beyond the present.

In their article "Toward a theory of episodic memory: The frontal lobes and autonoetic consciousness" (1997), Wheeler, Stuss, and Tulving describe the amazing human capability mentally to travel in time as a specific type of consciousness which they name "autonoetic consciousness."

> One of the most fascinating achievements of the human mind is the ability to mentally travel through time. It is somehow possible for a person to relive experiences by thinking back to previous situations and happenings in the past and to mentally project oneself into the anticipated future through imaginations, daydreams, and fantasies.
>
> (Wheeler et al. 1997: 331)

Mental time travel is mediated through a memory system connected to episodic memory (see Chapter 5). The activation of autonoetic consciousness is accompanied by a feeling of continuation and coherence in existence beyond the present, and between past, present, and the anticipated future. Autonoetic consciousness makes it possible for us to conceive the present both as a continuation of the past and as a prelude to the future (p. 335). This sense of coherence in the experience of life may, however, be disturbed because of brain damage as described by Tulving (1985). Furthermore, the experience of coherence may break down as a consequence of traumatic experiences (Horsdal, 2007a). Wheeler et al. recognize that the concept of autonoesis and the ability to mental time travel and the experience of coherence take us toward the domain of narrative. They write:

> Our discussion focuses on episodic memory, with the realization that this system of memory develops along with, and is perhaps related to, the emergence of other complex abilities, such as language and narrative skills, reasoning and problem solving.
>
> (2007: 343)

Autonoetic consciousness concerns more than the relationship to the past and to the developing capability for episodic memory (see Chapter 5). It is a precondition for our ability to plan, for our development of fantasies and ambitions for the future, and for the significant feeling of existence in time.

I want to propose that the development of autonoetic consciousness and the ability to mental time travel is also connected to the infant's actual physical travels and movements in time and space and, thus, connected to both interpersonal interaction and bodily experience. Repeated experiences of independent motion provide the infant with the potential to undertake new intended excursions, and mentally to replicate previous travels or imagine new destinations, targets, and possible experiences.[7]

Augustine's reflections on time

In the eleventh chapter of Augustine's *Confessions* we find the famous reflections on time, analyzed by Kermode and Ricoeur, among others. Augustine uses the example of the recitation of a psalm to discuss the extension of the attended present, encompassing the presence of the past, the present, and the presence of the future. In the act of reciting, the mind is extended to encompass a threefold presence. Ricoeur, in his analysis of Augustine, notes that attention in this way deserves to be called intention, as the transit of the future through the present to the past is an active transition by the attentive mind. Augustine says:

> Suppose that I am going to recite a psalm that I know. Before I begin my faculty of expectation is engaged by the whole of it. But once I have begun, as much of the psalm as I have removed from the province of expectation and relegated to the past now engages my memory, and the scope of the action which I am performing is divided between the two faculties of memory and expectation, the one looking back to the part which I have already recited, the other looking forward to the part which I have still to recite. But my faculty of attention is present all the while, and through it passes what was the future in the process of becoming the past ... What is true of the whole psalm is also true of all its parts and each syllable. It is true of any longer action in which I may be engaged and of which the recitation of the psalm may only be a small part. It is true of a man's whole life, of which all his actions are parts. It is true of the whole history of mankind, of which each man's life is a part (28: 38)
>
> (Quoted from Ricoeur, 1984)

I agree with Ricoeur, who continues this quotation by stating that "The entire province of narrative is laid out here in its potentiality, from the simple poem, to the story of an entire life, to universal history" (1984: 22).

We create meaning in temporal movements through a focus on a time span, short or long. Using our narrative competencies, we intervene in the flow of time and go beyond the fleeting moment of the present, extending our attention to the present by connecting with the past, the present, and the future in order to make sense of what is happening. The narrative format with a beginning, middle, and an end is a form of cognition we apply in order to create meaning in temporality as we try to interpret and understand life itself.

We are always here and now contextually situated with our bodies in the world, but we can expand attention beyond the present here and now and consciously direct it toward other instants and periods. How we interpret a period or an event depends on where we place our demarcations, our beginnings and endings. The reappearance of comparable contexts makes our world and its rhythms familiar to us. We learn to focus attention toward both long and short time spans from small instants to days and years, and we ritualize the transitions between some of the contexts. If we focus on the movement of the body in time and space throughout the journey of life it becomes obvious how we, at the same time, are aiming at the construction of meaning, unity and coherence, and mark the shifts of contexts. Each day is not only seen as a continuous flow but, simultaneously, as a number of different sequences in different contexts. Situated in our moving and changing horizons we can mentally expand and widen them by the recognition of other times and places. We can move quickly or slowly, stay for a longer period, or move on.

Narratives may be very short or extending from the first beginning to the end of times, but eternity itself is without history. "Always" is a negation of what is temporal, transitory, and perishable. Narratives can compress long periods to short stories or expand and develop short events, but they need the bounded temporal dimension between a beginning and an end. Mere chronology is not enough.

Emplotment and configuration of meaning

Applying the formulation of Lakoff and Johnson (1980) the linear, progressive movement, *chronos*, has become a metaphor to think and live by. Linearity is also a prevailing concept in modern Western thinking in relation to an understanding of the trajectories of life. Not least in the adoption of linear progression as an ideal model for life and development, a way of thinking which overruled the pre-modern cyclical model of conceiving life.

The chronological dimension of the story, its temporal extension from a beginning to an end is, however, not in itself sufficient for a narrative configuration of meaning. In line with the comprehensive analysis by Paul Ricoeur in *Time and narrative* (1984), a simple listing of events or happenings in chronological order is not enough to make up a story:

> A story, too, must be more than just an enumeration of events in serial order; it must organize them into an intelligible whole, of a sort such that we can always ask what is the "thought" of this story. In short, emplotment is the operation that draws a configuration out of a simple succession.
>
> (1984: 65)

The creation of meaning, the sense-making activity through the act of narration, implies more than a replication of an accidental sequence:

> [. . .] the act of emplotment combines in variable proportions two temporal dimensions, one chronological and the other not. The former constitutes the episodic dimension of narrative. It characterizes the story insofar as it is made up of events. The second is the configurational dimension properly speaking, thanks to which the plot transforms the events into a story. This configurational act consists of "grasping together" the detailed actions or what I have called the story's incidents. It draws from this manifold of events the unity of one temporal whole.
>
> (1984: 66)

Ricoeur analyzes Artistotle's *On the art of poetry* in his discussion of emplotment and the configurational act. The focus is on the dynamic process of making a representation of action, the activity of organizing the events into a coherent composition which transforms the accidental and discordant elements into a concordant meaningful plot. Aristotle makes a distinction between simple (episodic) and complex plots. Aristotle, whose work is directed toward fiction, states that a plot must exhibit what is necessary and probable – not what is necessarily true. He says:

> A complex action is one in which change is accompanied by a discovery or a reversal, or both. These should develop out of the very structure of the plot, so that they are the inevitable or probable consequence of what has gone before, for there is a big difference between what happens as a result of something else and what merely happens after it.
>
> (1965: 45)

The narratives we tell about our lives differ, of course, from works of fiction in some respects. Normally, we do not simply invent by use of playful imagination what we are telling about our lives, we do not have the freedom of the poet to compose our stories by introducing those imagined or selected elements which in the best way serve the purpose of a unified plot. Aristotle's book on poetry is normative. It is about how to execute the *art* of poetry. Nevertheless, in our daily lives we compose and construct stories of actual happenings, selecting, underscoring, and organizing incidents in order to make sense of what happened. Besides the inserted beginnings and endings, our narratives of personal experience are also marked by selection, sequence, hierarchy, and organization. We negotiate meaning, to use Bruner's apt phrasing (1986, 1990), by imposing a particular temporal and causal structure and a particular perspective, or by combining multiple voices and perspectives in our life story narratives. And when we are listening to other people's stories, we also negotiate meaning, expecting to find some kind of coherence within their narratives in the course of the telling, not unlike the process of reading a story.[9] According to Peter Brooks (1984), who is writing about fiction, we read or listen to a story from the beginning in anticipation of retrospection. We are reading the end into the beginning and the beginning into the end. During our reading we apply a pre-understanding which later may be either confirmed or rejected, which often changes on the way or is overthrown by an unusual turning point in the narrative. But we expect to find some kind of meaning at last in the retrospective interpretation. If a narrative is interrupted, or if the last pages are missing, our curiosity is frustrated. A beginning such as: "It was a cold and stormy night," or to use Sartre's own example (*Nausea*, 1938: 65) from his protagonist's complaint of the mere coincidences of life compared to fiction: "It was a beautiful evening in the autumn of 1922" (my translation) introduces the expectation of something special and significant to follow which adds significance to the beginning. To the annoyance of the narrator in Sartre's book, life does not seem so well-ordered or structured as a fictitious narrative or as a well-composed piece of music, without contingency and coincidence, of which life seems so full. Sartre's protagonist would like to be able to live life already configured from the beginning and not just in retrospect, but he admits "that you might as well try to catch time by its tail" (1938: 66).

Fortunately, we cannot do this. We can, however, in most cases, through a negotiation of meaning transform *chronos* into *kairos* and make sense of temporality by narrative means, through the configurational act, by inserting beginnings and endings and organizing the parts on the path between them.

But where to insert the temporal demarcation, which parts of experience to accentuate, which happenings to select and point out are open questions? Often, a certain story of what happened will not satisfy the listener or the teller her/himself, and another try may take place as an alternative emplotment, a reconfiguration of happenings. An authentic quest for meaning in the lives we are living replaces the creative imagination we apply in the composition of works of fiction.

The demand for honesty, authenticity, and meaning in narrations of lived experience emphasizes the dynamic character of the configurational act. Our narrative activity is driven by our need for meaning. Our endeavors to make sense of our lives impel us to try out configurations and plotlines in narratives again and again. Thus, we do not have just one story to tell about our lives. The physical journey we are traveling in life is individual, singular and unique, but numerous stories can be told about this journey. The idea of a "life history" is, therefore, problematic.

While the perception of a limited period, a time span, is a cognitive act connected to the experience of motion in space, the configurational act, by which we organize the elements of this temporal period into a narrative, is, at the same time, cognitive and symbolic. Emplotment involves symbolic reification.

Life story narratives are more than chronological sequences of happenings. They are more than linear enumerations of events, they are stories narrated in a quest for meaning tried out by the configuration of the happenings and actions and by the chosen perspective of enunciation. We select, accentuate, and point out certain parts of our experience in our, continuous, attempt to create a plot marked by necessity, verisimilitude, and plausibility. The interpretations of existence in our narratives have a dynamic character. Understanding is a process. Meaning making is *"performance."*

Narrative causality

Our quest for meaning has to do with more than reconciliation with the past. We want to make sense of what is happening here and now, and we would very much like to be able to predict the future a little, or "to colonize" the future, to use Giddens' expression (1990). A plot conveys a causal structure, exactly in opposition to mere succession (see Ochs & Capps, 2001). This happened as a result of something else. When we ask how or why something happened or how to interpret certain actions we are looking for causes including motives and intentions. Not only the actions, motives, or intentions of other people may now and then amaze, puzzle, or terrify us and call for interpretations, but also our own emotions and our motives for action may at times seem incomprehensible and invite narrative explanations.

Bruner, in his book, *Actual minds, possible worlds* (1986), contrasts two modes of thought, a logic-scientific or paradigmatic mode and a narrative mode of thought. The former is characterized by causality of the type *if x then y* while narrative thinking is about "the vicissitudes of human intentions."

> There are two modes of cognitive functioning, two modes of thought, each providing distinctive ways of ordering experience, of constructing reality. The two (though complementary) are irreducible to one another. Efforts to reduce one mode to the other or to ignore one at the expense of the other inevitably fail to capture the rich diversity of thought.
>
> Each of the ways of knowing, moreover, has operating principles of its own and its own criteria of well-formedness. They differ radically in their procedure for verification. A good story and a well-formed argument are different natural kinds. The one verifies by eventual appeal to procedures for establishing formal and empirical proof. The other establishes not truth but verisimilitude.
>
> (Bruner, 1986: 11)

It is Bruner's intention to criticize behaviorism and positivism from a constructivist point of view and to argue against a reduction of the understanding of human affairs through the application of logic causation. Bruner wishes to limit the concept of causality to logical thinking in contrast to narrative thinking, which he claims for the realms of human intention.[10] With the analysis of conceptual metaphors, including the concept of causes, in mind, stating that: "there is neither a single, literal concept of causation that characterizes the full range of our important causal inferences" (Lakoff & Johnson, 1999: 171),[11] I believe there is a strong case for considering a special kind of causation in the context of narratives.[12]

Ricoeur attempts to avoid the relativity of constructivism in our views on history by ascribing a *singular causality* to narrative (1984: 126, 2004: 182). "If he had not done this (x), (y) would not have happened." Yet, he finds that: "there is interpretation at all three levels of historical discourse: at the documentary level, at the level of explanation/understanding, and at the level of the literary representation of the past" (2004: 185). Although, there are cases where experience may prompt us to claim, that "this will happen, if" as a likely result of preceding actions whose effects will impact the future, it is important to emphasize that narrative causality is context dependent. Unlike a traditional scientific statement such as "water boils at 100 degrees Celsius," a narrative explanation is only by analogy applicable to similar happenings in other situations and in other contexts. We can never be sure that a certain proposed causation in a narrative will always be a matter of fact in a new situation. It is – on the contrary – tentative, and may yet be plausible, in the attempt to apply the ideal "necessity and verisimilitude" in causal emplotment.

Bruner (1986), Labov (1972), and Nair (2001) use the following example of a very short narrative: "The king died, and (then) the queen died."

We infer a temporal and causal connection between the two incidents. In this way a narrative differs from a simple sequence. Furthermore, we may infer explanations and causes of the death of the queen, perhaps an interpretation proposing that she died from grief and not from the same contagious disease as the king.

In spite of the fact that the point of many narratives is to reproduce old, familiar "truths" (cultural assumptions) about the state of the art of the world, it is important to emphasize that each single narrative is a situated, contextual expression. The tiny narrative above neither states that kings always die before queens, nor that queens always die of grief for their dead husbands.

The type of causation we apply in connection with narratives may be that of *abduction*, a raised hypothesis explaining a confusing state of affairs/phenomenon.[13]

We use narratives across contexts by analogy. We compare one course of events with another. One story makes us think of another, quite similar story, and we try to interpret what is going to happen by using our repertoire of stories as a source of knowledge. Narrative knowing is based on analogy, by comparing similar actions, happenings and incidents. We use analogy to transfer the explanations embedded in the causal emplotment of stories from singular occasions to new situations. And we use stories for negotiation of meaning (Bruner, 1990). The openness of narratives, their tentative explanations, mean that we can discuss narrative causality. Recognizing the possible interpretation in the chosen configuration entails a possible discussion of "how things add up." The narrative explanation of what happened may be seen and told from a different perspective. The demarcations may be changed in a retelling with another new beginning, and with other incidents highlighted. Our understanding may be revised; it has not been settled once and for all. If our explanations of what happens lead us into a blind alley, and do not make sense, we may try again, reconfigure happenings in the construction of other stories.

Our narrative repertoire from singular contextually situated tellings and about different happenings provides us with a number of cultural plotlines. Each plotline conveys a particular perspective (Ochs & Capps, 2001), but the assembly of different individual perspectives makes up our indispensable fund of narrative knowledge.

Just as more stories can have the same point, a happening or a course of events can be explained and understood in several ways in different narrations with different perspectives, plots or configurations. But, as Ricoeur indicates (1984) it is the configurations of the narratives that make us feel at home in the world.

Configuration in life story narratives

Ricoeur describes emplotment as a configuration of events (1984). This is true of some narratives, but the configurations in life story narratives are somewhat different. When we tell about our lives we tell from the perspective of the context of here and now, and we tell about ourselves in the various contexts of there and then in the past (or in the imagined future) embedded in interactions in the different communities.[14] We tell about ourselves in the family where we grew up, in kindergarten, and in school, on the street with playmates, with grandparents, and later on in different jobs, educational settings, or different cultural communities, and in new intimate relations. The life story narratives display a configuration of our experiences in all these communities, or places in both a physical and relational sense. Albeit, our physical journeys through life are individual as we are embodied in time and space, our individual journeys only make sense by virtue of the affiliations of the communities we participate in for longer or shorter periods during a life time.

We are placed in some communities by chance, or by force; some contexts are a matter of choice, and some of circumstances. In some places we are welcomed; in others we are just tolerated. Good affiliations and relationships are immensely valuable and important but cannot be taken for granted. We may even be marginalized or expelled from some communities.

Over the years I have collected and read hundreds of life story narratives, and it becomes very clear that the emplotment in this narrative genre consists of a configuration of the meaning of our participation in communities and the trajectory between them.

Within the telling of a certain period, in a certain place, in certain relationships, a particular outstanding event may be highlighted with the intention of producing more accurate sensuous impressions and representations of interactions. Also prototype events, interactions frequently repeated at this time and place may be accounted in connection with the different contexts of there and then.

While life story narratives often display dialogic negotiations between multiple voices, I still find it meaningful to talk of emplotment and a configuration of meaning in life story narratives. Lived experience can be configured in narratives from various perspectives, but also here we find the application of conventional cultural plots.

Life stories told in the middle of a crisis may fail to achieve a meaningful configuration of lived experience. As elaborated in Chapter 7, the experience of crisis may undermine previous configurations, and a new understanding and interpretation of existence depending on a re-configuration of meaning, cannot always be achieved right away.

Chapter 2

Vicarious experience

Representation of action (*mimesis*) and mirror-neurons

Aristotle defined tragedy as a representation of action which had six elements (plot, character, diction, thought, spectacle, and song); the most important element was the plot.

> Of these elements, the most important is the plot, the ordering of the incidents; for tragedy is a representation, not of men, but of action and life, of happiness and unhappiness – and happiness and unhappiness are bound up with action. The purpose of living is an end which is a kind of activity, not a quality; it is their characters, indeed, that make men what they are, but it is by reason of their actions, that they are happy or the reverse.
>
> (1965: 39)

I would argue that we can transfer this definition of tragedy to narrative; narrative is a representation, not of men, but of action and life, of happiness and unhappiness – and happiness and unhappiness are bound up with action. In our stories the emotional quality of the narratives is an inherent feature. Our interactions with the world are never emotionally neutral, and neither are the stories we tell of our interactions. The example from logical scientific causation mentioned earlier: "Water boils at 100 degrees Celsius," will hardly prompt an emotional expression such as: "How terrible!" or "How wonderful!" as stories often will. Stories about actions and happenings evoke emotions, we respond to them with feelings of joy or regret, pity, fear, or laughter.

Stories evoke feelings; we identify with the representation of interactions just as we, in a similar way, react to the interactions that we witness and perceive directly. Stories are, according to Bruner, "vicarious experience" (1986, 1990). In my aspiration to link bodies, minds, and stories in interaction, I propose that recent neuropsychological research may inform our understanding of this phenomenon. Theories of mirror-neurons may proffer new information both about our capacity for empathy and about our instinct for imitation and representation of action (*mimesis*), which Aristotle recognized over 2000 years ago:

The instinct for imitation is inherent in man from his earliest days; he differs from other animals in that he is the most imitative of creatures, and he learns his earliest lessons by imitation. Also inborn in all of us is the instinct to enjoy works of imitation.

(Aristotle, 1965: 35)

Our capacity for imitation is an important issue in the contemporary debate between philosophers, neurobiologists, neuropsychologists, and educational researchers due to the discovery of mirror-neurons in monkeys by Rizolatti and Gallese, and the subsequent research of the human brain.

If we want to survive, we must understand the actions of others. Furthermore, without action understanding, social organization is impossible. In the case of humans, there is another faculty that depends on the observation of other's actions: imitation learning.

(Rizzolatti & Craighero, 2004: 169)

In their article "The mirror-neuron system" Rizzolatti and Craighero present the neural basis of identification. Mirror-neurons were discovered in monkeys in an area of the brain called F5. The visuomotor neurons discharge both when the monkey does a particular action, such as pulling or pushing or grasping an object, and when it observes another individual – another monkey or a human – doing a similar action. A motor representation of the observed action corresponds to activations during active action and, thus, transforms visual information into knowledge (Rizzolatti, Fogassi, & Gallese, 2001), a mechanism which may form the basis for a direct understanding of actions (Gallese, Fadiga, Fogasse, & Rizzolatti, 1996; Rizzolatti et al., 1996). Neurons which would cause the muscles to execute certain actions are not activated – fortunately, we do not copy all the actions we observe – but what happens is exactly a representation or mirroring of the interaction itself. It is not the object as such that is significant but the action. An object alone, or a mimed or intransitive action will not activate mirror-neurons in monkeys, but the neurons will, nevertheless, discharge in situations where the action in question has not been fully completed, indicating that the monkey is quickly able to capture what the other individual is about to do. The understanding of the action in question is probably brought about by a correspondence between the representation of the observed movement and a representation of actions from the repertoire of movements of the observer which enables recognition of the action. In this way, visual information can create an understanding of what is going on.

Although mirror-neurons are only indirectly studied in humans, considerable research indicates that humans, unlike monkeys, are also able to understand and to code intransitive and mimed action. We are able to draw conclusions not only about what is going on but also about the intentions and motives behind the action in question. The mirror-neuron system makes it possible to try to predict the consequences both of the actions we are planning to do, and of those which others are doing, by means of an automatic process of simulation which neither presupposes a theory about what is happening nor is a conscious representation (Gallese, 2005). It may seem peculiar that we have to activate a pattern of movement in order to recognize an action, but in fact it is not so strange. Through the simulation of movements we gather information on the interconnectedness of the action, not just visual snapshots of what is taking place. The mirror-neuron system enables an experiential understanding of the observed interaction, which serves as a foundation for further cognitive and emotional functioning.

Together with Lakoff, Gallese has written an article in 2005: "The brain's concepts: The role of the sensory-motor system in reason and language" in which they argue that our cognitive understanding is based on bodily interaction with the environment. They emphasize that our imagination is also based on bodily interactions; we also simulate the actions we are imagining. The mirror-neuron system can be regarded as a motor-resonance system which makes up the neural basis for the human ability for imitation and, as such, is a precondition for the significant human capacity to learn through imitation.[1] Rizzolatti and Craighero (2004) identify two kinds of imitation learning by humans; substitution where a usual way of doing certain things is replaced by a new and better motion pattern, and the ability to learn a new motor sequence which is useful for achieving a specific goal, whether it is the ability to tie your own shoelaces or handle new gadgets. It may be possible that the representations of mirror-neurons help us to re-combine familiar motor patterns in new ways. In any case, learning through imitation is more advanced than learning through trial and error. You learn faster by imitating than by having to try out various behaviors again and again by yourself.

Furthermore, neuropsychologists describe mirror-neurons which discharge in response to the sound of actions. The mirror-neurons may represent a mechanism which creates a direct connection between the sender and the receiver of a message. Some researchers suggest a connection between the mirror-neuron system and the development of language in humans.[2] One hypothesis (Rizzolatti & Craighero, 2004) proposes that language derives from gesture in communication (pantomime) in the course of evolution. From this point of view, communication of gesture is further developed into an abstract understanding of sound but the representation of gesture does not vanish completely. There is evidence that humans possess an echo-neuron system activated with motor resonance when people are listening to verbal material. Speech-related motor centres are activated when we listen to verbal stimuli. Listening to action sentences thus engages visual motor-circuits similar to those active in the representations of actions. This shows precisely a neural understanding of identification and appropriation of vicarious experience in narrative practice.[3]

Emotions and the social brain

Emotions are very significant when we are trying to understand what is happening. We do not comprehend another person's emotional state or facial expression by rational reasoning but by virtue of a bodily simulation producing a spontaneous resonance (Gallese, 2005). "[W]e do not just perceive … someone to be, broadly speaking, similar to us. We are implicitly aware of this similarity because we literally embody it" (Vol. 1, p. 104). In this sense, a "we" precedes the distinction with self and other. Gallese speaks of "a shared manifold of intersubjectivity." Carr, Iacobini, Dubeau, Mazziotta, and Lenzi (2003) have also studied neural mechanisms of empathy in humans. They write:

> Taken together, these data suggest that we understand the feeling of others via a mechanism of action representation shaping emotional content, such that we ground our empathic resonance in the experience of our acting body and the emotions associated with specific movement. As Lipps noted, "When I observe a circus performer on a hanging wire, I feel I am inside him". To empathize, we need to invoke the representation of actions associated with the emotions we are witnessing.
>
> (2003: 5502)

In light of this field of research, several neuropsychologists refer to "the social brain" and "resonance circuits" (Johnson et al., 2005; Siegel, 2007; Cozolino, 2006).

> Mirror neurons and the neural networks they coordinate work together to allow us to automatically react to, move with, and generate a theory of mind of what is on the mind of others. Thus, mirror neurons not only link networks within us but link us to each other. They appear to be an essential component of the social brain and an important mechanism of communication across the social synapse.
>
> (Cozolino, 2006: 301)

Cozolino does not just emphasize resonance behaviors serving imitative learning, synchronization of group behaviors, and emotional contagion. We find an example of the latter phenomenon in a situation when a person is telling us something very sad and we respond by spontaneously imitating her or his emotional facial expression. Cozolino's expression: "communication across the social synapse" points to the idea of a parallel between the communication between neurons and the interaction and communication (verbal and non-verbal) between humans and the interdependence between the two. Just as the individual neuron in itself is not the focus of interest in the functioning of the brain, Cozolino suggests that it may be due to the biases of Western science – that lead us to think of the individual as the "unit" of study – that we have not been able to bridge the gap between neurons within neural networks and the individuals embedded in the social world. He continues to argue that such a model could provide a means of integrating clinical research and research endeavors in science, education, and mental health (2006: 301). How we communicate across "the social synapse"[4] using our senses and means of communication directly affects the development of our brains.

Cozolino considers the role of narratives for neural integration. Stories both teach lessons of culture and serve as a means of homeostasis, and of emotional and neural integration, as narratives require us to combine knowledge, sensations, feeling, and behaviors. He reminds us of the social and public elements of our individual stories: "These co-constructed narratives remind us that each unique story of our own contains elements of someone else's story, which contains elements of some else's story" (2006: 307).[5]

The theory of the mirror-neuron system links bodies, minds, and stories. It provides us with a neural explanation of our ability to represent, simulate, and imitate interactions, and the feelings they evoke. Not only do we possess the ability to go beyond the here and now, extend our focus towards the past and the future, applying our capability for mental time travel in order to make use of our own lived experience. We are, through our exchange of narratives, able to convey our lived experience to others. The mirror-neuron system, our echo-neuron system, and the resonance networks of our social brains make it possible for us to experience the stories we listen to almost as if they were part of our own lived experience.

A repertoire of vicarious experience

We identify emotionally with narratives of personal experience. When someone is telling a story of the path she traversed, she is mentally walking over the path again, and the empathic listener is vicariously walking with her. To tell a story about a difficult path to a responsive listener may be a way to repeat the route with someone instead of walking alone. If it is difficult to find the right words to express the mental time travel then our repertoire of narratives, including fictions, may be of use. As we anticipate new journeys in life, small trips or long ones, or as we mentally repeat the journeys we took – alone, or in a story told to others – we spontaneously activate embodied pre-motor simulation and imitation of actions and feelings. The demarcated time span of a story framing the movement from beginning to end gives us, at the same time, the possibility of creating internal coherence, meaning, and interconnectedness in the space of time using emplotment for a configuration of events. Symbolization provides a reification of experience. Due to the fact that a story is a symbolic representation in language[6] we may share our experiences across time and space. Through narratives we may set out mental time travels, real or imagined, and thus relate to and share our own and others' experiences. Stories can lift us above the perspective of here and now and make a cultural transmission possible, and bring about identification with experiences from other places in other times. Through imagination we may travel the path other people followed in time and space and so we can acquire a perspective and an interpretation of what happens, and models for understanding temporarily evolving courses of action we either participated in, or witnessed as observers, or as partners in communication. Although narrative modes of explanation of meaning and coherence are singular and situated, we are using the vicarious experience embedded in narratives as analogies and parables when we confront new experiences we do not immediately understand.[7] "Perhaps, it is similar to the time when ... or, perhaps, it is because she intends to ... etc." So, often we negotiate meaning on the basis of the narrative repertoire we have picked up in a continuous search for plausible meanings in between certainty and doubt.

Nair (2001) stated that narratives provided human beings with a remarkable evolutionary advantage. Narratives give us the opportunity to learn through vicarious experience. We may sit safely in an armchair and experience dangerous and life-threatening incidents through stories, we may be affected emotionally and scared by identification with the narrative, but we do not get physically hurt. So we safely acquire a large narrative repertoire of lived experience, way beyond what we could possibly assemble in our individual lives.

Chapter 3

Telling stories

Narrative dimensions in interlocution

Discussions of the characteristics of narrative, following established traditions inherited from literature and linguistics, used to focus on the story as an object, a text that could be studied in relative autonomy from its production and reception. However, over the past decades the pragmatic aspects have increasingly come to the fore, and narratives have been analyzed embedded in interlocution.

Bruner, when he defines the function of the story as being "to find an intentional state that mitigates or at least makes comprehensible a deviation from a canonical pattern" (1990: 49) is referring to Kenneth Burke and his dramatic "pentad" consisting of an actor, an action, a goal, a scene, and an instrument in his description of the elements of a well-formed narrative adding "trouble" – which consists of an imbalance between any of the five elements of the pentad. Bruner follows Burke in the focus upon deviations from the canonical that have moral consequences, and he notes that "[t]o tell a story is inescapably to take a moral stance, even if it is a moral stance against moral stances" (1990: 51).[1]

Labov (1966, 1972), from a structural viewpoint, lists six universal elements in his story-grammar:

1   Introduction
2   Orientation
3   Complicated action
4   Evaluation
5   Resolution
6   Coda.

Nair (2001), analyses narratives in conversations and presents a critique of this narrative grammar. She demonstrates convincingly how these elements are distributed between interlocutors. Thus, it is often the listener who makes the evaluation ("Gosh! Really! How awful!"), but also other elements, such as the introduction, may be produced by the listener. Nair provides good evidence for her critique of Labov's structural model for neglecting the context of narrative practice – the situation in which a narrative is told. Her own narrative grammar encompasses the following elements:

1   Temporal structure
2   Inference structure
3   Causal inference
4   Informational inference
5   Evaluative inference.

The concept of "inference" refers to the conclusions the listener must draw in order to comprehend the narrative. With the example of the mini-narrative from Chapter 1 in mind, "The king died, and (then) the queen died," it is the reader who produces the causal inference, the informational inference, and the evaluative inference. To a large extent, Nair is taking the perspective of the listener in her understanding of narrative, and she calls attention to the fact that narratives are co-constructed. "Trouble," or the problem and its solution, is also in focus in her contribution to narrative theory. She often compares narratives to "theory," possible models of interpretation and resolution.[2] In her book *Narrative gravity* she concludes with the following definition: "Crisis: to perceive or 'create' a problem – and by implication, to think of a solution. Narrative is an essentially emotive learning device in culture contributing to the theory of mind" (2001: 393).

While Bruner is describing the well-formed narrative in the quotation above, mundane conversational narratives of personal experience are the focus for Ochs and Capps in their book *Living narrative. Creating lives in everyday storytelling.*[3] The authors point to the difference between telling a story *to* somebody and telling a story *with* somebody else, and they describe the function of personal narrative: "to air, probe, and otherwise attempt to reconstruct and make sense of actual and possible life experiences" (2001: 7). In line with this, they examine narratives in terms of a set of dimensions "that a narrative displays to different degrees and in different ways" (p. 19). The dimensions are:

1   Tellership
2   Tellability
3   Embeddedness
4   Linearity
5   Moral stance.

At one end of a continuum you have a story: with one active teller, a highly tellable account, relatively detached from surrounding talk and activity, with a linear temporal and causal organization,[4] and a certain, constant moral stance (p. 20). And at the other end you find a narrative with: multiple, active co-tellers, a moderately tellable account, relatively embedded in surrounding discourse and activity, with a non-linear temporal and causal organization, and an uncertain, fluid moral stance (p. 23).

Although you may argue against the very open and wide definition in the approach of Ochs and Capps in favor of stricter definitions of narrative, some of their dimensions are extremely valuable for a broader understanding of narrative practices. The issue of tellership is very important. Together with the second dimension – that of tellability – we find here an entry into the significant discussion of voice. Who is allowed a voice? Who is entitled to tell what to whom in which situation? Who is allowed to listen? How should your story be composed in order to find listeners who will respond? And who is left in a narrative void,[5] devoid of meaning and sense? Not everyone is granted an active tellership nor a responsive listener; not everybody is granted partners for interlocution. The contexts for interlocution have crucial significance for the impact of narratives.

As mentioned above, Peter Brooks, in his analysis of fictions in *Reading for the plot* (1984: 23) noted that we read a story in anticipation of retrospection. We believe that we shall get the meaning of the story when we come to the end but, on our way, while we are following the story, we infer temporary interpretations of what is going to happen and of the point and meaning of the entire story. Something similar takes place when we are listening to verbal narratives in interlocutions. All along we project temporary storylines, provisional plots and interpretations which may be overturned by unexpected turns of the narrative. But, in contrast to the reading of a story, in interlocution our way of listening and our interaction as listeners may very well influence the story that is being told and somewhat change the narrative activity of the teller. Meanings are co-constructions.

Voice and tellability

The issue of voice and the question of "a well-formed narrative" are strongly influenced by the cultural framework of narrative practices. The conception of a well-formed narrative differs in various cultural contexts. Our capability for symbolization allows for an infinite variety of expressions, restricted only by cultural filters. The narrative dimension "linearity" suggested by Ochs and Capps (2001) could serve as an example of a culturally specific feature of a well-formed narrative in a Western context, whereas Latin American stories often display a more complex structure with secondary plots and tangled themes.[6]

The cultural dimension of tellability has to do with both emplotment and genre. We have several cultural plotlines at our disposal (Polkinghorne, 1988) in the repertoire of stories with which we grow up. Narratives are both created and understood from different cultural, social, and historical perspectives. The constraints of cultural and social narratives impact our personal attempts to make sense. Cultural pre-understandings affect our interpretive frameworks; therefore, we find different interpretations in different periods and places (Gadamer, 1965).

There are different kinds of stories, and stories can be told in different ways. The concept of genre can be applied to narrative in two ways. There are fictional stories, historical narratives, and narratives of personal experience which cover a wide spectrum from collective stories to individual stories, from the life story narrative, the autobiographical account of an entire life to narrations of small incidents, happenings, intentions, and ideas. Stories of personal experience may, just like fiction, be told as heroic dramas, as tragedies, *Bildungsroman*, comedies, fairy tales, or as anecdotes (Bruner, 1986, 1990; Denzin, 1989). Tellability depends on interpretive frameworks, on cultural conventions of configuration and genre, and, of course, on the thematic content of the story.

We often witness the culturally dependent dimension of tellability. Many of us have experienced the embarrassment of telling the wrong story in the wrong place to the wrong audience, the faux pas of narrative practice par excellence. A story told with relative success in one context may be completely inappropriate if retold in a different cultural setting.

Edward Bruner uses the term "dominant narratives" in *The anthropology of experience* (Turner & Bruner, 1986) in order to emphasize that narratives may be "units of power as well as of meaning" (p. 19). There is an aspect of power in the authority of the narrator regarding the question of who has the right (and the possibility and capability) to tell what in which way. New interpretations can be suppressed if they are in conflict with the norms of value expressed in canonical narratives.

This is not just a political or public issue, but something that influences personal interpretations of actions and happenings. Our need for recognition and acceptance from the people around us may influence our accounts and our interpretations.[7]

In *Acts of meaning*, Jerome Bruner (1990) describes narratives as "rhetorical justifications." Quite young children recognize "that what they have done or plan to do will be interpreted not only by the act itself but by how we tell about it" (1990: 81), they quickly learn, to use Bruner's concept, to recount the canonical cultural versions. Bruner also mentions the wish of most narrators to portray themselves in a good light (p. 83). I agree with him to the extent that a great many narratives of personal experience can be described as rhetorical justifications, mainly asymmetrical narratives (Ochs & Capps, 1996) where the listener is someone in a position to judge, reward, or punish the narrator because of her account. However, as I shall argue later, there is another kind of exchange of stories of vicarious experience; told and received in order simply to share the experience, not to judge or to justify what happened.

Another aspect of voice and tellability, as Ochs and Capps (2001, 1996) point out, relates to our wish as narrators to engage our listeners. We want our listeners to be responsive, and to maintain attention throughout the telling. Telling a story means that you want to hold the floor from the beginning to the end. Nair (2001) notes that we put our vulnerable selves at stake in narratives that she terms "fragile" because the listener may brush them off as boring, trivial, appalling or too imaginative.[8] Ochs and Capps stress the socializing factor of narratives:

> Differential control over narrative content, genre, timing, and recipiency is central to the constitution of social hierarchies. Narrative practices reflect and establish power relations in a wide range of domestic and community institutions. Differential control over content, genre, timing, and recipiency is also critical to the selves that come to life through narrative.
>
> (1996: 35)

In most Western countries the majority of children today are encouraged to tell stories in schools and in their families, but 50 years ago well-behaved children were "seen, not heard" in many situations. Ochs and Capps demonstrate the unequal distribution of narrative rights (2001). Children and sick people often do not have the same narrative rights as adults and healthy people. Enforced silence is a cultural instrument used in many situations which limits the narrative rights of some people and, in certain cases, cuts people off from a meaningful integration of experience.

Plausibility

It is problematic to talk about the truth of narrative because of the potential to create different versions of any one narrative, and the effect of the perspective from which any narrative is told. Bruner accentuates the "subjunctive" character of stories of personal experience (1986, 1990), the position in between fact and fiction, as a positive feature which makes stories viable for negotiation of meaning. He prefers to talk of verisimilitude[9] instead of truth when we are dealing with the narratives.

Following Ochs and Capps (2001), I want to adopt the term *plausibility*. The authors identify two conditions for a story to be plausible: coherence and authenticity. We try to achieve coherence in our narrations; a story that falls apart normally seems implausible.[10] The second condition, authenticity, is understood as an ideal we try to approach in our narrative endeavors. We continue to tell new versions of what happened until we find "the best fit." We may accept a certain interpretation of a course of events or of somebody's motives for action but, on second thoughts, we try out new narrative explanations, rejecting preliminary versions.

I want, however, to add a third element as a necessary component of a plausible narrative: "cultural re-embedding." By this concept I, again, want to emphasize the interaction between the partners of interlocution and the co-construction of meaning.[11]

The term "cultural re-embedding" links with Bruner's notion of narrative as a deviation from a canonical pattern (1990: 35). We are most likely – at least in a Western cultural setting – to tell stories about unusual happenings.[12] As mentioned above, an account of our most trivial actions is unlikely to engage our listeners. The experience of the unusual happening will in different degrees throw us out of our usual, familiar routine, and in this sense imply a disembedding from convention or tradition. In the act of sense making during the construction of narratives about unusual happenings we try out a reconfiguration in order to integrate the event; and a successful narrative which creates sense and meaning of what happened for both interlocutors means a re-embedding in a meaningful world (however provisional).[13]

Cultural re-embedding may, however, in a significant number of cases be in conflict with the former two conditions. Someone may tell a story in order to please the partner of interlocution, perhaps to obtain a certain goal or to avoid some unpleasant consequences; the story seems perfectly coherent, and it will be accepted (re-embedded) by the listener, in spite of the fact that it is far from being an authentic account. On the other hand, a perfectly true and authentic story may be rejected because it opposes the cultural conventions of the partner of interlocution. This can result either from a transgression of cultural norms of a well-formed, coherent narrative, or due to a display of material which the interlocutor for some reason – moral or otherwise – rejects. Stories may seem implausible and be rejected for several reasons. Many stories show rich veins of wishful thinking, or they provoke the listener because of an unacceptable view of the world, an ideologically objectionable interpretation of existence. Stories that in some cultural contexts are untellable, and stories told by narrators whose tellership is not recognized, are unlikely to be culturally re-embedded in interlocution and, thus, unlikely to be accepted as plausible accounts.

Narratives can be inauthentic and unreliable. Just as we have unreliable narrators in the works of fiction, unreliable narrators in stories of personal experience are not so rare a species. Often, examples of unreliability are due, as in fiction, to manipulations of the enunciation. You may claim you did, or did not do something, take the credit for somebody else's action, or disclaim responsibility and attribute the action to another person.

Disagreements about the accounts of "what really happened" are, nevertheless, generally fruitful. Due to the different perspectives of individual narratives we need to challenge the single perspective, and the single authoritative account. We also need to have our own plots challenged, from time to time. If our points of views are not opposed or questioned in interlocution, we may be caught in the narrow circles of our own delusions. Rigid cultural configurations may exclude other perspectives and other voices.

We should always keep in mind that, in our position as narrators or listeners, we are embodied and situated in space and time. Our interpretations of the world and of existence are contextually situated; we see, tell, and make sense of the past and of the future from the perspective of here and now, whether or not our stories are told with a point of view close to, or with a temporal distance from the protagonist of our stories. Perspectives on the past and the future are likely to change throughout life, along with a change of circumstances and situations, and along with the change of general knowledge.

The fact of our embodiment and our individual journeys through different communities and contexts in time and space affect the co-construction of meaning in plausible narratives. According to the neuropsychological theory of mirror-neurons and of the social brain, we vicariously experience the representations of actions and connected emotions directly when we are listening to narratives. However, we do not necessarily regard the actions and emotions we are representing and reflecting in the process of listening in exactly the same way as the narrator does, because we refer to our individual repertoire of actions and their emotional impact in this process. Our lifelong personal experience will attach specific meaning and emotional impact to certain actions and happenings, and not to others, due to differences in our individual history of interactions and to the way we are culturally embedded. We are not equally sensitive and we are not equally responsive, in spite of our social brains. Yet, we have the opportunity to learn something new every time we are listening to a story.

The cultural space in different contexts

Narrations take place in a cultural space between teller and listener. As symbolic acts, as reifications of lived experience, the stories come to life and are received in a cultural space which, like Winnicott's "potential space" or "transitional space" (1971), is neither subjective nor objective but both at the same time. The co-construction of meaning depends on the verbal and the non-verbal communication between the partners of interlocution in the cultural space, and on their implicit or explicit interpretations of the verbal and non-verbal interaction.

There are very different contexts for narrative practices, and different kinds of interaction in the cultural space in the various contexts.

As mentioned above, Ochs and Capps (2001) distinguish between stories told *to* somebody and stories told *with* somebody. Another major difference concerns the occasion for telling the story. Did someone ask the narrator to tell a story for a specific reason? Or is the story told on one's own initiative? In the former case, the range of different occasions and reasons for narration corresponds to a wide variety of reactions and interactions in the cultural space between the interlocutors. The previously mentioned possibility of asymmetries between them affects the interaction and may elicit rhetorical justifications or inhibit the communication.[14] Narrations on one's own accord, on the other hand, make demands on attentiveness, because a story is an utterance of some length which requires the floor for a much longer time than a single comment.

In conversations, one narrative often gives rise to another; sometimes the act of telling dominates attention as some people prefer to hear themselves instead of listening to others. Listeners may also appropriate other people's stories, and dominate the sense-making activity of other narrators. Attributions of meaning often take place in conversations as the listener supplies the narration of another person with the last words of an unfinished sentence. Very often, the narrator will accept this and herself repeat the suggested word and continue the narration from there. Meanings are co-constructed, and all listeners (as well as readers) fill in the gaps of the narratives in the act of comprehension and interpretation.

While rhetorical justifications may be a prototype of particular asymmetrical narratives, I want to suggest another prototype which offers broad scope for a more empathic response in the cultural space. When we meet a new person whom we appreciate we, spontaneously, want to share narratives of personal experience in order to share the part of our lives we lived apart, and the journeys we travelled without each other. In this case, the stories are responded to with open curiosity rather than with evaluation or condemnation. The stories are responded to as a gift, a privilege to be allowed to encounter. In our imagination we traverse different landscapes in time and space; and the narrative journeys provide us, through vicarious experience, with wider horizons. In this case, the narrative activity is rewarding for both teller and listener. Sharing the journeys through grim or sad periods in narratives with a responsive listener is less difficult than walking the road alone. Sharing the wonderful part is a form of celebration. The empathic and curious responsiveness in this prototype of narrative practice is the ideal to which I aspire in the process of collecting narrative interviews.

Chapter 4

The body, the brain, and experience

Recognition

Significant cognitive development takes place in interpersonal interaction before the development of the ability to tell stories of personal experience and actively enter the world of narrative.

From the beginning of life we learn to perceive and recognize certain interactions in specific ways with a specific emotional impact; we learn to share with others attention to new objects, we learn what is attractive or what is repulsive or dangerous, and we gradually learn to master our movements, memory, and language.

In order to consider these developments more fully, I want to introduce some of the discussions about cognitive development, consciousness and emotion, memory, interpersonal interaction, and communication. These are huge fields to cover, so this introduction is very selective with the emphasis on the literature which accentuates our interconnectedness.

> The environment is not an "other" to us. It is not a collection of things that we encounter. Rather, it is part of our being. It is the locus of our existence and identity. We cannot and do not exist apart from it. It is through empathic projection that we come to know our environment, understand how we are part of it and how it is part of us.
>
> (Lakoff & Johnson, 1999: 566)

In the living present we are constantly sensing, perceiving, encountering, and relating to our environment. Fortunately, everything that happens in these encounters does not just vanish into oblivion an instant later. We are able to retain and to remember something of what happens and thus we are able to learn from experience. If I close my eyes for moment, I recognize my surroundings and myself when I open my eyes again. Although we sometimes wake up in a foreign place and, for a moment, wonder where we are, normally we quickly orientate and recognize ourselves and our surroundings. Although we, and the world around us, are constantly changing, the changes are rarely so fast and radical that we cannot recognize any familiar elements.[1]

We do not know exactly how this happens, and the computational metaphors usually applied when we talk about encoding, storing, and retrieving information, are probably far too simple. We do not have files in our brains in the way a computer does; we do not even posses messy lumber rooms or deposits, though it often seems so when we are unable to "retrieve stored items" from experience.[2]

The computational metaphors have, nevertheless, an advantage in that they allow us to distinguish between the time of the original experience – the encoding – and the time of the recall of the experience. An example could be the smelling of honeysuckle flowers in a summer garden and the recollection of the scent as we are reading a text later (for example, *The sound and the fury* by William Faulkner, 1929). According to Carrol (2003: 201), a representation is an activation or reactivation of a neural pattern.

A theory of consciousness

While we do not know exactly what consciousness is, Damasio proposes a very interesting and useful theory in his book: *The feeling of what happens. Body, emotion and the making of consciousness* (2000).

He suggests two main assumptions: first, feeling and cognition are intimately connected;[3] second, consciousness of the world and of the self emerge in the same process: "the presence of you is the feeling of what happens when your being is modified by the act of apprehending something" (2000: 10).

The starting point is the body as a living organism trying to obtain some kind of homeostasis as a response to what happens. What happens inside, with or around the body releases emotions, which may be pleasant or unpleasant, and a second step is a feeling of this emotion. After this, the conscious representation or image of what happens emerges as the feeling of a feeling of an emotion. A feeling accompanies the creation of an image and implies a consciousness that it is *our* image; *we* are seeing, hearing, touching or recalling something. No happenings are emotionally neutral.

Damasio makes a distinction between "core consciousness" – what is happening here and now in the fleeting moment – and "extended consciousness," which implies memory and extends beyond the passing moment:

> Core consciousness is a simple biological phenomenon; it has one single level of organization; it is stable across the lifetime of the organism; it is not exclusively human; and it is not dependent on conventional memory, working memory, reasoning or language.
>
> (2000: 16)

Extended consciousness extends both to the past and to the future at the same time as the awareness of the here and now is present. Accordingly, he makes a distinction between a momentary core self, constantly born and reborn, and a temporally extended self connected to the lived past and imagined future, an autobiographical emerging self depending on memory.

Consciousness and attention are not the same. Focused attention which can be temporally extended beyond the transient is conscious, while momentary and peripheral attention may be either conscious or unconscious. Very often, many things are happening at the same time. There are different levels of attention. We may direct our attention to the text we are reading, At the same time, perhaps, we register the buzzing of a fly, the light, a fatigue in the leg which make us change our position, an association comes to us, a feeling of hunger appears, and so on.

Damasio describes "core consciousness" as a simple wordless narrative about what is happening to an organism when it interacts with an internal or external object.[4] The conclusion of the narrative is the reaction to the encounter, the modified condition of the organism (p. 168). The feeling of the transient core self comes from being the protagonist of this narrative. He uses a metaphor from T.S. Elliot: "you are the music while the music lasts," about the core self and continues:

> Something does last after the music is gone, however; some residue does remain after many ephemeral emergences of core self. In complex organisms such as ours, equipped with vast memory capacities, the fleeting moments of knowledge in which we discover our existence are facts that can be committed to memory, be properly categorized, and be related to other memories that pertain both to the past and to the anticipated future. The consequence of that complex learning operation is the development of autobiographical memory, an aggregate of dispositional records of who we have been physically and of who we usually have been behaviorally, along with records of who we plan to be in the future. We can enlarge this aggregate memory and refashion it as we go through a lifetime. When certain personal records are made explicit in reconstructed images, as needed, in smaller or greater quantities, they become the autobiographical self.
>
> (pp. 172–3)

Although Damasio discusses the creative significance of language acquisition for temporally extended consciousness in humans and the autobiographical self, he does not find that language is a necessary condition for consciousness. He ascribes even extended consciousness to other living creatures without language, such as certain mammals. And he assumes that words and sentences refer to non-linguistic concepts, actions, happenings, feelings, and relations: "The words and sentences of healthy and sane humans do not come out of nowhere, cannot be the de novo translation of nothing before them" (p. 185). Damasio argues that the defenders of the thesis of language as a precondition for consciousness only refer to extended and higher forms of consciousness. They do not consider his concepts of core consciousness as a foundation for a later developed extended consciousness. The implication of the thesis of language as a necessary condition for consciousness is, he argues, that we deprive babies and animals of consciousness. Furthermore, we do not fall asleep, experience absences of sentience or become unconscious when we do not focus our attention.

Core consciousness precedes evolutionary and individually extended consciousness, and is a fundamental prerequisite of extended consciousness. At the same time, it is extended consciousness that gives the resonance of past and future to core consciousness (p. 119). Double processing is needed for extended consciousness:

> Extended consciousness occurs when working memory holds in place, simultaneously, *both* a particular object *and* the autobiographical self, in other words, when *both* a particular object *and* the objects in one's autobiography simultaneously generate core consciousness.
>
> (p. 222)

> Extended consciousness goes beyond the here and now of core consciousness, both backward and forward. The here and now is still there, but it is flanked by the past, as much past as you may need to illuminate the now effectively, and, just as importantly, it is flanked by the anticipated future.
>
> (p. 195)

In this description we come close to the temporal concepts discussed in Chapter 1 in connection with Augustine and Ricoeur, and to the concepts of autonoetic consciousness that allow us to experience the present in connection with the past and the future with some degree of temporal continuity (Wheeler et al., 1997).[5] Extended consciousness allows us to expand attention beyond the narrow frame of the present situation and mentally to travel forward or backward in time and, at the same time, still be present in the present.

Damasio is well aware of the limitations of conscious knowledge. He lists our ignorance of:

1   all the fully formed images to which we do not attend;
2   all the neural patterns that never become images;
3   all the dispositions that were acquired through experience, lie dormant, and may never become an explicit neural pattern;
4   all the quiet remodeling of such dispositions and all their quiet renetworking that may never become explicitly known; and
5   all the hidden wisdom and know-how that nature embodied in innate, homeostatic dispositions.

He concludes: "Amazing, indeed, how little we ever know" (p. 228).

Many things happen which we will never know about. Our past interactions with the world have, nevertheless, a decisive impact on how we see, meet, and react to the world we encounter today.

The significant role of feelings in neuroscience is of incredible importance (Watt, 2003; Turnbull, 2003) and expands the field of cognitive science. The recognition of the significance of feeling has opened the way for a growing interest in the body and in the impact of interpersonal interaction.

Brain plasticity and the influence of culture

Modern neuropsychology, including Damasio's theory of consciousness, strongly resists the sharp distinctions made in the past between body and soul, and the physical and mental dimensions. The brain is, of course, a part of the human body, and (together with the central nervous system) processes bodily phenomena, impressions from the surrounding world, and psychic content of various kinds.[6]

The distinction between cognitive development and cultural interaction is now much less marked. The brain is conceived as a complicated system of dynamic processes, shaped by experiences forever in a state of change "in continual emergence with a changing environment and the changing state of its own activity" (Siegel, 1999: 17). Experiences of interpersonal interactions are thought particularly to influence the development of the brain and the mind. According to Cozolino, evolutionary genetic changes are too slow to explain all the rapid and radical changes from generation to generation, so the impact of cultural learning becomes increasingly obvious. He says:

> The human brain is an "organ of adaptation" to the physical and social worlds; it is stimulated to grow and learn through positive and negative interactions. The quality and nature of our relationships are translated into codes within neural networks that serve as infrastructure for both brain and mind. Through this translation of experience into neurobiological structure, nature and nurture become one.[7]
>
> (Cozolino, 2002: 16)

Our brains grow a lot in infancy. From the birth of an infant until the age of four the brain grows from 350 grams to 1.250 grams, which is 80 percent of the weight of the adult brain. Certain parts of the brain are not fully developed until adulthood; and the brain changes throughout life.

Neuropsychology can, within limits,[8] inform us of what happens in the brain when we interact with our environment. Neurons communicate with each other across synapses in an electro-chemical system with the aid of neurotransmitters. More than 60 different chemicals affect the neurons, some of them promoting and others inhibiting synaptic connections. Neurons develop dendrites, which can connect to thousands of other dendrites from different neurons. Neurons have to connect to each other across the synapses in order to develop and grow through activation. They form neural networks, and the brain "learns" through changes in synaptic strength. Neurons may be fired or not fired in a certain mosaic pattern. Which neurons are fired is a result of our encounters with the world. Every minute the brain makes millions of calculations in milliseconds in order to produce a coherent experience of our interactions with the environment. We do not become overloaded, however, because many of the processes are unconscious (Gazzaniga & Heatherton, 2006). The interactions create quite consistent patterns in our abilities, experiences, emotions, memories, and dreams, but new learning will modify the synaptic connections within the networks.

Conversely, synaptic strength may be consolidated in a process called "long term potention" (LTP), with the result that postsynaptic neurons are easily activated. Also, the amount of myelin, which promotes the speed of synaptic connections, grows gradually over the course of a lifetime. While existing connections are strengthened, new connections are created. New neurons may emerge throughout life (a process called "neurogenesis"), but a surplus of neurons which are not active may vanish.[9]

The environment plays an enormously important role in neural development, physically[10] and socially. We are able to learn all our lives, but plasticity becomes somewhat reduced as we grow older. The number of neurons is reduced, while existing neurons may grow like oak trees. The function of a modified neurogenesis may be that a larger amount of early learning can be maintained. Dendrites that are changed according to new experience are, perhaps, more capable of a refined learning if they are modified and not exchanged (Cozolino, 2002: 69).

There are critical or sensitive periods in the course of development, but also possibilities for the repair or restoration of certain kinds of damage caused by an unhealthy environment (Gazzaniga & Heatherton, 2006). Learning in the sense of integration of neural networks is, according to Cozolino, promoted by moderate arousal which implies an increase of attention, in contrast to too much stress which disturbs and inhibits integration and consolidation. Many functions are carried out unconsciously. We normally pay little attention to our breathing, and we perform many tasks and movements without conscious attention (Cozolino, 2002: 129). If we can manage our interaction with the environment, our being in the world, without major problems then we have much more space for focused attention. If all our attention is directed towards disturbing problems here and now, or directed towards disturbing images from the remembered past or the anticipated future, the capacity to be flexible in our responses decreases (Schall, 2001; Cozolino, 2002: 144).

Unfortunately, the environments in which children grow up are not equally responsive to their needs. The interactions across the social synapses result in different developments of the social brain. Johnson et al. (2005: 600) state that the maturational approach "does not successfully explain some aspects of human functional brain development," and they propose as an alternative viewpoint "interactive specialization," implying that "cognitive functions are the emergent product of interactions between different brain regions, and between the whole brain and its external environment" (p. 601).

Actions, happenings, and social relations

Lived experience includes action and suffering. There is an exchange and a reversibility of roles (Ricoeur, 1992). Damasio focuses on what happens to us, the feelings of apprehension, and the response to what happens. In our interchange with the environment we also initiate actions, provoke reactions and responses from others. We learn at an early age that some of our actions have results; also, that all actions are not equally predictable.

As previously discussed (Chapter 2) the assumed existence of mirror-neurons forms a bridge between our interactions with the environment and the actions and happenings we observe. We observe what happens to others and what others are doing, and this affects us in a way that is similar to the response to our own interactions. We respond to observed interactions according to our experience of interactions. The continuous development of our brains depends on the character of interactions, our unique repertoire of perceived interactions. We have an individual body, but we are socially dependent on one another, regulating each other's biological condition, regulating disturbances and fear; we are interconnected and interdependent in biological, social, and psychological processes. Our well-being, social engagement and social motivation depend on interpersonal interactions (Cozolino, 2006). Cozolino's theoretical point of departure underscores the significance of non-verbal communication. He points out that the shape and contrast of color of the human eye facilitates our perception of gaze direction. We react to the size of pupils, to blushing, and to different emotional facial expressions, movements, rhythms, as well as to smells.

It may be a result of our Cartesian inheritance that we have clearly underestimated the importance of non-verbal communication. At least, we often fail to make explicit the main part of this tacit knowledge. Part of non-verbal communication goes on without conscious awareness, but we react to that non-verbal communication and our responses are frequently prompt. We have learnt a lot, implicitly and explicitly, from experience in social interaction, not least in infancy when our brains were not full-grown, and this learning affects our later reactions. We affect and regulate each other's feelings by means of our facial expressions, actions and words. Particular chemicals are released in our brains during communication; this is why we are literally at risk of becoming socially addicted in some relationships. In a discussion on mother – infant interaction, Cozolino suggests "that proximity of the mother is translated into the biochemical language of opiates" (2006: 117). We possess neurochemical systems that reward interpersonal care. During conversations we often repeat each other's words and gestures.

Cozolino suggests that the function of the mirror-neuron system may bridge the space between the sender and receiver of a message and strengthen emotional resonance and mutual understanding. Simulation, imagination, and anticipation of the actions and sufferings of others play a significant role in social interactions, promote identification and the ability to create a mental representation of others' thoughts, feelings, needs, and intentions.

As we shall see in Chapter 8, the level of interpersonal interconnectedness in communicative acts has implications for the construction of a narrative life story interview.

Representation of events

In their research on the mirror-neuron system and the interaction between this system and other networks of the brain, Iacobini and his colleagues found that the context is of significance for the comprehension of an action (such as grasping a cup from a table in a context of either having breakfast or clearing the table after breakfast) (Iacobini et al., 2005). The mirror-neuron system connects to other brain networks as we spontaneously compare new apprehensions with our repertoire of experienced interactions. Mental representations of events have been discussed at length in the literature on cognitive development using different concepts such as RIG (representation of generalized interactions) (Stern, 1985, 2009), scripts (Schank & Abelson, 1977), and MER (mental event representation) (Nelson, 1996). Repeated interactions are contextually demarcated and experienced with beginnings and endings.[11]

According to Nelson, the infant is able to generalize patterns of experience in the events and contexts, pleasant or unpleasant, in which she participates[12] and, gradually, to develop models of the world on the background of these patterns of experience. The infant acquires sociocultural meanings through collaborative construction. In 2005, Nelson says: "In a larger perspective, the individual (brain, body, mind) and the social world form an interdependent transactional system that is in a constant process of organization" (Nelson, 2005a: 117).

Nelson defines an event as an organized sequence of actions with a certain purpose (eating breakfast or having a bath). A single action such as picking up something or chewing something does not count as an event.[13] She points out that the infant learns social rules in social interaction with objects.[14] An event includes actions, objects, and persons. A ball is, perhaps, perceived as something you play with and roll rather than as a circular object. She implies that children make their concepts both from function and form, but that function often is central. The repeated event – such as having breakfast – has a temporal structure. You may, in accordance with Roman Jakobson (1960), talk of a syntagmatic structure in opposition to a paradigmatic structure;[15] but paradigmatic categories play a part in different events, for example the different kinds of food eaten at breakfast. Nelson talks of "slot filler categories." Events include routines, rituals and play and invite imitation and the use of symbols. The perspective of here and now will gradually be transformed in the direction of a symbolic, mimetic system of representation.

In a discussion of Nelson's approach to language and cognition, Tomasello (2002) argues that infants who learn to understand the meaning of verbs through participation in ordinary interactions acquire a foundation for a complex syntagmatic construction at the same time. The verb "to give" contains in a functional event perspective someone who gives, an action with an object, and a receiver. In this way, linguistic grammatical categories can be seen as a further development of non-verbal understanding.[16]

Children learn to compare and find resemblances among repeated events and to draw thematic connections (a bone is connected to a dog, for example) and connections among exchangeable paradigmatic categories related to events. We should, however, bear in mind that children in their interactions also learn early on to apprehend, categorize, and organize according to aesthetic and affective preferences.

Proto-narratives

Trevarthen researched communication with infants over many years. He observes that:

> It is the nature of human consciousness to experience being experienced; to be an actor who can act in relation to other conscious sources of agency, and to be a source of emotions while accepting emotional qualities of vitality and feeling from other persons by instantaneous empathy.
>
> (1993: 121)

He underscores the difference between interaction with physical objects and with other living creatures, which feel, intend, and act. Social interplay involves alteroceptive perception. Trevarthen suggests that human learning is based on a special kind of curiosity which is intersubjectively regulated: "Emotions generated and perceived intersubjectively appear to have a unique function in regulation of learning and memory" (1993: 156). Feelings regulate the development of social communication as the participants find a common world. Social intelligence is not exclusively human, but humans are able to further develop communicative skills through narratives.

Mary Catherine Bateson (1975) named the communication between mothers and infants "proto-conversation." Proto-conversation is mediated by eye contact, vocalizing, hand movements, and movements of arms and head, and they express interpersonal closeness and complementary or synchronic feelings. There are many senses at work: smell, sound, touch, sight, and, not least, rhythm and timing are of great significance. Trevarthen terms proto-conversations "narratives of feeling" and compares them to a musical duet: "These behavioral particles are organized in a stream of emotional signals, which can have the equivalent of syntactic organization or narrative structure – they may be described as an '*emotional narrative*'" (1993: 151).

The absence of emotionally attuned communication makes the infant withdraw, freeze, or express confusion or anger. Depressive adults caring for infants are likely to cause reduced communicative competence. Video recordings of successful interaction replayed with a displaced timing, so that the infant is not met and responded to in the appropriate rhythm, show a very significant negative reaction to this problematic "communication."

Trevarthen (1993) describes the proto-conversations as a forerunner of learning by guided participation (Rogoff, 1990). But, as we acquire language and are able to communicate about interactions and feelings from non-present situations, we must emphasize that interlocution is far more than an exchange of words:

> Conversation, the main traffic of human social understanding and meaningful cooperative work, is full of an immediate interpersonal vitality that goes beyond, or beneath, the words ... Everyday conversational discourse is not held together by cognitively tidy grammatical rules or abstract theoretical explanations but by empathic cooperation of an immediately

persuasive, "phatic" kind. Interpersonal relationships in the family and in society are certainly supported on this level of direct, intuitive, and emotional communication.

(1993: 159)

Several other researchers (Feldman, Greenbaum, & Yirmiya, 1999; Papousek & Papousek, 1995; Schore, 1994, 2003 among others) have described non-verbal communication between infants and their caregivers.

Face-to-face interactions, emerging at approximately two months of age, are highly arousing, affect-laden, short interpersonal events that expose infants to high levels of cognitive and social information. To regulate the high positive arousal, mothers and infants ... synchronize the intensity of their affective behavior within lags of split seconds.

(Feldman et al., 1999: 223,
quoted after Schore 2003: 13)

Prompt responses indicate, according to Schore, unconscious communication.[17] The contingent response of the sufficiently good caregiver implies that she regulates the level of arousal and thus reduces stress in the infant. Regulated interactions create not only a feeling of safety but are also a condition for curiosity "that fuels the burgeoning self's exploration of novel-socio-emotional and physical environments" (Schore, 2003: 16).

Evidently, regulation of affect influences motivation. We want to explore what is pleasant and reduce unpleasant emotions. The feelings which we spontaneously and unconsciously read into a given relation in a given context will influence our motivation to become involved in the interaction. Obviously, this has consequences for learning, and influences the degree of curiosity and openness with which we may spontaneously encounter the world. Mutual adaptation, or the opposite, happens very fast and generally implicitly, but it leaves a trace of the emotional impact of the interaction. Schore quotes Lieberman (2000) in saying that what we call "intuition" is an application of our implicitly acquired knowledge (see also Glaser, 2003: 147).

According to Siegel (2001a: 69) a responsive collaborative interaction is more important than stimulation for a healthy development:

The non-verbal interactions of caregiver and infant can be proposed to be the most important elements that help to create a secure attachment between the infant and the caregiver at the beginning of life.

(2001: 84)[18]

The main goal of a collaborative and responsive communication is for the infant "to feel felt" by the other.

Both Cozolino and Schore maintain that this kind of communication, involving a direct contact between the right hemispheres of both partners, is of decisive importance for the development of the infant's brain toward a more coherent and complex organization of consciousness.

An impoverished environment may cause damage to cognitive and emotional development; problems of understanding others' emotions, reduced empathy and regulation of affect, and reduced curiosity. Some children are unlucky enough to grow up in environments where the space of the social synapses is a dangerous minefield, which urges only to withdrawal or rage (Cozolino, 2006). Damage to the development of the social brain may cause different kinds of pathology and influence our health and trust. If you feel that the world is a dangerous place you may hesitate to become involved in new learning. Fortunately, the lifelong plasticity of our brains opposes the determinism. Responsive learning environments and collaborative interactions may repair previous damage, perhaps even with the help of narratives.

Joint attention

Tomasello (1993: 174) makes a distinction between the early proto-conversations between infant and caregiver,[19] which he terms "primary intersubjectivity," and "secondary intersubjectivity" referring to the interpersonal interplay which takes place after the occurrence of "the nine-month miracle." The concept of "the nine-month miracle" is a description of the great leap forward when the infant is able to follow the gaze of another who invites the infant to joint attention toward a new perspective, for instance by pointing at something. Within primary intersubjectivity the focus and the "object" of the communication are the partners of the "dialogue," the communicative act in itself. By the age of eight to nine months, the infant is able to adopt the perspective of someone else. This initiates a joint point of reference to something new, something that may now be attended to through interaction with someone who has a different perspective. At this time children begin to notice what adults are doing with different objects (social reference), and to imitate actions. Children attend to others with communicative movements and they begin to understand people as emotional and intentional agents. Before "the nine-month miracle" an infant and an adult can, of course, simultaneously attend either to each other or to some object, but the infant cannot at the same time attend to the adult's relation to the object.

To be able to see "through the gaze of another" implies a new perspective on the self. The infant will gradually be able to see herself with the eyes of another. The ability to follow a different perspective in joint attention is crucial for language acquisition. This important step in human communication is the basis for deixis, situating an utterance in communication within a context of here and now, you and I, and this and that: the joint point of reference.[20]

Preverbal communication provides significant cultural tools for infants. They learn about rules for turn-taking, and the different ways of maintaining others' attention. Throughout life we develop more and more cultural tools that help us to improve communication and to construct and negotiate meaning (Bruner, 1996). Continuously situated responsive encounters are a precondition for new understanding. A crucial point is how often the individual is invited by others to joint attention to a different perspective or is responsively met when inviting somebody.

Chapter 5

Memory

Different kinds of memory

Before I begin to explore how children learn to tell stories, another significant precondition must be discussed: our ability to remember. If we could not remember anything, we would not have anything to tell. But what is memory? How much do we actually remember? And is our memory reliable?

> Memory is the primary form of all mental representations: Other forms such as concepts, categories, schemas, imaginations, dreams, pretence, plans, conjectures, stories, even language derive from memory in some way.
> (Nelson, 1996: 152)

The precondition for recognition mentioned in the previous chapter depends on some kind of memory. Memory is a vast field of research and I am approaching it, with my background in the Humanities, only through the literature. Milner, Squire, and Kandel provide a review of memory research in their article "Cognitive neuroscience and the study of memory" (1998), where they emphasize the relationship between memory and learning[1] and suggest that:

> the synaptic connections between neurons mediating behavior are not fixed but can become modified by learning, and that these modifications persist and can serve as elementary components of memory storage.
> (Milner et al., 1998: 454)

Learning as a result of our interaction with the environment occurs in a lifelong perspective. The plasticity of our brains probably indicates that the brain structure "is unique to each individual and dependent on each individual's experiential history" (p. 463).[2]

We are, however, not consciously aware of everything that happens. We only explicitly remember an infinitesimally small part of what happened but, fundamentally, it does all matter. Implicit memory plays a significant role and may even affect our explicit memories.

Milner et al. (1998) refer to a patient who, after experiencing brain damage, was not able to retain any experience in memory beyond the time his attention was focused on the particular occurrence. He remembered events prior to his accident, but everything that happened afterward he forgot a minute later. Nevertheless, he was able to learn new skills by practice – in spite of the fact that he had no recollection of having practiced them before. But he was unable to learn new things which required explicit memory. This introduced the idea of implicit memory; and experiments showed that not only motor skills but also emotional learning connected to habit learning took place independently of explicit recall.

Tulving and Lepage sum up:

> there are many forms of memory, from habituation and simple classical conditioning to the loftiest thoughts that one can have based on what one has learned. Interestingly, most of these forms of memory, contrary to public consensus, have nothing to do with the past. Instead, most forms of memory and learning studied in many areas of life sciences have to do with the present and the future, not with the past. The single exception is episodic memory.
>
> (2001: 209)

The main distinction is between implicit and explicit memory (Tulving, 1972, 1983, 1985; Tulving and Lepage, 2001; Siegel, 1999, 2001b; Wheeler et al., 1997). Implicit memory is sometimes referred to as procedural memory or non-declarative memory.[3]

Implicit memory is present at birth, or even before, and is active throughout life. Implicit memories are not accompanied by any internal experience of recall, but they may accompany explicit memories with, perhaps, inexplicable impressions and feelings. A major part of what we learned and what we know is implicit; we are not aware of using previous experience. Implicit memory includes more than tacit knowledge. Many of our assumptions and ideas about the state of the world are shaped by implicit memory (Schacter & Scarry, 2001). Implicit memory is more about our ways of being, acting, and reacting than about conscious knowledge. Siegel (1999: 29) includes mental models, behavior, sensations, and feelings in implicit memory. He gives the example of a child who, very early in his life, was bitten by a dog without any conscious recall of the incident. This child may subsequently show fear of dogs without knowing why. Siegel calls the brain an "anticipation machine" constantly scanning the environment in an attempt to find out what is happening and what is going to happen. Previous experience forms new models of expectation. We do not have to start anew at each encounter. Generalizations from repeated interactions are the essence of implicit learning. Implicit memory, which is sometimes termed procedural memory, is, as Cozolino points out, context-free and lacks source attribution (2002: 90).

In contrast to implicit memory, explicit memory requires conscious awareness and focal attention for "encoding" (Siegel, 2001b: 1000). Explicit memory involves conscious awareness that we are remembering something. Obviously, language acquisition strongly supports explicit memory.[4] According to Tulving (1972) explicit memory consists of semantic memory (memory of facts, words, graphic, etc.) and episodic, autobiographical memory.[5] Semantic memory develops prior to episodic memory. Wheeler et al. write:

> Because the procedural memory system is stimulus driven and requires environmental support, organisms can demonstrate procedural learning only when the appropriate stimulus cues and behavioral supports are present in the environment. When semantic memory emerges, the infant becomes capable of mentally representing and operating on the part of the world that exists beyond immediate perception. Semantic knowledge coexists and does not replace the procedural memory system.
>
> (Wheeler et al., 2003: 343)

Semantic memory is about our knowledge of things and names and propositional facts, not personal experience. It is a fund of knowledge we continuously upgrade, directed toward the present and the future rather than the past (Tulving and Lepage, 2001); and we have no awareness of the source of this knowledge, as we do not recollect ourselves in time and space within the context of what is remembered. Nevertheless, this fund of knowledge is not always accessible when we need it; we may know that we know something, but at this specific moment we cannot remember it, and fail to retrieve what we are looking for.

Episodic, autobiographical memory does not develop until the second year of the infant's life. Wheeler et al. write:

> It is the kind of memory that renders possible conscious recollection of personal happenings and events from one's personal past and mental projection of anticipated events into one's subjective future. As such, it is the memory system that mediates time travel.
>
> (2003: 332)

Autobiographical memory involves a sense of self at some time in the past (Siegel, 1999). There are lots of things "we just know" about the world, and there are specific episodes we recollect, remembering ourselves situated in the past. According to Wheeler et al., to episodically remember an event is a capacity that comprises more than just memory; it encompasses autonoetic consciousness and the capability for mental time travel. The development of autonoetic consciousness and of autobiographical memory does not happen automatically, simply as a result of maturation. As Siegel points out (2001b: 1002) the quality of attachment and interpersonal communication with caregivers enhances the development of autonoetic consciousness. In the following chapter, the cultural impact on autobiographical memory will be discussed. From a developmental perspective, an event may be remembered first implicitly, then later by the semantic memory system that allows conscious recognition, and, finally, as a contextually localized episode.[6] Infantile amnesia, our lack of personal recollections from early infancy, is ascribed to the immaturity of the episodic memory system and autonoetic consciousness. Siegel (1999: 44) mentions limited narrative capacity in order to explain infantile amnesia.

Autobiographical memory should be regarded as a (significant) part of episodic memory. Besides autobiographical memories of experience, our participation in narrative practices eventually allows for a recollection of explicitly remembered episodes told by others, stories about ourselves or stories about somebody else appropriated as vicarious experience.

Klein et al. (2004) list three conditions for a memory to be experienced as an autobiographical memory:

1   the capacity for self-reflection
2   the feeling of personal ownership of one's actions, and
3   the ability to think in a temporal way about personal occurrences.[7]

As we acquire autobiographical memory and the capability for mental time travel, it becomes possible to go beyond the confines of the situated context. We may travel from here and now to there and then, and our capability to understand what is going on and to confront what is going to happen is immensely expanded as we can, because of this mental time travel, consciously negotiate meaning with a background of lived experience. Recollections of episodes communicated through narratives of vicarious experience add to this capacity. Telling about events enhances our episodic memory as well as when we engage in silent, non-verbal repetition.[8] In the communicative exchange of stories of personal experience we also become embedded in cultural communities and create social ties.

Both episodes of vicarious experience and personal autobiographical memories have a narrative structure as we use a narrative organization to make sense of a demarcated period of time. Not all of what we tell – and remember – about ourselves and our lives is, however, episodic. We summarize, generalize, use bits of categorical or generic knowledge memory, and we continuously develop our implicit patterns and mental models of the world.

The different kinds of memory work together. Siegel suggests: "We sense, perceive, or filter our explicit memory through the mental models of implicit memory" (1999: 43). Previous explicit memories are, perhaps, later forgotten, or become part of our implicit habit system. I also want to argue that some episodic knowledge eventually may become part of the general fund of semantic knowledge. How the different kinds of memory work together comes to the fore when we have to unlearn and relearn. We often apply very different devices simultaneously in order to memorize new procedures or codes.[9]

A recollection of an episode a couple of years ago may illustrate the different kinds of memory. I visited a newly divorced neighbor who had moved to another town and bought a standard house, similar to one I had lived in 35 years previously. As she was showing me her house I spontaneously remembered the period 35 years ago when I was living in a similar house. My recollections of myself in this context were distinctly embodied; I knew exactly how to move around in her house, where to expect and find the lights in the bathroom. When we entered the kitchen, which had a small table, I suddenly remembered having listened to the radio, broadcasting the landing on the moon in 1969, sitting at a similar table in a similar kitchen; a typical autobiographical memory of an outstanding event. The view of the stove triggered memories of cooking red pepper sauce in a cast-iron frying pan. I had made that sauce several times back then so this was not a recollection of a singular event but a summary of several occasions, a so-called prototype memory. During my visit many different memories were evoked, but my biggest surprise was how accurately my body remembered how to move about in a specific environment after such a long time.[10]

The act of remembering

> Memory is central to mental functioning and plays a key role in numerous aspects of our everyday lives. Recollecting the concert we attended last week, recalling the plot of a favorite novel, acquiring the knowledge and skills to perform a new job – each of these and countless other cognitive feats depend on the effective operation of our memory systems. Without memory, our awareness would be confined to an eternal present and our lives would be virtually devoid of meaning.
>
> (Schacter & Scarry, 2001: 1)

The influence of culture, including language and narratives, on memory is immense. Ricoeur states: "It becomes legitimate to suppose that it is always in historically limited cultural forms that the capacity to remember (*faire mémoire*) can be apprehended" (2004: 392). Material objects may serve as triggers, and the availability of interested interlocutors plays a decisive role in determining what we remember or forget. Both the context of "encoding" and of "retrieving" an episode influences the capability to recall the event. What we remember or forget also depends on the frequency of recall. Some memories are spontaneous, others we have to search for; some are voluntary, while others are not.

Ricoeur (2004) discusses the difference between spontaneous recollections and memories we actively search for and hope to find. How memories are triggered by associations is a very interesting issue, in connection with both developmental psychology and cultural psychology and learning. Social practices of remembering take place between caregivers and infants, between family members, friends, and colleagues, and in many other interpersonal relationships. We evoke and supply memories in interpersonal interaction and create, simultaneously, a common history and collective versions of the past.[11]

I mentioned earlier that we do not possess a hard disc with files full of stored information nor a messy lumber room with fragments of the past in our brains.

As early as 1932 Bartlett stated that "the past is being continually re-made, reconstructed in the interests of the present." The present situation, the inter-personal relations and the social context we are embedded in, together with our current knowledge, affect our memories of the past. Cameron, Wilson, and Ross (2004) researched the distortions we are likely to create, "the presentism bias," which makes us look at the past differently. People are, for instance, likely to assume that they learned more from a course or an education than they actually did in order to flatter their present self. This is no surprise in a culture like ours with its emphasis on personal, progressive development. Ross and Buehler (1994: 14) suggest that we are likely to rewrite our stories when they do not fit our contemporary ideas any longer.

> In a well-known analogy, Neisser (1967) compared the act of remembering to the paleontologist's task of reconstructing a dinosaur from a few pieces of bone. The paleontologist's reconstruction is guided by the fossil remains, as well as by his or her current understanding of biology and dinosaurs. The same remains might have yielded a quite different reconstruction 100 years earlier, because of shifts in scientific knowledge. Similarly, people reconstruct and interpret episodes from their pasts by using the bits and pieces they retrieve from memory together with their current knowledge and under-standing of themselves and their social world. When relevant knowledge and understanding changes with time, so too might memory even if the informa-tion retrieved remains constant.
>
> (Cameron et al., 2004: 207)

The probability that the retrieved information does not remain constant, but changes a little every time it is retrieved, makes "the presentism bias" of even greater significance.[12] Siegel, who defines memory storage as "the change in probability of activating a particular neural network pattern in the future" (1999: 25) and who adds: "[i]f the pattern is fired repeatedly, the probability of future activation is further increased" (1999: 24), has used the metaphor of a path in high grass trodden by repeated walks as an image of the changes in synaptic con-nections created by several recalls. We are likely to follow our footsteps and, eventually, a path will appear. We do not, however, place our feet accurately, like we did during the earlier walks (personal communication). Frequently retrieved memories, thus, correspond to increasing synaptic strength in the neural net-works in question. Siegel says of our reconstructions of the past:

> This reconstruction process may be profoundly influenced by the present environment, the questioning context itself, and other factors, such as cur-rent emotions and our perception of the expectations of those listening to the response. Memory is not a static thing, but an active set of processes.
>
> (1999: 28)

The lack of the accuracy of our memories, due to the continuous processing of previous impressions, is, of course, a problem for the reliability of testimony.[13] But the continuous processing of impressions has very positive results for the way we function in our interaction with the environment. Hyman (1999) suggests that our flexible memory is a good thing as our world and we ourselves are constantly changing. There is a more pressing need to adjust to the changes than to remember old versions of our surroundings. Another advantage has to do with the emotional intensity of certain memories. Freud has already pointed out how the emotional intensity of painful memories is gradually reduced by many repeated recalls (1920). Doris Lessing (1972) created a forceful image of this phenomenon in her novels about Martha Quest. The protagonist tells about a painful event to which she, after a long time span, is finally able to return; and now the act of remembering is like putting her hand into very hot water, realizing that she is able to withdraw her hand when the burning of the water gets too painful.

This shows exactly how this voluntary, conscious withdrawal from a painful memory is not possible as long as the emotional intensity of the implicit and explicit memory is so powerful that the present is flooded by the past. Traumatic memories are so painful as long as they are not integrated into a more meaningful configuration of experience because they continue to appear with the original intensity, unmodified by the normal continuous processing and the desensitization which accompanies it.[14]

We can have too many memories as well as too few. Ross and Buehler (1994: 219) quote Nietzsche's (1874/1983) observation: "It is possible to live almost without memory … but it is altogether impossible to live at all without forgetting." Ricoeur reminds us with a subtle irony that, as we grow old, we have more memories but a reduced capacity for remembering (2004). The issue of forgetting has implications for a narrative theory. Both the beginning and the end of a human life are beyond our individual capability of conscious recollection. We have to rely on others to complete our individual stories; as individuals we are definitely cut off from an absolute completion. Our individuality is founded on, and intertwined with, interpersonal relationships. Our stories include the stories of others, just as we are part of the stories others are telling.

The cultural narratives will influence not only how we tell about our lives, but also how we remember our lives. Memories we can tell to others are dressed in language and hold an embodied, emotional, and sensuous quality.

The famous Swedish novelist Kerstin Ekman plays in one of her books *Gör mig levande igen* (*Make me alive again*) (1996) with the connotations of the constructed word: "re-membering." The concept of fragmentation: disjecta membra (the fragmented members or limbs) is contrasted with the act of remembering (and telling), as putting together pieces of what was, in order to make it whole and alive again in the story.[15]

Chapter 6

Early interactions

Transitional space and symbolization

Autonoetic consciousness allows us to be aware of our protracted experience across subjective time and to perceive the present as a continuation of the past and as a prelude to the future (Wheeler et al., 1997: 335). This experience of continuity is a result of a responsive interaction between infants and caregivers, as discussed in Chapter 4 with reference to Trevarthen (1993), Schore (2003), Siegel (1999) and Cozolino (2002, 2006). According to Winnicott (1971) trust in the future is built up from many repeated instances of satisfactory interactions. A sense of continuity is gradually established across a number of not too serious disruptions of attentive presence. From being together with familiar caregivers, the feeling of belonging and of feeling felt emerges in the infant. Winnicott describes the importance of a transitional object in this process, a comforting object which symbolizes the secure presence and attachment. The transitional object is neither just a subjective idea nor an objective thing; the point is that it is both. The condition for its continuous existence and function is that we refrain from trying to solve the paradox, whether it was something the infant made up, or found. It exists and works because the infant found it and made it up at the same time.

The transitional object is established in the intermediary area between magical and symbolic thinking. Winnicott speaks of the potential and transitional space between caregiver and infant that leaves room for differentiation and the development of the use of symbols. What is internal can be made external, real and working, by articulating it using social symbols. The image of the mother audibly expressed can make her appear in person. Expressing the two words "Daddy – comforter" in the middle of the night can make the father get up and bring the infant the lost comforter. The acquisition of a common code is so great an achievement that it almost feels magical; magical in the same way as the transitional object, which was a self-made symbol from where the infant enters the world of culturally coded, common symbols of which "mum" and "dad" belong to the first. Hallucinations remain private, but the use of cultural symbols allows us to encounter our imaginations from the outside, as perceived through our senses; and then we can share our internal worlds with others in symbolic play, in narratives, and in other cultural activities that unfold in time and space.

We are familiar with the pleasure and enjoyment that infants show when we are naming the different elements in the environment, when they gain access to the common denominators, just as we are familiar with the pleasure of sharing experiences throughout life. By the common codes of symbolization, I and you become attached to each other in a potential space. The use of symbols transforms the original transitional space into a space of cultural communication. The use of symbols also gives access to a cultural space beyond subjectivity and objectivity, something we simultaneously find and create.[1] Communication in play and narrative enables a sense of community with the other, provides a feeling of a mutual experience, and of a mutual construction of and participation in internal and external reality. What is symbolized may be repeated, re-experienced, re-narrated, and materialized, for example as a text or a picture, available for later repetitions in a cultural system of signs so that we can establish a sense of belonging across the passing of time.

"What is that?" is soon replaced by "Why is that?" in order to capture and test cultural explanations, causations, and motivations. Soon the young child has access to the negotiation of meaning and sense making by entering the world of narrative practices. When we enter into narrative we move from the feeling of what happens towards the meaning of what happens.

From here and now to there and then

Vibeke Grøver Aukrust (1995) researched the development of narrative competence in a kindergarten in Norway. She investigated the communication between the young children and the staff which took place while the children had their diapers changed. With the youngest infants the staff initiated little narratives of here and now explaining what they were doing.

> Oh! You are all wet, so we'll give you a clean diaper. First we take off the pants, then we'll give you a wash, then we'll dry you, and then you'll get a clean diaper, and then we put your clothes back on.

This kind of communication with children, in which nurses are also skilled, provides information about a sequence of actions and offers some security during the interaction.[2] By and by, the little narratives in the washroom included a longer time span extending from: "And afterwards we are going to read a book" to "conversations" about what took place the day before and about what was going to happen tomorrow. Gradually, the young children began actively to participate in the conversations. Aukrust explains how the staff attributed meaning to the infants' exclamations. The adults supplied and added words and sense to what the children tried to express, and ascribed some interpretation of the infants' contributions.

Very often, caregivers verbally interpret pre-verbal infants, finding causes for their changing moods, their intentions and reactions, and overtly express their interpretations. Children's acts of meaning and their attempts at sense making are appropriated in various degrees until the children are able to claim a different perspective and interpretation.[3] Aukrust also found another device used by the staff; that of overhearing what the infants were trying to say. In this way, the young children were socialized to tell narratives in culturally compatible ways. As they grew bigger they learned to tell stories about something which was new to the interlocutor, instead of telling something she already knew. Young children have no objection to telling or to listening to the same story again and again. It is obvious that young children love repetition; to them so much of the world is new, so little is familiar.

The expression "narrative appropriation" I owe to Peggy Miller and her colleagues (Miller et al., 1989: 302): "When caregivers tell stories about the child or intervene in the child's storytelling, they are implicitly appropriating the *child's* experience overlapping with their own."

There is good evidence for this suggestion. However, one may argue that personal experiences are always colored by the cultural environment in which we live. Small children, however, quite often passively accept an adult's interpretations of their experiences and feelings, even though they do not always feel "right," either because they lack the capability verbally to express an alternative viewpoint, or because a less attentive environment with highly asymmetrical power relations suppresses the child's own voice.[4]

I was supervisor of a Danish study on the application of narratives in kindergartens and preschools. The staff made picture books with the children using photographs from everyday life in the institutions in order to support children's memory, sense of coherence and narrative skills. But the study showed that the adults appropriated the children's experience to a very high degree, as they wrote short sentences to signify what the photos represented. When the children were asked what was shown in the photos, they had quite different ideas about their meanings.

Miller (1994: 164) studied the culturally specific narrative environments that children inhabit. Children are included in narrative practices in different ways; stories are told *around* the children, *about* the children, and *with* the children, and all three types of stories influence children's self-perception.[5] Children's participation in narrative practices gives access simultaneously to the experiences of other people and to events and happenings they are not able to remember themselves.

One of the most closely studied infants was Emily, whose dialogues with her father and subsequent soliloquies at night-time were recorded between her eighteenth month and third year (Nelson, *Narratives from the crib*, 1989, see also Nelson and Fivush, 2004).The development in her narratives was studied by a number of prominent researchers and has since been taken up in several books on narrative (see, for example, Bruner, 1990; Ochs & Capps, 2001). I agree with Bruner, when he suggests that she was doing more than simply reporting what happened but was "trying to make sense of her everyday life" (1990: 89). Her narrative advances were driven by a need to create meaning. Sometimes several versions were tried out in order to find a satisfactory explanation of why things happened in particular ways. It is very interesting to see how she eventually makes use of temporal markers like "because," "always," and "and then" and gradually masters temporal sequencing in her narratives.

Double processing, being simultaneously here and now and there and then, is a necessary condition for narration beyond the proto-narrative of a mere sequence taking place in the present. Wolf (1990) talks about the development of an authorial self, sufficiently independent of a given situation to select different voices and perspectives. In a dialogue between a mother and a two-year-old boy who had just returned from kindergarten, Wolf shows the child's ability to change context (1990: 191):

Mother:	Here give me the mittens.
	(J holds out his hands and his mother tugs off the mittens.)
Mother:	Those are wet. Did you play in the snow this afternoon?
J:	We made a snowman. A big one.
Mother:	Yeah? Did you give him a face?
J:	Rocks … eyes.
	(Outside the late afternoon train rolls by.)
J:	Train's coming. [*He listens for a minute and then looks back to his mother.*] And sticks for his arms.
Mother:	No wonder these mittens are sopping.

Wolf describes how children, eventually, learn to edit their expressions, and to apply multiple voices and perspectives. Children become narrators who can represent the "same event" in different ways, they learn to change context, engage in symbolic play, enter and leave fictions and imagined worlds, and to move freely between here and now and there and then. But before they reach this level they learn to remember and to tell stories in culturally specific ways.

Memory talk

"Remembering is a skill, first learned by young children in social settings. We all begin, in childhood, by remembering with and for other persons; only later are we able to spin narratives just for ourselves" (Neisser, 1994: 11). Fivush (1994: 136) expresses the matter in these terms: "By examining the ways in which adults structure conversations about the past with their children, we can begin to explore how children come to represent and understand their own experiences."

The title of Catherine Snow's contribution to the book *The self in transition* (Cicchetti & Beeghly, 1990), "Building memories: The ontogeny of autobiography" is significant in this context. She assumes the notion "that an individual's self is a socially constructed and socially maintained phenomenon." Parents contribute to the selection of incidents to include in the auto/biographies, and to the selection of canonical versions of those incidents (1990: 214). She says:

> In collaboration with their children to tell and retell stories about personally experienced events, parents are building up a system of narrative memories that elaborate upon (if they do not replace entirely) the memories of events as originally experienced.
>
> (1990: 221)

She points to a significant issue concerning the narrative development in the interactions between parents and children – the amount of shared knowledge. Adults' support of early narrative endeavors depends on the amount of shared knowledge. It is so much easier to understand what the young child is talking about if she is referring to a shared experience. And it may be difficult to make sense of an account from a different context. This problem increases in cultural contexts such as the Nordic countries which have a very high level of employed women because the children, from an early age, spend several hours in institutions; the transfer between two different contexts, the family and the pedagogical institution increases the problem of communication and shared knowledge across the two communities of practice.[6] Development of autobiographical memory and narrative competence thus depends on how much time the young child spends together with adults who collaborate with the child in telling about what has happened (and what is going to happen), and on the amount of, and conditions for, shared experience.

Collaboration on memory talk between young children and parents has frequently been researched in an American context (Fivush & Reese, 1992; Reese & Fivush, 1993; Fivush, 1994; Farrant & Reese, 2000; Fivush & Vasudeva, 2002; Nelson & Fivush, 2004;[7] Nelson, 1993, 2005b; Engel, 1986; Hudson, 2002, McCabe & Peterson, 1991; Miller, 1994; Miller et al., 1989; Ochs & Capps, 2001 among others).

Fivush and Reese distinguish an "elaborate" style of communication and a "repetitive" style of communication. Parents who belong to the elaborate category engage in long conversations with their children, give a lot of details and unfold the stories to support the children's memory. They may include emotional aspects, telling not only about what happened but also of the actor's emotions, and they emphasize what makes sense and creates meaning. Repetitive parents, however, do not provide supporting background information but focus on repeating the same questions in order to elicit "the right answers." The categories are, however, not completely distinct in practice. Repetitive parents tend to become more elaborate as the children grow older and provide more information, but the different styles may, nevertheless, result in unequal development of autobiographical memory and narrative skills.

The authors also maintain that parents are more likely to engage in memory talk with girls than with boys and more often use more emotional expressions in the narrative endeavors with girls. The co-constructed narratives (in American white middle-class settings) display culturally gendered differences (for example, modeling distinct appropriate emotional reactions for girls and boys respectively).

Our memory is influenced by multiple recollections and by the social conditions in, and culturally specific ways of telling about, the past. Miller (1994: 175) highlights Bartlett's observation that "reconstructive memory work is socially distributed." And the narratives from autobiographical memory are deeply immersed in other people's stories. When I ask interviewees to tell me about their first memory, I frequently get the reply that they are uncertain if they actually remember this specific event, or if it is something they have been told by their parents. Some of the stories *about* the child, and *around* the child easily become part of the autobiographical narrative. Some "family stories" are repeated on many occasions; they create affiliations, and shape identity and autobiographical memory in the same process.

Using fiction

Young children are not only exposed to, and invited to, co-construction of narratives of personal experience – including family narratives from the time before the child was born and narratives from her youngest days before the development of autobiographical memory; from an early age children grow up with narratives from the realm of fiction. In contemporary society the production of books for children is enormous,[8] but storytelling also played a significant role in pre-modern oral societies.

Fictional narratives enter young children's repertoire of stories along with personal narratives of vicarious experience. They fuel children's imagination and supply personal narratives in specific ways. Fictional narratives give access to a variety of "possible worlds" (Bruner, 1986). Often, fictional narratives contain intense emotions and may cause strong emotional reactions in the listener. They supply an everyday exposure to themes and issues which may go well beyond what is normally talked about between children and adults.

Another important aspect of the function of fictional narratives is the poetic impact. Bretherton (1993), making reference to Stern (1985), discusses the shortcomings of language concerning a richly faceted representation of lived experience. She states: "On the one hand [language] makes experience more sharable with others, but on the other hand it may drive a wedge between experience as lived and as narrated" (1993: 257). In my view, fictional narratives, on the contrary, may enhance the acquisition of new linguistic possibilities. The aesthetic language of narratives and their poetic impact may provide possibilities for adequate, sensitive, and sensuous expressions of experience. Furthermore, not only do we use language to find a way of expressing our feelings and experiences, but, simultaneously, language influences and shapes our feelings and experiences. Fictional stories fuel children's creativity and imagination. The decisive factor is the richness of the narratives of everyday communication and the quality of the repertoire of fictional narratives. If the theory of the mirror-neuron system is correct, narratives – including fictional narratives – have a considerable impact on the developing minds of the recipients.

A wonderful story of a young child's use of a fictional narrative is reported by Miller, Hoogstra, Mintz, Fung and Williams in a chapter of *Memory and affect in development* (1993). "Troubles in the garden and how they get resolved" discusses the function of the retellings of "The Tale of Peter Rabbit." The little boy, Kurt, is almost two years old when he is introduced to this story of Beatrix Potter. Peter Rabbit soon becomes his favorite story, and during the next four or five weeks he repeatedly requests that the story is read aloud to him. During this period he produces five different retellings of the story. In these retellings he, in various degrees, includes himself and his personal experiences from his grandparents' garden. The retellings produce alterations from the written story and culminate in a reconfiguration of the plot. The reconfigurations move towards a gradual solution of the conflicting elements of the story. In the later versions, Peter Rabbit no longer violates the human cultural norms for gardening (that you should not destroy anything but are to plant and care for what is growing). He is no longer naughty so he has no conflict with his mother; on the contrary, he is with her and the other little rabbits all the time; the mother is holding his hand. Thus, he does not fear what happens in the garden anymore, and in the last version even the conflict with the terrifying Mr. McGregor is resolved as the former enemy is planting parsley in the garden with the rabbits. All the fears from the written story have eventually been eliminated in Kurt's edited retellings.

In the analysis of the retellings, Miller et al. refer to Bakhtin's concept of multiple voices and the idea of borrowing a voice from somebody else and populating it with other motives. Besides the many fine explanations of Kurt's strong involvement in the story, whose conflicts parallel his emotional experiences and the threats of disruption to his secure relations with his mother and grandparents, I find in the presented material one more conflict that may explain the little boy's preoccupation. Peter Rabbit's mother forbids Peter to play in McGregor's garden because his father lost his life there and ended up in a pie. If this could happen to the father, it may also happen to the mother. The fear of losing the mother is voiced in some of the versions. In the second retelling, both Mother Rabbit and Peter are run over by a car, and several versions show an ambiguity in the voices, both relating to Kurt and Peter and to Mother Rabbit and Peter's mother. This fear completely disappears in the last version in which all of them are planting parsley together; it is even allowable and acceptable to eat parsley from the garden.[9]

I remember another instance of reconfiguration from my own early childhood. I had been frequently exposed to fictional stories and also to spontaneous creative productions of imagined narratives, so it was quite natural that I should try to create fictions myself. I had learned the letters of the alphabet, but I did not know how to read. So I put down lots of letters in an arbitrary order in a notebook, illustrated the stories, and read them aloud to my brothers. One story was about a girl who fell into a pond; a drawing depicted the main event. As I read the story aloud, my brother provided me with the puzzling information that I, by chance, had written the word "cheese" on one of the pages. The authority of the elder brother who went to school and knew how to read and write was overwhelming, so I had to somehow make a cheese fit into the story of the girl who fell into a pond. I remember that this challenge caused me trouble. I, finally, succeeded in producing a reconfiguration and a retelling that included the cheese, but as the code of writing was private, the plot of the story is long gone.

Chapter 7

Narrative competence

Features of narrative competence

From the early proto-conversations through the fascinating landscape of symbolization, children participate in communication with their caregivers, listen to stories, engage in memory talk and gradually acquire narrative competence. Obviously, the narrative environment in which children grow up is of inestimable significance. The cultural environment may or may not be supportive. Some children grow up without much interpersonal communication, others are lucky enough to be in an environment full of responsive interaction and rich narrative activity.

The focus on the acquisition of narrative competence is slowly gaining more credence. In *The culture of education* (1996) Bruner suggested that, in spite of its significance, the understanding of narrative competence was still inadequate. Over the years, the role of narrative has appeared in some educational and pedagogical settings, and in educational research.[1] But there is still a very long way to go before the acquisition of narrative competence becomes an integral part of the curriculum for teachers, not least preschool teachers, and is considered a natural part of the upbringing of children. The inquiry into narrative competencies and their impact may, hopefully, open the way for this development in the curriculum of teacher education.

During one decade of research I have tried to pin down the features of narrative competence, inspired by the writings of Bruner and Siegel in particular,[2] and by empirical narrative research (see Chapter 12).

I propose that narrative competence involves:

- autonoetic consciousness
- articulateness
- integration of experience
- regulation of emotion
- sense making
- identity work
- future planning
- different perspectives

- negotiation of meaning
- open-mindedness
- attentiveness
- understanding other minds
- community building
- dialogical communication
- reflexivity
- analytic ability.

I shall discuss these mental and interpersonal functions one by one.

Autonoetic consciousness

The awareness of existence beyond the present, the temporal consciousness of being embodied in a world across the past, the present, and the future, has already been mentioned in the first chapter of this book. It is a necessary condition for the following functions, and a capability acquired in the second or third year of life, depending on the interpersonal environment in which the child grows up. Autonoetic consciousness may temporarily deteriorate in the case of severe trauma (Wheeler et al., 1997; Horsdal, 2007a).

Articulateness

A very significant aspect of narrative competence is the development of children's command of language and articulateness. The power of expression is the first condition for having a voice. And this is learned by practice. The samples of life stories indicate that skilled narrators very often grew up in a storytelling family. The power of expression matters if people are to exercise their rights as citizens. Articulateness concerns more than fluency and diction; the scope of what may be expressed – emotions, sensations, thoughts – depends, to a high degree, on this aspect of narrative competence.[3]

Integration of experience

As long as everyday life proceeds as usual, we can follow familiar routines unquestioned and unchallenged, relying on implicit knowledge, traditional explanations and habits. Modern life in contemporary society is, however, characterized by rapid changes and unforeseen events. When something is happening which we did not expect, our scheme of things may fall apart; when our picture of the world is shaken we may have to reconfigure our interpretation of existence. Narrative competence is the best resource we have to navigate in the space between rigidity and chaos.

As mentioned in Chapter 5 on memory, the flexibility of autobiographical memory assists us in recognizing what is "the same" in spite of minor changes.

We recognize a path we followed some time ago despite some changes in the landscape. We have to accept change continually. Children grow up, people grow old, neighborhoods are torn down, and new blocks are built. In between, dramatic events occur in our lives: separation, illness, loss, as well as happier events. We have to integrate all this into our models of the world. "Creating coherence is a lifetime project. Integration is thus a process, not a final accomplishment. It is a verb, not a noun," Siegel says (1999: 336). "As integration occurs, the creation of coherence represents the flow of states of the system on the 'fertile ground between order and chaos' – a path of resonance with a balanced trajectory between rigidity and randomness" (p. 322).

The capacity for integrating radical change and constructing a meaningful spatiotemporal coherence depends on responsive communication and co-construction of narratives. We all know from experience how narrative competence and a responsive environment facilitate the integration of disturbing transformations. It is so much easier to be reconciled with violent change if we have someone with whom we can discuss what has happened.

Regulation of emotion

Metaphors such as "I was out my mind," "I was not myself," and deliberations on possible causes of unexpected emotional reactions indicate some of our difficulties with the integration of different emotional mental states. The construction of reasonably coherent narratives supports the integration of deviating incidents and thus helps us to accept a "self" (oneself or the self of another) which may be variously sad, happy, angry, warm, and distant in different situations with high emotional impact. The story of Kurt is an excellent example of the regulation of emotion through narrative enactment. In a commentary on Miller et al., DeHart asks if the narrative form in itself provides a tool for the regulation of emotions (1993: 118). Personally, I am sure this is the case, considering the emotional and embodied aspect of narratives. Oppenheim, Nir, Warren, and Emde also propose a relationship between regulation of emotion and narrative. When children construct narratives it helps them to tackle potential conflict material and construct prosocial themes (1997: 284).

Sense making

Making sense of what happened before and what is happening now, and how these things are connected, is the essence of our narrative endeavors. As a narrative provides a situated perspective on occurrences and actions it gives us *a* solution to a problem, *an* explanation of cause and intention of an action, *a* construction of meaning. We do not just repeat the past or start anew from nothing. We need to make sense and to apply analogical thinking when we confront "deviations from a canonical pattern" (Bruner, 1990) or simply initiate interactions with an unfamiliar world in new places, and as newcomers in communities of practice. We all know the temporary worries or despairs when we cannot "make things fit together," when "it does not add up," and when things fall apart as we cannot make sense of what is going on and why. Our narrative repertoire with its variety of cultural plotlines is our primary toolbox for understanding the world and our interactions with it. We use stories as parables, possible models for future actions (Turner, 1996). But narrative competence involves more than just a selection of the best fit among cultural configurations of meaning. Sometimes we have to construct and create new meaning in opposition to dominant beliefs. Sometimes, unfortunately, atrocities and violence may occur which are utterly senseless.

Identity work

This concept emphasizes – in line with "integration" – the dynamic aspect of identity.[4] Identity work is about becoming. When we encounter transitions in the trajectories of our lifelong journeys we are confronted with the question of identity: How will this transformation influence my interpretation of self? What self will emerge in interactions in new places, new relationships, and new situations? And how will this emerging self connect to, or transform, prior interpretations and constructions of self and identity?

Interpersonal relationships are an integral part of identity. Although the grand narrative of Western modernity focuses on the individual and emphasizes individual autonomy and individual choice, we are fundamentally interdependent and interconnected. Identity work encompasses both the temporal aspects and the interpersonal relationships in old and new contexts. Thus, we cannot restrict ourselves to having at our disposal a number of roles to play in various changing contexts. Identity is primarily a narrative construction, based, however, on embodied experience in interaction with the environment. Insufficient narrative skills leave the narrative construction of identity exclusively to others.

Future planning

If we do not know who we are, where we are, or how we got here, our ability to plan for the future is practically non-existent. We cannot really make plans for what we are going to do in the future if we are mentally overwhelmed by present problems or preoccupied by anxiety-provoking memories of the past. In a traditional society, people had fewer choices to make; many would simply follow the in footsteps of their ancestors. Today, we have to choose all the time, and we feel individually responsible for making the "right" choice. Furthermore, long-time planning is less safe than in a more traditional society. It is unlikely that you can plan your career as a child or adolescent and remain on the same path until retirement. Walter et al. (2002) talk of "yo-yo-ization" when they describe the contemporary transition from adolescence to adulthood. And this example of the frequent need for re-planning only refers to working life and lifelong learning. In other parts of our lives we also have choices to make and plans to consider.

Different perspectives

The possibility of telling different stories from different perspectives about the same event helps us to comprehend that we, as embodied human beings situated in time and space, cannot survey the world, and the truth of the world, once and for all from an omnipotent perspective. To quote Mary Catherine Bateson:

> The quality of improvisation characterizes more and more lives today, lived in uncertainty, full of inklings of alternatives. In a rapidly changing and interdependent world, single models are less likely to be viable and plans more likely to go awry. The effort to combine multiple models risks the disasters of conflict and runaway misunderstanding, but the effort to adhere blindly to some traditional model for a life risks disaster not only for the person who follows it but for the entire system in which he or she is embedded, indeed for all the other living systems with which that life is linked.
>
> (Bateson, 1994: 8)

Negotiation of meaning

Different perspectives allow us to combine multiple models of the world, and therefore enable us to negotiate in the never-ending pursuit of meaning in between authenticity and doubt "in the fertile ground between order and chaos" (Siegel, 1999). Narratives have, as Bruner (1986, 1990) states, a "subjunctive" character that makes them especially suitable for negotiation of meaning. Narrative causality deals with abduction – a hypothesis put forward to explain a puzzling phenomenon – but confined to the temporally unfolded event or course of events (see Chapter 1). In *Sources of the self. The making of modern identity*, Taylor talks of "the BA principle" in favor of tentative truth claims: the Best Account so far (1989).

Open-mindedness

Of course, negotiation of meaning presupposes an open mind toward different perspectives, toward new ways of looking at things, and new comprehensions of actions and happenings. Access to an abundance of narratives – not least personal life story narratives that provide us with the opportunity vicariously to accompany the life-journeys of other human beings – is a viable short cut to an open mind. Together with fictional narratives, they support our imagination. At the same time, a responsive environment, supportive of curious explorations, and securing a safe emergence is equally indispensable for the development of an open mind. The interconnectedness of the stories and the cultural space in which they are told and listened to remains inseparable.

Attentiveness

Not only should children learn how to tell stories, but they should also learn how to listen. From everyday experience we all know someone to whom it is far more important to hold the floor than to allow others to finish what they are saying. Older people tell in their life story narratives how they, as young children, sat in a corner or under the table and listened to stories when guests arrived. They sometimes learned to listen rather than to express themselves. Today, in some environments, almost the opposite is the case. Listening attentively, with an open mind, to what the other is about to tell with patience and empathic respect for the other's right to a voice, and with curiosity concerning the unknown path we are travelling during the story, is a distinguishing feature of narrative competence.

Understanding other minds

The literature on developmental psychology frequently deals with young children's gradual capability for understanding that others may have a different view of things, a different knowledge of things, and different feelings from themselves. The point here is not to enter into these discussions,[5] but simply to underscore how a rich narrative practice assists children in this development.

Community building

Sharing narratives builds communities. We create a common past through narratives and establish affiliations through our stories. Stories accomplish a sense of belonging to families, institutions, organizations, to physical or to imagined communities. Shared stories constitute a common fund of collective knowledge and memory. Narrative is the glue that makes us stick together, and join each other on our future journeys through the sharing of our dreams and plans.

Dialogical communication

Within this concept I intend to combine some of the features and implications of narrative competence mentioned above, such as open-mindedness, attentiveness, understanding other minds, and negotiation of meaning, in order to point to a type of communication that differs from arguments which you want to win, or statements that you only put forward to prove your superiority, or as a rhetorical means to accomplish some goal. Dialogical communication does not necessarily end up in agreement. To listen attentively and with empathic respect to another perspective on the world does not imply that you should appropriate the interpretation of existence of your interlocutor. The aim of a dialogical communication is not consensus but a widened horizon, a more comprehensive interpretive framework. It is a way of encountering the other. Both the sameness and the otherness of the other's expression of experience contribute to a more spacious mind.

Reflexivity

Several sociologists (Beck, Giddens, & Lash, 1994; Giddens, 1990) talk of reflexivity as a core concept in contemporary society due to emancipation from the traditional ways of living. We are, it seems, increasingly personally responsible for making appropriate choices in order to achieve a successful and purposeful life. Without reflexive renegotiations of identity and autobiography it is impossible to accomplish this.

Reflexivity is, furthermore, a concept that plays a role in professional and organizational development and in learning. If we want to improve practices and perform better, or if we want to find out if our actions are in line with our intentions, or if we have to work together in teams, or simply with new partners, we need to reflect on our actions and on their implications. Practice is, in general, executed as tacit knowledge. When we need to make implicit embodied types of behavior explicit to ourselves or to others we depend heavily on narratives.

Finally, reflexivity is another word for "metacognition,"[6] which simply means the ability to think about how we think, to consider the range and conditions for our interpretive frameworks, to think over the implications of our perspectives, and to take heed of the historical and cultural influences on our convictions.

Narratives provide us with possible meanings about what happens. Narrative competence allows us to consider the limits of our knowledge.

Analytic ability

The ability to analyze stories is highly significant in order to realize what and how meanings are constructed; for example, by looking at points of view, moral impact, voices, themes, plot, and genre. In the same way as articulateness is acquired, analytic ability is learned through practice. The immense impact of narratives regarding our interpretations of self and existence and the way we make sense of the world around us makes analytic ability a very important skill. If we cannot critically analyze the stories by which we are surrounded we become easy victims of manipulation and expressions of power relations.

Pedagogic intervention

Compared to the amount of literature discussing interactions between parents and young children and the impact of those interactions on narrative competence (Pillemer & White, 1989; Miller, Potts, Fung, Hoogstra, & Mintz, 1990; Nelson, 1991; Fivush & Reese, 1992; McCabe & Peterson, 1991; Fivush, 1994;

Farrant & Reese, 2000; Fivush, 2004; Nelson & Fivush, 2004, and others), the literature on the acquisition of narrative competence in kindergartens, preschools, and schools is much less comprehensive (Baumer, Ferholt, & Lecusay, 2005; Schwartz, 2003; Mouritsen, 1996; Trahar, 2006; Beattie, 2009, among others). I have already mentioned the interaction between staff and infants in the kindergarten, discussed by Aukrust (1995), and Ochs and Capp's fine book, *Living narrative* (2001).[7] Considering the importance of creating a cultural space in pedagogic settings for development of narrative competence with a focus both on the comprehension and on the production of narratives, I hope to see, in the years to come, a substantial increase in studies relating to this field of research. The call of contemporary society for creativity and innovation may, perhaps, inspire educational initiatives directed towards the support of children's imagination. There is a distance to cover from the mere recognition of the significance of narrative in educational contexts to the development of pedagogic knowledge on the acquisition of narrative competence. Beattie's art-based narrative pedagogy is an important step in this direction.

Several authors discussing narrative practices in education focus on the co-existence of delimiting and emancipating narratives (see, for example, McEwan, 2004 and Gergen, 2004[8]). Of course, narratives of all kinds coexist, but we should pay particular attention to the ambiguities in narrative practices in education. What is the character and form of these practices? What is their function? When I went to school, many years ago, a regular exercise was to write an approximately correct reproduction of a text read aloud by the teacher in order to secure the transmission of cultural, canonical narratives. Today, free narrative productions are more prevalent, in both oral and written form. However, Michaels in McCabe and Peterson (1991) presents depressing examples of negative pedagogic interventions between teachers and pupils, resulting in a "dismantling" of narrative performance due to a mismatch between narrative styles and teacher expectations. "If students are to be evaluated as competent speakers, thinkers, or writers, they must come to control or 'take ' the school-based norms and discourse forms into their own texts" (1991: 301). She analyzes how Afro-American and Latin-American children, socialized with episodic topic-associating narrative styles do not match White teacher's linear topic-centered styles of discourse, and shows how the Black children consequently are interrupted and misevaluated. Michaels concludes that, as we learn to narrate orally and in written form "we acquire not just words or constructions, but ways of making sense, ways of valuing, ways of drawing inferences, as well as perspectives on purposes and audiences for communication" (1991: 345).[9] Anyone who is familiar with the great works of fiction from other continents will be well aware of the fascinating varieties in narrative constructions which are much more complex than the linear topic-centered account.

As a researcher I was attached to a Danish project with the aim of equipping professionals in preschools and schools with methods to support children's narrative potential. After watching video-recordings of the interlocutions between teachers and children, I noticed with surprise the asymmetry in the interaction between the children and the teachers. In order to make my observations explicit to the teachers I came up with a new concept to pin down the communicative genre of the teachers in their "dialogues" with the children: "Appreciative interrogation."[10] The teachers defended themselves by commenting that they normally talked – including to their own children – in this way, questioning the children in an appreciative way. The idea of narrating themselves instead of questioning in order to elicit new stories had never crossed their minds, although adults normally exchange stories when they communicate with one another.

It is good, but not sufficient, that young children have books read aloud to them, that they have access to narratives presented in other media, that they eventually learn to read, or that they are asked to tell the adults stories. Far too often, the child returning home after school is asked, "What happened at school today?" and replies: "Nothing, really"! The cultural environment in which children grow up – both within the family and in educational institutions – strongly affects when and how we tell stories and what and how much we will tell to whom. In an impoverished narrative culture, narratives are only demanded in order to explain why something went wrong. To assist narrative competence, stories should be shared because of inclination, delight, or need. Listening to good storytellers and experiencing the joy of narrating is a good start for the production of stories.

Telling stories in different genres, and from different perspectives, and applying different voices, or discussing their points of view and moral impact, could easily be part of the normal communication between children and adults in different contexts.

Narrative breakdown

As mentioned above, we continuously have to integrate change since life does not stand still. As Beattie puts it:

> Creating a narrative is a process of making sense of a life in the midst of that life and within the wholeness of the life as it is currently understood. It is a process of synthesizing and integrating what is known, of merging the knower and the known, and of making something new.
>
> (2009: 63)

Siegel (2001a) emphasizes the space between rigidity and chaos in the process of narrative integration. He makes a distinction between "a cohesive narrative" which insists on a rigid comprehension of events, and "a coherent" narrative, the dynamic process of creating coherence, which, as mentioned, is an ongoing process, not a final achievement.

We normally negotiate small discrepancies between the narrator I, here and now, and the "me" from long ago in terms of change and transformations ("I have changed a lot since my youth"). Short-term discrepancies due to unusual mental states may be referred to like this: "I was beside myself," or "I was not myself." Apparently incompatible experiences call for sense making in communicative encounters, but if we have a rigid understanding of how things are, and a rigid configuration of the narratives of self and existence, we become more vulnerable in the face of alarming contradictions as our rigid interpretations may break down and leave us in chaos.

Lampinen, Odegard, and Leding have described a phenomenon (2004: 233) which they name "diachronic disunity." Some people seem to experience a loss of diachronic unity as they feel they have changed so much over the years. They apply a metaphor of discontinuity instead of continuity and feel unable to establish a narrative connection between present and past selves. The authors refer to Tulving (2002), who claims that mental time traveling implies a mental time traveler. Diachronic disunity may be related to dissociation and lack of integration. The essentialist conviction that we possess a nuclear self with a stable unity may inhibit the integration of contradictory experiences.

Traumatic experiences may cause temporary deterioration of autonoetic consciousness and the feeling of existence in time (Horsdal, 2007b). Agnieszka Bron (2000) drew my attention to a quotation from Ewa Hoffman's book, *Lost in translation* which accurately expresses this experience:

> I can't afford to look back, and I can't figure out how to look forward. In both directions, I may see a medusa, and I already feel the danger of being turned into stone. Betwixt and between, I am stuck and time is stuck within me. Time used to open out, serene, shimmering with promise. If I wanted to hold a moment still, it was because I wanted to expand it, to get its fill. Now, time has no dimension, no extension backward or forward. I arrest the past, and I hold myself stiffly against the future; I want to stop the flow. As a punishment, I exist in the stasis of a perpetual present, that other side of "living in the present," which is not eternity, but a prison. I can't throw a bridge between the present and the past, and therefore I can't make time move.
>
> (1989: 117)

Ewa Hoffman applies the same metaphor as Siegel (1999) to communicate the experience of stasis: "The prison of the present," and she points to the most significant cause of this unbearable narrative breakdown, the inability to bridge the past and the present.

The – albeit transient and tentative – construction of narrative coherence ensures the feeling of meaning which is indispensable in negotiations between different emerging selves in changing circumstances. A loss of meaning and sense exposes us to chaos and makes us freeze. We find ourselves imprisoned like Kafka's protagonist K. in *Der Process* (1925/1935). Beike, Kleinknecht, and Wirth-Beaumont (2004: 148) refer to Conway and Pleydell-Pearce (2002) and their view that "emotional memories could reinstate (past) signals for action" (p. 271) which would be maladaptive in the present environment. This may happen after a traumatic experience due to disintegration. Kolk (2003) explains:

> Memory is an active and constructive process: the mind constantly reassembles old impressions and attaches them to new information. Memories, instead of precise recollection, are transformed into stories that we tell ourselves and others, in order to convey a coherent narrative of our experience of the world. Rarely do our minds generate precise images, smells, sensations, or muscular actions that accurately replicate earlier experiences.[11]
>
> However, learning from individuals who have been diagnosed with PTSD confronted us with the fact that, after having been traumatized, particular emotions, images, sensations, and muscular reactions related to trauma may become deeply imprinted on people's minds and that these traumatic imprints seem to be reexperienced without appreciable transformation, months, years or even decades after the actual event occurred.
>
> (2003: unnumbered volume)

Building the bridge between the past and the present through narrative integration enables us to live fully in the present. To be present, here and now, to sense, experience, and participate attentively in what happens is difficult if the present is flooded by disturbing and confusing fragments of the past, or by fears of the future. Though it may sound like a paradox, the capability for mental time travel and the experience of being fully present here and now are reciprocally intertwined.

In his book on neuroscience and human relationships, Cozolino (2006) wrote a chapter on narratives and neural integration in which he argues that narratives, besides serving the function of teaching cultural lessons, serve as a means of homeostasis and integration of brain functioning (p. 303). Stories are told and listened to in a temporal sequence but understood as a whole, which is why linear and Gestalt processing, respectively taking place in the left and in the right hemisphere, are brought together and so join activity in both hemispheres, which seems to facilitate integration. Narratives combine explicit memory, general knowledge, sensitivity, emotions, and behavior. Cozolino underscores the evolutionary value of narratives, neurally and socially. Stories contain conflicts and solutions, thoughts and emotions and help us associate dissociated elements of our mental luggage. We learn to find new connections using each other's stories, telling and retelling together. If we are left alone without someone to talk to who cares to listen, we are very exposed, and may be left alone with fragmented and anxiety-provoking experiences.

Integration of experience takes time. Very often, troubling experiences have to be retold again and again in order to find a new configuration that may ensure a more coherent narrative.[12] Cozolino concludes:

> We need each other and our stories to discover ourselves, regulate our emotions, and heal traumatic injuries. Humans serve as external neural circuits that we can use to help each other bridge dissociated neural networks, provide us with new ideas, activate feelings within us that we may be unable to access or have forgotten to remember. When loving others link their brain with ours, the result is a vital integration. We can use our interpersonal resonance, intuition, and empathic abilities to help and heal one another. Human brains have vulnerabilities and weaknesses that only other brains are capable of mending. For human beings (and neurons) relationships are a natural habitat.
>
> (2006: 307)

Chapter 8

The narrative interview

A review of applied research

My interest in the features and functions of narrative, and in the acquisition and impact of narrative competence, grew alongside my fieldwork as a researcher doing biographical research in educational contexts.[1] During two decades of immensely rewarding work with life story narratives I have developed a methodology for biographical research with regard both to the construction and the analysis of the narrative interview, informed by practice and theoretical inquiries. During this time I have met so many inspiring narrators and learned so much from the experiences they have communicated. Before I explain the methods I have developed for doing biographical research I will present a brief overview of the different projects in which I have applied life story narratives in various ways.

The first collection of life stories[2] was published as a textbook for foreign students studying Danish language and culture. I collected 25 life stories with Danes born between 1893 and 1968 representing different social and local backgrounds. Out of the polyphony of individual stories grew a cultural history of social change and identity in Denmark in the twentieth century. Some years later, within the framework of a large research project running from 1997–2000, I continued collecting stories in order to analyze the change in interpretations of self and existence throughout the twentieth century, with a special focus on lifelong learning, identity and democracy. This project resulted in three books and more than 20 articles.[3] One book: *Livets fortællinger* (Life story narratives, 1999), covered the theoretical and methodological approach, another: *Vilje og vilkår. Identitet, læring og demokrati* (Will and circumstance. Identity, learning and democracy, 2000a) the analysis of 120 narrative interviews. In later chapters I shall return to the findings from this project and from some of the following inquiries. In 1999, I took part in a Nordic project using narrative interviews to research the outcome of participation in liberal education related to democracy in Norway, Finland, and Denmark. I also interviewed refugees in a project researching democracy, citizenship and the meeting of cultures.[4] I participated in a European project researching vocational guidance for foreigners.[5] In a further European project in the Grundtvig Socrates program we sought to identify competencies for active citizenship.[6] This involved narrative interviews with young active citizens from Hungary, France, Finland, and Denmark to look at the competencies they possessed and, in particular, how they had been acquired in the perspective of biographical learning. All the life story narratives I have collected and analyzed were handwritten as they were told, as I shall explain below.

I have carried out several evaluation projects in order to research learning outcomes arising from participation in development and research projects. For this, I interviewed young girls with am immigrant background at a folk high school, librarians working with lifelong learning, staff in social care and health care, staff (psychologists, teachers, managers) working with children who lived in institutions, as well as other researchers.[7] Furthermore, I had the privilege of closely following a large number of life story interviews collected by my PhD students, such as interviews with children, adolescents and adults who had received special education, teachers working in special education and students in different programs of professional development.

While this is not an exhaustive list of research projects it should convey the scope and focus of my research. In summary, the main areas of interest are adult education, lifelong learning, professional development, identity, democracy, and intercultural understanding.

Whilst undertaking these research projects I have also sought to expand and develop my theoretical understanding of narrative and of narrative research.[8]

Over that period I developed a method for collecting life story narratives that differs from other existing approaches.[9] I have taught a number of courses on the application of this method in a wide variety of contexts: PhD courses in Denmark and in other Nordic countries, in different educational contexts, and, in psychiatry, in European projects within Education and Culture, and in organizations trying to improve intercultural understanding.

Methodological considerations

Collecting a narrative interview is one kind of communication across "the social synapse."[10] It is an interpersonal interaction that takes place in a cultural space between the interviewer and the interviewee. The former is receiving a gift during this performance as the narrator consents to share her experiences and to allow the listener to accompany her on the journey she is traveling. Gifts should be treated with care and respect. They are freely given; and, to expand the metaphor a little, it is bad manners to force somebody to give a gift, or to complain about the content or the wrapping.

As researchers, we should not treat our interviewees, or the products of our interaction with them, as objects – neither from an ethical nor an epistemological point of view. "Respondents" or "informants" should not be regarded primarily as containers of information that we need in order to accomplish our research, but as human beings whose voices we are grateful to hear, and whose experiences we are grateful to share because they can expand our knowledge of the social, cultural, and phenomenological world we inhabit, widen our horizons and vicariously take us along different paths in space and time.

As researchers in education or cultural studies, we are not evaluators or judges of the narrated biographies, and neither are we therapists who should assist the narrators in the construction of a better story,[11] or try to find hidden causes and explanations in the fissures of the narrative.

But we are, or should aim to be, confidence-inspiring, attentive, and responsive co-constructers of meaning, who, being very aware of our ethical obligations, are diligent in our efforts to minimize the possibility of any manipulation or distorting appropriation of the experiences of the other.

These considerations have methodological implications. But before elaborating on those I will propose a definition of a life story narrative:

> A life story is a situated narrative – a spatio-temporal experientially embodied construction of self and identity in a social world and an interpretation of existence including world view, values and attitudes.

A life story emerging from a narrative interview is an account constructed from the answer to the one and only question posed: "Please, tell me about your life from the beginning until we are sitting here today."

The very first consideration to take into account is whether or not the researcher has the necessary human maturity, courage, and responsive attitude to set out on the journey of vicarious experience in biographical research. We can never know in advance where we are going; and we have to follow all the way, we cannot quit and turn round before the story has come to an end.

Making contact

First of all, we have to consider who to interview and how to establish the initial contact. Obviously, the answer to the first question depends on the type of research. Biographical research covers many different fields (research in education, organization, health, sociological studies, to mention just a few). The number of interviews also varies from samples of more than a hundred interviews to case studies involving only a few stories. The second question depends on the first. In some projects, certain methods for making contact are more appropriate than others.

When I first started to collect life stories 20 years ago, I began by asking my friends and acquaintances. And I always suggest to my students that they carry out a test interview with someone they know in order to try out the method and become familiar with the role of the interviewer. As I wanted a broad representation of different social and regional backgrounds and ages, I continued my search by asking everybody I met if they happened to know some good storytellers. I traveled all over Denmark and contacted a lot of people. Sometimes, I could agree to conduct an interview at short notice; in other cases, when I came across more vulnerable people, I suggested that I could come back in a fortnight or so in order to give them more time to prepare or to decide whether or not to take part.

In later projects I have often used intermediary contacts, e.g. teachers in adult education who could ask their students for volunteers to tell me their story. Another way of making contact is the snowball method; you ask the present interviewee if she knows somebody else who would like to be contacted. When I interviewed members of the immigrant community I often used intermediary contacts, who could assure them of my integrity and respect. This also was necessary when I interviewed young criminals who had very little trust in journalists and reporters.

In other projects I have advertized for interviewees. Actually, over the years many people contacted me on their own account as they wanted me to write their life stories.

When the volunteers have agreed to take part in the research it is very important that they are thoroughly informed about the procedure for the interview, how it is carried out, the rights of the interviewee, the right to quit at any stage, the degree of anonymity, the interviewees' right to have their stories back for proof-reading, and the assurance that nothing will be used without their consent. Also, it is significant that the interviewees are aware of the context of the research, the topic, the intentions, and the applications of the research, although this, obviously, will affect the story that is told. Finally, the interviewees should be informed of their right to choose the place for the interview. Most of the life story narratives I have collected were told in the narrator's private home. I guess this is the place where most people feel at ease. Alternatively, interviews were conducted at the workplace, in educational institutions, in organizations, social institutions, etc. The interviewees sometime ask in advance how long time the interview is going to take. This is largely up to the narrator, but I usually reply to managers and leaders who have a tight schedule that it is likely to be a couple of hours. My own limit for attention and writing is six hours a day.

Compiling biographies

When interviewer and interviewee meet face to face, the information on procedures and rights, etc. mentioned above should be repeated so the interviewee is perfectly clear about what is expected from her. I am very careful about expressing that my interest is to listen to *her* voice, to *her* experiences, to *her* interpretations. It is not a question of what is relevant to me, but what is relevant to the interviewee in her attempt at the construction and negotiation of meaning. This is important since many interviewees – as most narrators – want to engage their listeners and deliver what they think is expected from them in order to make the performance and the time spent together worthwhile. We live in a culture where the life stories of the rich and famous are published. Ordinary people's biographies are rare, and in everyday life very few people seem have time to listen to longer tales. This is why the researcher often hears comments like: "I do hope this is something you can use," or "I am not a very special person." Conscientious interviewees are likely to try to come up with the "right" answers and to present themselves to their audience as a little bit better than they, perhaps, feel they really are.

To avoid this bias, thorough preparation is essential. The other, equally important condition is to go along with the narration all the way to the end without any kind of intervention or interrupting questions during its course.[12] Any form of inquiries eliciting more details or elaborations should not in any way interrupt the telling as this will lead the configuration and emplotment astray. From the beginning of the story until the end, it is completely up to the narrator to choose what to tell, in which order and how; it is completely up to her to decide what is significant or insignificant, as it is completely up to the narrator to omit what she does not want to tell. The configurational act is the narrator's responsibility alone. It goes without saying that if the intention of the narrative interview is to learn about the narrator's interpretation of self and existence or about the meaning of experience and its impact, questions – whether they are part of an interview guide or just of a clarifying nature – will interfere with the construction of meaning through the act of plotting during the telling.[13]

As mentioned above, I, and my students, write the life story narratives by hand.[14] In the beginning, I did this in order to avoid bringing a lot of technical gear into people's homes that might disturb the narrators (many of whom in my first project were quite elderly and not used to modern gadgets). I could sit anywhere with a notebook and a good pencil. But I gradually realized other advantages of handwriting, some of which I found it rather difficult to explain in the beginning. Besides the obvious advantage of being so busy writing and following what the narrator was telling was that I was prevented from intervening and from posing disruptive questions during the performance. My being occupied with attentive listening and writing removed the possibility of any embarrassing pauses in the narrative flow of the teller. I did not in any way stress the narrator when she needed time to reflect. Quite the contrary, breaks and pauses in the telling were welcomed as they helped me to keep up with the pace of the narrator. But there was more to it than that. I used to say that I simply liked to let the stream of words go through my fingers and through my body on their way to symbolization on the paper. I felt this way of doing it created a fertile cultural space between me as a biographer and the narrator who was telling her story. Much later, the theory of the mirror-neuron system and the concept of the social synapse seemed to suggest some explanation of what is going on in this cultural, transitional space. Conceiving and writing each word and sentence as it is told activates motor circuits similar to those active in the representations of actions and events, representations which also shape the emotional content of the events. Simultaneous telling and writing also underscore the phatic dimension of the communication including the "immediate interpersonal vitality that goes beyond, or beneath, the words" (Trevarthen, 1993 – see Chapter 4).

In this attentive listening and writing I am mirroring and reflecting the actions, happenings, and emotions in the story. In order to be able to write verbatim every word that is being told I have to be extremely observant and attentive and present here and now. Capturing the narrator's words and meanings, and simultaneously putting them on paper, is so tense a performance that you cannot allow yourself to drift away for a second. And the performance of symbolization from feelings and thoughts to words on paper implies a close cooperation in a mutual rhythm like that of a dance. As an interviewer I have to try to keep pace with the teller; on the other hand, she has to adapt her narration to the speed of my writing. Of course, the narrator has been carefully instructed in advance to tell slowly enough for me to be able to follow. The reduced pace of narration allows for more reflection about what to say and how to put it. The joint rhythm is tested on the way. Normally, the narrator attends to the movements of my fingers; when I stop writing a paragraph she may continue, or I will look up from the paper and look at her signaling that now we may go on. If I happen to miss something, I put a mark on my page to remind me to come back to this later *after* the story has come to an end. In a few cases, however, I have to ask a very eager narrator to slow down her stream of words. This rhythmic collaboration emphasizes the vicarious experience. The work of the interviewer is almost like a midwife assisting in the delivery of life story, but contrary to the life stories produced through semi-structured interviews the teller alone composes the selections and configurations of the story. The transitional space becomes a space of safe emergence. It is safe for the narrator to reproduce and revive past landscapes and relations as she visits memory lane with someone else accompanying closely all the way, who – by means of the slow cooperative rhythm – assists silently and empathically in the sense-making process.

Once the narrator shows that we have come to an end by saying something like: "I think, that is it," or "Here we are today," then I can fill in any points I have missed using my notes marked in the margin, and ask: "You said something about taking a course in book-keeping I did not quite catch." But I do not ask for elaborations, and I do not ask about ellipses in the narration. Of course, writing down a narrative by hand, as it is being told, is a skill to be learned. With time you discover ways of making abbreviations in order to speed up the writing, which you, of course, must be able to read afterwards.

The initial – and until completion only – question: "Please, tell me about your life from the beginning until we are here today," has a fixed end, but not a fixed beginning. It is up to the narrator to determine where to begin, and the starting points vary enormously. While someone will begin telling about her great grandparents, another person begins her story with a family narrative about her birth, or when she started school, or in medias res, beginning the story by introducing a very significant event that happened at some point, or by introducing a close relationship. Sometimes, in the preparatory phase, I have mentioned "your first memory" as one of several possibilities, as I know from experience how the first memory is a fantastic trigger that often initiates a continuous flow of autobiographical memories. Life story narratives are by no means necessarily chronological or linear if the narrator is free to compose and configure the story on her own; and there is a great variety between very detailed events, and quickly passed periods, and ellipses even within the same narrative.

The interviewer is, however, responsible for some editing and interpretation. The pauses in the telling are transformed into signs: commas, full stops, new paragraphs, dashes, etc. I will carefully reproduce unfinished sentences without adding anything but a dash; but some of the hesitating interjections of which oral speech is so full, are not reproduced in the written story. The handwritten story thus appears a little less confused, more readable and meaningful to the narrator when she gets the fair copy of her story back for proof-reading, revision, and recognition. This extremely gentle editing during the writing of the story is, in fact, another advantage of this methodological approach. This advantage, first of all, is of an ethical nature; but the basic idea of doing biographical research in order to understand how people try to make sense of their lives through narrative configurations of experience is strongly supported by this approach.

As I already indicated, in this way of doing biographical research it is an indispensable rule that the teller of the story, the interviewee, has the full right to revise, accept, or reject the story altogether. After the interview, the interviewer makes a fair copy of the narrative and sends the file with the fair copy (or a print-out) to the narrator so that she can decide if she can recognize and accept her story. She is free to correct misunderstandings, to add something she later found important, to delete passages she regrets having told, to cover her identity as much as she wants, or to withdraw completely and remove her interview. Not until I receive the acceptance from the interviewee do I feel free to use the interview, to quote or to publish parts of it, or the story as a whole. It is essential to secure agreement that the interviewee acknowledges the life story narrative as her own, as a fair representation of how she tries to make sense of her life at the particular stage when it was made.

In contrast to my approach, most biographical research is produced by transcriptions from a tape-recorder. My method varies from this in several aspects. Many transcriptions of recorded interviews are very careful to incorporate more details of the communication: length of pauses, all types of interjection, laughter, whispering, shouting, etc. in order to support the validity of the analysis, or as a complementary analysis of ruptures, inconsistencies, incoherence, and contradictions.

Even the most careful transcription, however, cannot encompass all the non-verbal and verbal interaction that takes place during an act of communication such as making a life story interview. The interviewee does not get anything back after offering her gift and, if she gets a copy of the tape, this is not, in any way, something she can influence, check, and correct. Careful transcriptions do not guarantee a correct reproduction: I have often encountered misinterpretations of recorded and transcribed biographies when I was assessing theses and papers.

Another difference between recording and writing a life story as it is told concerns the reactions of the listener. As the tape is running the attentive interviewer tries to encourage the narrator and to assure her of attention by small phatic exclamations ("um-um"). The interviewer who is writing does not have to prove her attention, which is obvious. Nevertheless, in both cases facial expressions and body postures reveal reactions to what is told. I am convinced from many years of experience that writing the story as it is told is an approach which really supports the narrator's sense of feeling felt.[15]

Furthermore, it is worthwhile taking into account that producing a fair copy of a handwritten narrated interview (or one written on a laptop) is so much faster than making transcriptions from recordings.

Although, the main point of doing narrative life story interviews from my methodological approach is the interest in the meaning-making of the teller, in her configurational act rather than a focus on all the ruptures which appear in normal, fast oral speech; and, although, the slow speed of the telling and all the little pauses that are necessary as the narrator has to keep in pace with the writer, allow for a lot of reflection on the way, and for preparation of more well-formed sentences, for inexplicit choices of what should be expressed and how, many narrators are still amazed that their narrative is not more coherent. Some narrators, when they receive their fair copy, are even a bit embarrassed that they do not have a more fluent diction. I wonder how they would feel if they saw a transcription of recorded, normal, oral speech, which usually is far less eloquent. But in spite of my focus on coherence and sense making, all the life stories have multiple voices and negotiate meaning as they are told. They display choices of beginning, selections, exclusions, and competing perspectives.

Telling a life story narrative may be a very emotional event. Refraining from interventions, such as questioning on particular themes or periods, or inquiries into ellipses, etc., during the narration as well as focusing on narrating as a sense-making activity, reduces the risk of crossing personal boundaries. As researchers, we are usually neither therapists nor close friends, and we are certainly not qualified to act as such. What we can do, however, is to frame the interview and influence the interaction in a way that supports the integrity of the interviewee as much as possible.

First of all, when you enter somebody's home for the first time it is important to act with some delicacy and sensitivity. It is a good idea to tell something about yourself and what you are doing before you start interviewing. Openness, small talk, or the establishment of some common ground between interviewer and interviewee, is a good beginning – as well as allowing time for coffee or any other refreshment that the narrator may wish to serve.

Likewise, when the narrator has finished her story, the researcher should take her time to "elaborate on the coda" that is, to come back to the ordinary familiarity of here and now, especially if the mental time travels of the narration traversed painful territory. It is the researcher's responsibility to check that the narrator regains and restores emotional stability before she rushes out of the door. Again, small talk and discussions of what will happen next support this interaction. Applying the metaphor of taking someone by the hand on the mental journey through the (story of the) life course, you should not let go of the hand too abruptly, but gently and unambiguously, always keeping in mind that we are researchers and decent human beings, not a new friend or a therapist.

Fair copy and proof-reading

As mentioned above, it is very easy to produce the fair copy of the narrative interview as long as you are able to decipher you own handwriting. Afterwards, it is sent back to the narrator for proof-reading and acceptance.

The written version of the narrated life story is a reification of what was told. It exists outside the mind of the narrator, and beyond the moment of telling. Thus, the narrator can encounter her story from the outside at a different time and use this opportunity for reflection and negotiation of the self and the identity, and interpretation of existence which have been co-constructed during the narrative interview and the production of the fair copy. In this way, a small part of the gift she gave by telling her story is returned, and several interviewees have expressed appreciation of this opportunity that supports the process of sense making in which all of us are engaged.

The narrators' requests for corrections or alterations vary considerably. The vast majority only want to correct small misunderstood matters of fact, such as the spelling of a location or a date. A few express concerns about how statements they have made about people would be received by the people concerned. Perhaps they regret their depiction of certain relatives or friends and fear to give offence, should their account be made public. Maybe they feel embarrassed to make public some expression of weakness or vulnerability, or maybe they find that the self-image presented in the story is not very flattering. But the latter examples only account for a very few and, perhaps unsurprisingly, mainly people relatively high up the social ladder, who are concerned about their presentation and performance in public. People from the opposite end of the social hierarchy seem generally not to be afraid of presenting disadvantageous deeds and characteristics openly and honestly to the public. I sense that they are grateful that someone cares to listen to them and to give them a voice. Among the large number of interviews I have collected during the past 20 years, only two people, both well-known to the public in little Denmark, chose to withdraw altogether. One of them said that he had read the story every evening for a whole week, and that it had given him the opportunity for much reflection upon his life. He appreciated having told his story; he just did not want to have it published.

In contrast, there was an occasion when I had fully expected someone to withdraw from a research project. I had interviewed five young girls from minority backgrounds at a folk high school. One of them, a girl from Bosnia, told a terrifying story about how her entire family had been violently abused during the war in the former Yugoslavia in the 1990s. I intuitively sensed during her narration how important it was that I emanated a feeling of security and tried to express non-verbally that I was able to contain the atrocities she was telling me about in order to secure a safe emergence. When I returned home I was exhausted and felt quite vulnerable. A week later, as I returned to discuss the proof-readings with the young girls, the Bosnian girl asked me if we could go and talk together in private. I thought she wanted to withdraw, perhaps regretting having told such terrible things about herself and her family as she knew that the interviews, or part of them, would be published; and I would certainly have understood this. But I was wrong, she did not want to withdraw, she just wanted to thank me. She said it had been extremely difficult for her to narrate the story, but that she had felt a great relief afterwards. I replied that the fact that she had been able to tell this story in a fairly coherent way proved that she was on her way to getting on with her life. She gave me a hug and we departed.

These two examples suggest that the transitions we have encountered in our lives call for reflection, sense making, and creation of meaning, and that a narrative interview may assist in this process.

Interview variations

In many research projects the construction of the life story by a narrative interview was undertaken and followed by a structured qualitative interview. This may be carried out immediately after the life story narrative, or the researcher may return another day for the second interview. If the research project has a specific focus it can be advantageous to put a number of specific questions to the interviewees in order to ensure that this issue is thematized and discussed. If I use this method I will ask the same questions of the whole sample of interviewees. Some interviewees are likely to continue the narration of their story in response to the questions, others will simply reply in a more disconnected way. In all cases it is interesting to compare the answers to the questions with the biographical interview. The multiple voices, the negotiations of meaning, the nuances and ambiguities of the life story narrative decrease in the answers, which, in some cases, are much more unilateral, politically correct, and "appropriate." An interviewee, who in the supplementary questions was asked about significant cultural values today, replied that "tolerance" was a very important value. However, in her narrative life story interview she told about the insurmountable problems at Christmas as her family-in-law had different customs and the two families could not agree on how to celebrate the feast.

Another variation is the repeated biographical interview, in which the researcher will come back to the narrator once more or several times to continue the narration. This variation allows for a more thorough process of meaning making if the interviews are carried out within a relatively short time span or a longitudinal research if the interviews are collected at larger intervals. A very interesting project researching adult learning was carried out in Germany; Hof and Fischer sought out respondents after 20 years who had been interviewed during the 1980s and carried out new biographical interviews in order to study the different interpretations of participation in learning contexts depending on their former and current life situation.[16]

Thematically confined narrative interviews are more suitable in some research projects. For example, I have asked for stories of learning in a lifelong perspective, stories about the use of, or participation in, specific contexts in a lifelong perspective (e.g. libraries). There is considerable advantage in adapting the ordinary qualitative interview into a narrative interview by asking questions that invite storytelling so that the respondent can unfold a temporal dimension and elaborate and unfold the answers. In a longitudinal evaluation project with an emphasis on learning, I interviewed the participants with an interval of two years. Three questions made up the first encounter: "Please, tell me about your present position and areas of work," "Please, tell me about the journey you traveled in order to get here," and "Please, tell me about your vision for the future?" When I returned two years later, I asked specific questions concerning the process during the intervening two years and the outcome, and ended by repeating the last question from the first meeting about the visions for the future. A comparison between the two visions and how the field was talked about gave an interesting insight into the learning that took place during the time of the project (see Horsdal, 2008b).

The situated interview

The narrative interview is a performance in a transitional space between the teller and the listener/writer. The biographical narrative constructed by this performance is, obviously, a contextually situated life story. We have many stories to tell about our lives, and we tell different stories at different times and different places to different interlocutors.

The researcher has to take into account the situated context of the biographical interview. This includes:

1   The here and now in which the story is articulated is the time of enunciation and the point from which both the past and the future are conceived.
2   The narrative interview is constructed within the framework of research. The agenda of the researcher and the type of study will, obviously, influence the narrative. If the interviewer or researcher is known to the interviewee, if prior to the interview they have interacted professionally or privately, mutual understandings and inside knowledge may mark the narrative both in regard to what is said and how it is said, and what is omitted. Asymmetric relationships between interviewer and interviewee may also have an effect.
3   The present life situation of the narrator influences the telling. If she recently had a divorce, lost a relative, experienced severe illness, got a new job, moved to another city or country, or if any major transition has occurred, this will, inevitably, show in the form of the interpretations of self and existence in the story. Present crises may affect the degree of coherence of the story.
4   The wider context also matters. In many life story narratives you see traces of recent political changes, elections, disasters, issues of public debate in the media, etc.

5   Collective, cultural narratives mark the life story interviews. Political or religious convictions, grand narratives about progression and growth, individualism, or narcissism, all kinds of beliefs and ideologies leave their stamp on stories. Interpretations of significance of gender, race, or social class may also play a role in the interviews. Cultural narratives may also result in life stories told in specific genres.

6   The narrative competence of the teller matters. Interviewees, like all of us, grow up in different narrative cultures. Some are used to telling stories about personal experience, and some are not. Some are accustomed to the telling of anecdotes. Some are acquainted with limited versions, interrogations by authorities or narratives about specific themes and incidents in therapeutic settings.[17] If the interviewee has previously told her life story in another context, her familiarity with this special narrative genre shows in the narrative interview. For interviewees with very little narrative competence, both the act of remembering and of sense making is extremely difficult.

7   Finally, what the interviewee actually remembers – including autobiographical memory, semantic memory, and implicit memory – of her experiences, sensations, and of what she has learned from others will determine the narrative.

As we shall see in the following chapter on analysis, the situated context of the narrative interview influences the life stories in significant ways. Both interviewee and interviewer are, during their encounters, situated at a specific point in their lives and in a wider cultural context.[18] Furthermore, their collaboration and the co-construction of a narrative interview will be influenced by the extent of shared knowledge. If they know each other beforehand, some issues may not be explicitly expressed. On the other hand, different sociocultural experiences may result in a lack of common knowledge, as the narrative construction of collective identities may be quite divergent in different cultural contexts (see Cortazzi and Jin, 2006). However, in spite of the risk of intercultural misunderstandings, narrative methods offer a great opportunity to access intercultural knowledge as vicarious experience. Furthermore, we all have a great deal in common as human beings on the experiential level in spite of our different cultural narratives and interpretive frameworks.

Chapter 9

Interpretation and analysis of life story narratives

Pre-understanding

Pre-understanding is a concept derived from hermeneutics.[1] As we are listening to or reading a life story narrative we, inevitably, interpret the story within the context our own experience and narrative repertoire; there is no way to detach ourselves completely from the interpretive act. Even the mirroring of motor-circuits and emotions representing the narrated actions and events takes place on a basis of prior experience. We *identify* with the stories we hear, and the projections and identifications are so obvious and happen spontaneously and often without our conscious awareness. Communication implies the duality of identification and difference. We try to understand others in recognition of their individuality; at the same time, we can never exclude ourselves from the understandings and interpretations. Consequently, the exercise is not to avoid this identification but to be explicit and conscious about the way and the extent to which we interpret the narrative according to our present situation, personal dilemmas, and cultural narratives. Just like the interviewee who is telling about her life we are, as interpreters, always contextually situated. We can try to be observant of how this will influence our interpretations; and we can train our interpretive and analytic skills, and be more aware of analytical methodologies and tools.

Most of the points listed in the previous chapter concerning the situated interview also apply to the researcher in her analysis of the narrative interview:

1   The analysis is carried out at a certain point of time within a context of a particular research project which, obviously, determines the analysis of the narrative material. The atmosphere and impressions of the encounter between the interviewer and interviewee during their collaboration may influence the analysis.
2   The present life situation of the researcher may influence her comprehension of the narrative interview.
3   The wider context also matters.
4   Collective, cultural narratives influence the basic assumptions and implicit understandings of the researcher (for example preconceptions of good science or good research).
5   The analytical competence and experience of the researcher and her narrative repertoire will influence the research.

The methodological approach to be presented in the following is mainly herme-neutic and is inspired by literary narrative analysis. Narrative interviews are not hard core data in a sociological sense to be used for an objective study of reality. Life story narratives do not open a window to life itself and to factual events but represent situated interpretations of life and experience. The concept of one single life history is far too narrow; our sense making is tentative, and life story narratives change over time just as we do and the world around us.

Life stories are "fictional facts," Denzin argues (1989: 76), symbolic expressions and ambiguous, like life itself:

> Stories then, like the lives they tell about, are always open-ended, inclusive and ambiguous, subject to multiple interpretations. Some are big; others are little. Some take on heroic, folktale proportions in the cultural lives of group members; others are tragic; and all too few are comic. Some break fast and run to rapid conclusions. Most slowly unwind and twist back on themselves as persons seek to find meaning for themselves in the experiences they call their own.
>
> (1989: 81)

On the other hand, a life story narrative cannot mean just anything. Albeit, there is not one true or exhaustive interpretation of a story, all readings are not equally good, and some typical readings may even distort the purpose of life story nar-ratives in research.[2] In our culture, the psychological characterization of the individual self is a very common framing; an interpretation that constructs an individualized, psychological portrait of the narrator seems to be a natural incli-nation for many readers of biographical narratives. The focus in my approach is not the individual person – how she or he *really* is beyond the surface – but how the narrator tries to make sense of lived experience through her narration.

Life story narratives differ from fictional narratives in more than one sense, which is why the application of "tools" from literary analysis has to be adapted to this specific discursive genre. Life story narratives are not stringent composi-tions to the same extent as fictional stories. The tension in a work of art in rela-tion to its framing and boundaries due to a tight composition is far more striking than in the more casually configured life story. A tightly composed work of art may vibrate against its own limits, it has no "dross of coincidence," while the narrative interview – in spite of the time for reflection – is a first attempt to cre-ate meaning in a specific situation. In the life story, some narrative threads may be initiated and left again without conclusions. Associations may lead the narra-tor along byways; and emotional experiences which are difficult to put into words can influence the story a great deal. Nevertheless, the hermeneutic axiom of understanding the parts according to the whole, and understanding the whole according to the parts also counts in the interpretation of life story narratives. Not until we come to the end of the narration are we able to see the impact of what is told and how and why in the course of telling. This has sometimes caught my curiosity during the process of listening to and writing down a narrative interview. I wonder why, perhaps, a certain episode, all of a sudden, is elaborated so much and look forward to the end of the story when I shall find out why this particular episode at this time of telling was so significant. The personal context of the situated interview discussed above is often decisive in this respect.

Another difference between works of fiction and life story narratives concerns the fact that there is some kind of "history" behind the life story narrative. There is a physical journey behind the biography, the journey that the narrator traveled in time and space during her life, a journey that to some extent is revisited as mental time travel by narrative means. The narrative is constructed on a background of memories and thoughts about what happened in real life on this journey of transformation. The story is an attempt to negotiate the meaning of what happened; and what is told about this during the narrative may have very different implications for the narrator outside and after the construction of the life story narrative than would be the case with an invented fiction.

The first thing to take into account in the analytic process as indicated above is the situated context of the narrative interview. The life story interview is made at a certain point of time, in a specific context within a specific framework of research by the collaboration of two individuals. Afterwards it is transformed into a text that can be analyzed. A complete analysis of the narrative life story includes an analysis of the *context* of its production as well as of the constructed *text*. Therefore, if the researcher wants to accentuate a particularly interesting part of the narrative, both the *co-text* (the surrounding text within the interview viewed as a text) and the *context* of its construction as an interview[3] should be taken into account in the analysis.

Time and space

Temporality is one of the main distinguishing features of narrative. First of all, narratives unfold in time and cover a space of time. Analytical methods which ignore this aspect, like some of the methods from structural text analysis,[4] fall short of grasping the central temporal feature of narratives. I agree with Ricoeur (1984) and Polkinghorne (1988) in their criticism of structuralism for reducing temporality to a binary logic; this critique, however, should not include all structuralist studies of literature. Jonathan Culler in his foreword to the English edition of *Narrative discourse* (Discours du récit) (Genette, 1980 (1972)) calls Genette's book "a culmination of structuralist work on narrative," and Genette's work introduces a conceptual framework for narrative analysis which I have found extremely useful with regard to biographical narratives.

Genette, who uses Proust's novel *Remembrance of things past* as an example of the application of the analytical tools, suggests a construction of the sequence of the story and a comparison between this and the narrated sequence. This is useful in the analysis of a life story narrative. The distinction between narrated time and story time[5] enables us to form a survey of the composition of the life story narrative: the sequence, order, and hierarchy of what is told in the biography.

How and where do people begin their stories, and where do they end? In which order are they told? Few stories are merely chronological accounts. Where do they pause and linger and elaborate events? Where do they jump, leave something out, skip a period entirely or cover a decade by a single remark? Answering those questions can assist the interpreter in achieving a general view of the story, and here Genette's concepts can be used as an analytical tool that helps us to "open" the text.

Following Genette, we can use the biographical narrative to construct the chronological sequence of the events narrated. In a biographical narrative this is a construction of the physical journey in time and space that the narrator traveled or imagines she will take in the time to come.

First, the story as it is told is divided into parts, where each part constitutes a single context in time and space. Genette writes about dividing the narration into single events, but as a life story narrative is composed by many things other than events, and primarily consists of narrations of contexts, communities of practice and relations in which the narrator participated or was a member at some time during her life, (cf. Chapter 1, Configuration in life story narratives) this exercise is somewhat different. In between the narrations of the different contexts and communities of "there and then" – the family, the school, the grandparent's house, a holiday, etc. – the narrator may jump in her narrative to here and now and discuss or negotiate the narrated context from the point of view of the present. In this case, we have another part in time and space of the narrated sequence to note in order to construct the survey of the narration. Each of the divided sequences is given a number, 1, 2, 3, etc. Shifts marked by time adverbs, *then*, *when*, *before*, *after*, *while*, *in the meantime*, can help to distinguish the parts as well as other kinds of shifts in the narration.

At this point, the construction of a chronology can be made; a new sequence marked with letters, A, B, C, from the earliest date of the narration to the latest. Now, the two sequences can be compared. In a simple linear and chronological story the narrated sequence and story sequence overlap (1A, 2B, 3C ... etc.) while in a more complex story the comparison will display a different sequence (such as 1F, 2C, 3K, 4F ... etc.).

The comparison between the narrated sequence and the constructed chronology enables a clarification of the *order* of the telling. A clarification of the order of narrated experiences assists the conceptualization of the narrator's configuration. We notice flash-backs, flash-forwards, and ellipses in the narrated life story. The life story narrative may cover a time span longer or shorter than the life of the narrator. Some narrators begin their storytelling about their ancestors, while others limit themselves to their own existence. Simply the length of the timeline, drawn from the earliest event mentioned to the latest which may be in the distant future, tells us something about the interpretation of self and existence and of important affiliations. The significance of kinship has changed over time. The community of family, relatives, and ancestors had a greater impact on the identity construction in traditional society; however, grandparents still play a very significant role in many young people's stories. The timeline of a narrative also depends on the narrator's age as the time span of lived life and of an imagined future obviously is different for the older narrator and for the adolescent. If the teller lived a long life, she has many experiences and memories to represent, and she is likely to create meaning of the past time in a slightly different way compared to the young narrator who, presumably, has most of her life ahead of her. Despite their age, some narrators are considering the future while others may conclude their story years before the time of the telling, leaving an empty space in the most recent period of their life as though nothing really happened in all that time.

It becomes clear how much space the different parts of life, the different contexts take up in the narrative. Genette talks about the *duration* of an episode; in the narrative interview we shall find a great variety between detailed and elaborated accounts of certain contexts while other periods of life are quickly passed, summed up in a few sentences, or completely excluded from the narration. The different chapters of a life are not equally comprehensive in the narration. A fortnight may take up an hour in the telling and cover several pages, while a period of ten years may be totally omitted and appear only as an ellipse in the telling. Some incidents may be told several times in the story. We can consider the concept of *frequency* when the narrator returns to a certain issue or incident in the story.

The concepts of *order*, *duration* and *frequency* enable us to find out when and where the narrator is in her story. The study of the temporal aspects of the narrative also reveals something about the narrator's conception of time: it may be cyclic, linear, or fragmented.

Time and place are closely connected. The point of departure is always here and now, the actual context in which we are situated and embodied. Whether we tell about our past, or of the imagined future, we do so from the point of view of enunciation, although our stories encompass other voices from other times in the related narratives that become part of our own stories. Retellings as well as memories are, however, recalled at the time of the telling exactly in order to serve the sense-making process in this moment.

Through the emplotment of the story, the here and now of the time of the telling connects to there and then, the other chapters of our life story narrative lived in different contexts in different places in different communities. Places are not just the physical surroundings we experience with our senses in interaction with the environment but always also a matter of relationships. In our analysis we can examine in what detail and how comprehensively they are described, and how they are emotionally evaluated. Physical places may just be a framing for activities or ascribed symbolic meaning, positive or negative. The affiliations are never neutral.

Participation in communities of practice

The next step in the analysis of life story narrative draws inspiration from a quite different area of research. In 1991, Lave and Wenger published *Situated learning* and discussed the implication of legitimate peripheral participation in different learning contexts.[6] The focus in their work was on the social interaction of participants in a community of practice and how this could change over time as the peripheral newcomer was gradually transformed and, perhaps, became a more established member of the community. This focus can be transferred directly into the life story narratives, and I find the concept *legitimate peripheral participation* very useful in order to clarify the relationships and interactions in the narrated contexts.

Apart from the communities we create ourselves when starting an NGO, a business, a collective, or by getting married, most of the communities we become related to, or part of, during our lives were already there prior to our entrance. Some contexts were a matter of choice; in other communities we landed by chance or fate or circumstances. Entering a new community as a newcomer is, in many ways, like entering a stage on which a play is going on with rather fixed roles and scripts designed prior to our appearance. Yet, the arrival of a newcomer – think of a new baby born into the family – may significantly change the interaction of the participants already there.

We are members of some communities, such as families, or we may be employees of an organization, for a very long time; however, the interactions between participants may change considerably over time, as well as the number of participants in the community. In other communities our participation is brief. Yet, transient encounters may be of significance in the story.

Do we feel ourselves to be legitimate participants of a given community? Naturally, a newcomer is a peripheral member, but will she continue to be so, or gradually move in a centripetal direction? The issue of inclusion and exclusion appears in this context. It struck me that a majority of narrators end the account of a given context by a negative or a positive evaluation: "This was really an awful place!" or "That was a wonderful time!"[7] And the evaluations, to a very large extent, depend on the interpersonal relationships and interactions.

In traditional society people were born into a community, they had to adapt, they had little personal choice, and it was a matter of great consequence to leave the community voluntarily, and even more so to be expelled. On the other hand, you did not have to prove your legitimacy. In most cases, it was given. In contemporary society personal choice and individual responsibility for making the "right" choices have increased immensely. This implies a higher degree of negotiation of choices, of meaning, and of affiliations, mirrored by the life story narratives. You are more vulnerable if you have to prove your legitimate participation all the time and everywhere.

Most of us, today, travel from context to context, from community to community. We participate in different communities of practice, not only one by one in the course of life, but simultaneously as family members, employees, friends, associates, partners, students, etc.

We all know from experience the feeling of entering an unknown community of practice for the first time. Normally, we hesitate a little on the periphery in order to find out what kind of place we have entered. Knowledge of appropriate cultural codes can be very useful. At a party where we know very few of the other guests, the convention of shaking hands – if this is appropriate in the given culture – and engaging in conversations with other participants can be a way into the company away from the peripheral position. With this in mind, the number, variety, and diversity of different communities of practice which we encounter in contemporary society underscores the importance of (inter)cultural knowledge and transparency. Narrators tell about where they have felt accepted, and where they felt miserable and scared. Interviews with refugees who experienced exclusions in more than one sense represent stories which deepen our understanding of the significance of legitimate participation and creation of affiliations. The negotiation of identity becomes extremely problematic when a person feels isolated from legitimate participation.

The affiliations to the various communities of practice created from interpersonal interaction fuel the sense of belonging which roots the narrative construction of identity. Narratives may also reveal affiliations to imagined communities;[8] a sense of belonging to a nation or to a spiritual or religious community that becomes part of the narrative construction of identity.

The analysis of the accounts of the different communities of practice in the narrative interviews thus involves scrutinizing the concept *legitimate peripheral participation*; a discussion of participants, how they are characterized, how the interpersonal interactions develop, how the issue of affiliation or the opposite is treated, as well as the explicit and implicit evaluations of these chapters of life.

The communities of practice can, in line with the original research by Lave and Wenger, be analyzed as learning sites. We learn through interaction in the various communities in which we participate throughout life. We learn in the family, in institutions, in educational settings, on the street among friends, at different work-places, etc. The life story narratives give access to the experiences of learning in all those communities. The interviews reveal how the different communities of practice are considered as learning environments. Was this particular learning site a good and safe learning environment, or the opposite? How about the learning outcome? What did the narrator claim to have learned from her participation in this particular community? We also learn about the impact of the learning environments on the future. Very often the impact is substantial. Did participation in this context encourage further learning or the opposite? Autobiographical narrative interviews are an outstanding source for research on the experience of lifelong and life-wide learning. What I term "biographical learning" (see Chapter 12) refers to the narrated experience of learning in the various communities of practice in which the narrator participated throughout her life (until the time of the narration). The range, scope, and quality of the individual person's biographical learning, as well as its significance in the interpretations of experience, may vary substantially.

Besides the significance of interpersonal interaction in various communities, some contexts are places with a great impact for various reasons. Acute sense impressions of embodied interactions, recognitions of the beauty of landscapes, symbolic accentuations of places from "enchanted spots" to the heavy weight of cultural traditions color the stories.

Voices, persons, relations

A very significant part of the analysis of life story narratives consists of an examination of the multiple voices within the narrative in order to clarify who is speaking and from which perspective. First, we have to distinguish between the interviewee as a person in flesh and blood from the context of the interview, and the authority of enunciation within the text. During the interview the narrator decides what to tell and what to suppress. She decides which voices to include; she authorizes the retellings, and presents the perspectives and points of view of the narration.

The interviewee telling her story to the researcher is represented in the text both as the *narrator* and as the *protagonist* of the story. The narrator is telling about herself – the protagonist – from the moment of the enunciation, and she can tell about her former self with a variety of distance and proximity. If the point of view remains at the present moment of telling, the distance in a chronological biography will gradually decrease from the beginning to the end of the story where it dissolves the time difference between story time and narrated time in the statement: "And here we are today." But, as mentioned before, few narratives are strictly linear; normally, the narrator alternates perspectives and viewpoints. "I" (now) can tell about "me" (then, when I was a little girl), and I can tell about this little girl by adapting her perspective from my memory, trying to show what she experienced, felt, did, thought back then, or I can tell about this little girl as I view her experiences, feelings, actions from my present perspective (as well as adopting positions in between). I can also, as an autobiographical narrator, adopt other people's perspectives of this little girl, the protagonist of the story. Very often, there are shifting positions of identification, distance and retrospection. The narrative may be blended with other voices: direct or reported speech and fragments of cultural narratives and fictions. A typical example of shifting perspectives within a single passage due to a combination of remembered fragments, later considerations and pieces of factual knowledge can be seen in the following quotation:

> I remember I was in my pram in the bottom of our garden. I imagine my mother must have felt tired on such a Sunday afternoon. How could I know it was Sunday? I don't know. I worked myself half way out of the harness, and then the pram fell over, and I was lying on the graveled path. I vividly remember the flowers along the garden path. Spiraea, fuchsia, periwinkle and some yellow flowers that open up in the sun and close in clouded weather. I was lying there, scratching the ground. I was not afraid. I cannot remember if I was picked up. I guess I was between 2 or 3 years old.
>
> (Woman born 1909) (my translation)

A shift in tense from past to present often indicate a dissolution of distance as the narrator is "reliving" the event she is telling about. The researcher should observe any type of shift in the narrator's voice, in distance or mood, or in use of personal pronoun. The narrator may use *I, you, we, one*, or a third person indicator speaking about the protagonist and include other people's stories about herself. The polyphony of voices appears as the narrator negotiates meaning, sometimes acting rhetorically as an interlocutor in a dialogue. A distance from a specific event may appear in the use of another pronoun, in application of irony, or in an anecdotal account of a problematic happening, indicating that this has been retold a number of times and has found a fixed rhetorical format.[9]

The narrator may use a pronoun other than "I" to signify the protagonist, or she may use the pronoun "I" but the voice – and the point of view – belong to somebody else:

> Always, in joking as in earnest, I was told that I was a bird that had fallen into the wrong nest. They said I had been mixed up. I should have shown an interest in reasonable things such as money and economy.
>
> (Woman born 1945) (my translation)

Sometimes the narrator makes a shift from "I" to "we." How, when, and in what connection "we" appears in the narrative is of significance. "We" may be used to express affiliations, common intentions, common actions or common values.[10] Or you can tell about communities and relationships maintaining the "I" in spite of common activities. The pronoun "we" may be used either to underscore affiliations or as an attempt to relieve the protagonist of some pressure. The application of "we" can even be ironic if the narrator wants to distance herself from a prevailing collective viewpoint. A thorough analysis cannot just consider the personal pronouns at their face value but should try to clarify how and why they appear in particular ways in the life story. Scrutinizing the voices enables us to clarify and begin to understand the rhetoric of the narrator.

It is interesting to notice if the protagonist is primarily depicted as an actor who is doing things and making things happen, or as a passive object in the situation. We can tell about ourselves as heroes, and as victims suffering endless misery. Life story narratives display several literary genres. However, the multiple voices in most narratives may give rise to a more complicated or mixed picture of the interpretation of experience.

The different voices play two main roles in the life story narratives; one is about characterization of persons – not least of the protagonist – and the other is about the negotiation of meaning, of values of cultural narratives, and both serve the construction of identity through the narration.

In the following quotation from a biographical interview with a woman who for many years suffered from kidney failure, a reported voice serves as a common characterization of the narrator (indirectly), of her mother, and her grandmother:

> It is difficult to be little and weak. I didn't allow people to get close. "I can manage," I said. It is hard for strong women to show they need help.

The first years I was on dialysis my mother came along every time. During the many hours we had to talk about something. Then she told me about my grandmother who always in a thunderstorm would sit down by the window and say to her children: "Look at the lightening! Isn't this great! There is nothing to worry about." Then one day, when she was old, she phoned my mother and asked if she would come over as she heard thunder and she was so afraid. "You were never afraid of thunder," my mother said. "Yes, always," grandmother answered.

In a way, my mother told her own story while I was in dialysis.

(Woman born 1960) (my translation)

The quotation above illustrates an example of identification. Application of different voices may serve the opposite, marking a distance between the narrator's opinions and others' as in the example above of the woman "in the wrong nest."[11]

The negotiation of meaning and values emerges from the following quotation:

The college works as a springboard for something else. You don't really know what you want – you tried the university – maybe two or three times. This is typical of many students at college. What, really, do I think myself? What do I want? Well, maybe you have an obligation towards society. My father always maintained that.

(Woman born 1979)[12] (my translation)

The narrator may include voices from relatives, from neighbors, colleagues and friends, from collective narratives, public media, from idioms and from poetry, hymns and songs in the construction of identity and in her characterization of others in the life story narrative.

It is significant to know who is mentioned and how. Presenting the name often indicates a significant other. How are the different persons in the story represented? From which point of view? Do we encounter their behaviors, their remarks, or even their thoughts? How are the relationships described? Constructing the other is one of the ways of constructing yourself. Both the characterization and the function of other persons in the life story narrative should be taken into account.

Finally, the communities of practice from the previous part of this chapter will be revisited. The analysis of voices, persons, and relations is closely connected to the analysis of the interactions, affiliations, and developments of the various communities of practice related in the story.

An apprentice who had a bike, and it was stormy, and I asked if he would go with me in my car, and then he says something about me being a wrong color, but I had to drive him home. Compared to what people say in the street it hurts more if they know me, and we have been working together.

(Man born 1976) (my translation)

This quotation comes from an interview with a refugee from Somalia. His gradually acquired ability to cope with bullying, offensive remarks, and discrimination in different communities of practice from school to various workplaces takes up a significant amount of space in the narrative, signifying the difficulty of establishing a sense of belonging in these contexts.

As the narrators configure the biographical story on their own, the weight of some persons or the opposite, the peripheral touch of someone or their complete omission can be remarkable. I have interviewed old men who never mentioned their children in their life story.

Themes and configuration

Frequently, analyses of life story narratives confine themselves, or at least give priority, to a thematic analysis. Of course, we should distinguish the different themes in the story; determine which issues take up space and weight in the narrative. The framing of the study will, to a certain extent, influence the themes. In a study on liberal education, the interviewee is likely to prioritize her participation in different non-formal educational arenas, but a narrow restriction to those issues in a life story narrative would simply indicate that the interview has not been well prepared. If the interviewee who was asked to tell her life story from the beginning up to the present confines her story strictly to the theme of research in order to avoid any "irrelevant" topic she has, perhaps, misunderstood what was wanted from her.

Prior to the thematic analysis we may try to discern which discursive elements the text displays. In other words, what is the "stuff" of the narrative? We may find accounts of actions, intentions, plans, happenings, dreams, feelings, evaluations, causations, rhetorical justifications, descriptions, arguments. Life story narratives, obviously, contain episodes from autobiographical memory, but also prototype memories, bits of factual knowledge from semantic memory, memories prompted by material objects or photographs, bits of remembered conversations or retellings, etc. What kinds of statements are comprehensive or scarce? What is positive or negative in the telling? Narratives contain attitudes and values implicitly and explicitly. And cultural narratives – political, philosophical, spiritual, and social interpretations of existence – pervade the stories and color the accounts. Collective visions of "the good life" (Taylor, 1989) may be negotiated in individual stories as a cultural framework of sense making. Very often, narratives show a clash of values.

The thematic ordering of the narrative is interesting, especially in combination with the development and configuration of the story. The point is not only to distinguish the themes that occur in an interview but to realize how they are organized in the course of the narration and in the emplotment. Normally, in a Western cultural setting, a life story narrative describes a development, an evolution, some kind of change or turning points. Very few life story narratives show no trace of development or change, as temporal change is a fundamental aspect of narrative itself. One example was a narrative interview with an old woman suffering from senile dementia.[13] As her short-term memory was not functioning very well she quickly forgot what she had already told, and thus repeated the same theme over and over again, a theme of relations and affiliations between her siblings, her husband and herself in her childhood as well as later on. Another interview, unusually[14] confined to almost one theme – economic improvement – still showed a development of gradual and constant improvement.

During a life story, particular themes may prevail in the narrative: loss, death, playful interactions, survival strategies, close relationships, etc.

Bruner (1987) once noticed that auto-biographical descriptions of one's childhood often had the character of prophesy. The "lively" child in the story grew up to be a "lively and active" adult. Precisely because we try to make sense of our lives from the point of view of the time of enunciation, we select and recall memories that "fit" the configuration of meaning we are constructing. Therefore, it is not so much prophesies as the other way round, a retrospective selection from the time of the present that we experience.

If we happen to interview people in the middle of some kind of crisis this, of course, may influence the narrative tremendously due to the difficulty and need to make comprehensible the deviations from expected circumstances. At a later stage, when the crisis has been overcome, it may be represented in the narrative as a turning point. Fictive narratives normally have turning points. We initially expect this or that to happen, but a crisis or turning point that often solves or mediates a conflict reverses our expectations or fears as we reach the end of the story. Very often, life imitates narrative fiction – at least in the narratives of lived experience. Frequently, a miserable period or a crisis is retold from the distance with the comment that it was an instructive experience. The narrator "learned something." This interpretation, which mitigates the circumstances, is part of the larger metaphor that *life is a school* (Lakoff and Johnson, 1999); an often shared understanding in Western culture of life as a learning process in which we, through actions and sufferings, gain more knowledge of the vicissitudes of the human plight and intentions. An overriding element of a thorough analysis is to pin down the identity construction in the narrative and the interpretations of existence.

Changes may occur in different forms. What has changed? The narrator herself or the surrounding world? Changes of the world (technological, moral, material) are a frequent theme in the stories of older people. Change in itself may be viewed as a threat or as a possibility. Also, the relationship between self and others, or the individual and the social may be subject to change in the narrative discourse. When considering change and transformations we may try to find out how this came about, was initiated, and if a transition for the better or for the worse was the result. Explanations of what happened which we note as narrative causations from one stage to another are a very significant part of the configuration.[15] When we try to explain emotional states, effects, and actions we make use of narrative strategies. We employ causations, not in a logical-scientific sense but as expressions of probabilities, discursive demonstrations of psychological, moral, or social necessities. In the narrative configuration forms of narrative causalities are constructed that produce particular expressions of probability and necessity. Therefore, a registration of themes in the narration, an observation of how comprehensive or transient they are, combined with an analysis of the function of the different themes in the configuration of the narrative, may support an understanding of the complexity of the narrative.

Metaphors

Analysis of metaphors gives a most fruitful access to insight in life story narratives. I do not restrict the term to figurative, ornate tropes but include metaphors in the broad embodied sense, as demonstrated in the works of Lakoff and Johnson (1980, 1999), Johnson (1987), Lakoff and Turner (1989). In perception and representation of experience we make use of conceptual schemas and a large number of primary metaphors we can combine into more complex metaphors, poetic as well as quite ordinary, which we use for reasoning and for expression of emotions and experiences. We say, for instance, that we are "in high spirits" or "feeling down" (*high is up* is a metaphor based on bodily orientation), or "time flies" (*time is motion*, based on movement in space), "I cannot grasp what you mean" (*understanding is grasping*, based on object manipulation).

As discussed in Chapter 1, *life is a journey* is the metaphor based on our physical trajectories in time and space that captures the basic feature of life story narratives. This metaphor has numerous derivations that we find in the stories: *getting a position, reaching a destination, to be held back, making progress, standing on two feet, changing track, feeling balance, jumping from one thing to another, facing obstacles,* etc. They inform us of significant elements in the interpretation of existence. Life may be interpreted as a purposeful journey, or as a journey of transformation. And the route taken may be interpreted as a matter of fate, of coincidence, of compulsion, or of choice. The alternations between the opportunities to rest and stay and the obligation to move on are of significance. As many of those everyday metaphors are based on our embodied interaction with the world, they are widespread across languages, but there is also a cultural basis for our different expressions and use of language. This, of course, can cause problems when we have to analyze narrative interviews translated from one language to another.[16]

A close reading of life story narratives often reveals an inclination to use a group of specific metaphors indicating interpretations of the self, of interactions, of proclivities or preoccupations. One may search for frames while another wants to transcend the frames.

A mixed or apparently contradictory use of metaphors may help us to discover complexities. For example, this narrator who is telling about a new job says:

> And now, all of a sudden I had to stand there and prepare my teaching five days a week. I might have put a bucket beneath each armpit that is how much I was perspiring. I was so scared I was about to faint … Somehow we survived. This was really the biggest challenge of my life, and yet, the best thing I did apart from getting married and having children.

I must have felt like a chicken breaking out from his eggshell. I got plenty of use for the creative side of my personality. Again, it was a completely different world. It was just like coming home.

(Woman born 1961) (my translation)

Up to this point the narrator has represented herself as a person looking for security, safety, and familiarity. But she manages to break out from the shell into a different world and still able to feel like coming home. By the application of metaphors, she illustrates her learning process and its result: the ability to feel at home in a bigger world.

Samples of stories

Usually, in applied research a number of interviews are collected, sometimes a limited sample, sometimes a very large collection. Individual stories may be accentuated in the analysis as "case studies," while the remaining narratives are represented in the analysis in a less detailed way. We should, as researchers, how-ever, be very conscious about how we represent our interviewees and their lives, also in our analysis of the material. Many people dislike the feeling of being reduced or fragmentized, as often happens in analyses based on coding of the material.[17] A comprehensive analysis of the individual life story interviews is likely to do more justice to the complexity of human life. The methodological "tools" described above can be used to open the texts that we as researchers have constructed together with our interviewees, in order to become familiar with the narratives in their complexity, and prepared to complete an analysis according to the objectives of our inquiry, which is not based on sloppy or care-less readings or misinterpretations. Some researchers choose to collaborate with their interviewees on the interpretations, especially where there are a number of rounds of interviews, or the interviews are part of a longitudinal study.[18] The ethical responsibility of the researcher for the representation of the human beings whose lives and stories she has been studying remains of paramount importance throughout the research from the interview stage to the presenta-tions and publications of the research. Working with narratives should convinc-ingly teach us the ethical significance of how people are represented in various texts, journals, and archives. This also applies to the final research product, the narratives from the field (Van Maanen, 1988; Czarniawska-Joerges, 1995) based on our narratives of the field.

Although I might miss a good point in my analysis of some applied research by obeying the simple rule of respecting each interviewee, this is far better than to risk having abused in some way or another the openness and confidence of the narrators.

Samples of narratives invite a comparison of differences, variations and simi-larities on a many different levels, some of which will be illustrated in the follow-ing chapter. Common cultural narratives emerge from the multiple voices of individual life story narratives as we shall see in the next chapter.

Chapter 10

Cultural identity

Cultural narratives

From the polyphony of samples of life story narratives common cultural narratives emerge. Patterns of interpretations of self and existence stand out from the multiple voices in biographical research. Turning the perspective toward the individual life story narrative we see, as discussed in the previous chapter, how personal stories are immersed in cultural narratives. In the analyses of each story we discover how the individual narrator negotiates meaning between different cultural narratives; and comparative analyses of samples reveal common features as well as distinctive nuances and variations between the different stories. We recognize interpretations of existence, basic assumptions and encounter common narratives of gender, social class, and ethnicity, as well as narratives of political and religious or geographical affiliations. We uncover narratives of transformation. In a narrative approach to identity, the cultural and the personal are closely intertwined. Charles Taylor points to the significance of language and to the social character of meanings, and their influence on human values:

> There is no way we could be inducted into personhood except by being initiated into a language. We first learn our languages of moral and spiritual discernment by being brought into an ongoing conversation by those who bring us up. The meanings that the key words first had for me are the meanings they have for *us*, that is, for me and my conversation partners together. Here a crucial feature of conversation is relevant, that in talking about something you and I make it an object for us together, that is, not just an object for me which happens also to be one for you, even if we add that I know that it's an object for you, and you know, etc. The object is for us in a strong sense, which I have tried to describe elsewhere with the notion of "public" or "common space."[1] The various uses of language set up, institute, focus, or activate such common spaces, just as it would appear the very first acquisition of language depends on a proto-variant of it, as seems indicated in the pioneering work of Jerome Bruner.

So I can only learn what anger, love, anxiety, the aspiration to wholeness, etc., are through my and others' experience of these being objects for *us*, in some common space.

(Taylor, 1989: 35)

We become culturally embedded through participation in "common" or "cultural spaces" and acquire social and cultural meanings in communication. We are continuously surrounded by cultural narratives that influence our interpretations of self and existence: as Somers and Gibson phrase it: "all of us come to be who we are (however ephemeral, multiple, and changing) by locating ourselves (usually unconsciously) in social narratives *rarely of our own making*" (1994: 59). Kerby also emphasizes the connection between the personal and the cultural narratives:

> The stories we tell of ourselves are determined not only by how other people narrate us but also by our language and the genres of storytelling inherited from our traditions. Indeed, much of our self-narrating is a matter of becoming conscious of the narratives that we already live with and in – for example, our roles in the family and in the broader sociopolitical arena. It seems true to say that we have already been narrated from a third-person perspective prior to our even gaining the competence for self-narration. Such external narratives will understandably set up expectations and constraints on our personal self-descriptions, and they significantly contribute to the material from which our own narratives are derived.[2]
>
> (1991: 6)

Cultural narratives, however, change over time as the analysis will show, and they are frequently contested or negotiated by the participants, though more so in some sociocultural contexts than in others. The rate of circulation of cultural narratives has seriously declined during the past 50 years. As Charles Taylor (1989) argues, our interpretive frameworks have become problematic in Western modernity. However, Lyotard's prophesy or statement from 1979 that the "master narratives" would disappear and leave us with only small, individual narratives has proved to be wrong (Lyotard, 1979). The modernist narrative of individuality and the narrative of progression and growth still seem to be influential examples of grand narratives in our culture. Lyotard is, however, right in assuming that master narratives are no longer indisputable.[3] They are, increasingly, contested and negotiated, but some people still take a lot of grand narratives and hegemonic or dominating discourses for granted in their interpretations of lived experience. In applied biographical research we are able to follow the change in cultural narratives and to discern what kind of memories different people in different contexts choose to narrate, or to retell and embrace as part of their ongoing identity construction.

We keep connections with the past and relate to each other through narratives as well as through material objects. We tell and retell, give and receive gifts, inherit and keep stuff, or discard or forget, both in public by establishing museums and archives or in personal life as elements in a continuous construction of identity.

Circumstance and choice

Prior to the Danish study on identity, learning, and democracy based on a sample of 120 life story narratives (see Chapter 8), I had published two books with collections of life stories in chronological order (about 25 in each volume), beginning with the oldest and ending with the youngest narrator (Horsdal, 1991, 1998). The plot of those two volumes showed to an astounding degree how the interpretations of self and existence had changed in accordance with changing social conditions and changing cultural narratives during the course of the twentieth century; so the samples of stories could be read as a cultural history of identity in this period. The change may be summarized as a transformation from a representation of life as a common destiny due to given circumstances to a matter of individual choice and responsibility.

Therefore, I decided to divide the large amount of material from the 120 narrative interviews into three generational groups in order to support the process of containing this entire extensive sample in its complexity for the final analysis. I wrote a chapter on each of the groups, the first encompassing the narratives from people born before the Second World War with the heading: *In those days they did not ask what you wanted* (a quote from one of the stories). It must be emphasized that the 120 interviews were collected during the 1990s and analyzed by the turn of the century.

The first chapter represented a sample of old people who grew up in a traditional society. As the stories were told at the end of the twentieth century, the view of the past is underscored by both positive and negative aspects of a fairly stable society characterized by vicinity, scarcity, family dependency, necessity, hard manual work, little education, and local affiliations that has now largely vanished.

For those with property and work, the anchorage in the local the environment often stretched backward through several generations. They had stayed in the same place, in the same professions, upholding traditions and supporting ties of kinship through family narratives. Among the narrators were several farmers who represented the sixth or seventh generation on the property regardless of the size of the farm; but also in other professions the continuity was explicit. Grocers, independent merchants, carpenters and coopers tell about being the fourth or fifth generation following in the footsteps of their forefathers.

Until the middle of the twentieth century, property and self-employed work secured a high degree of stability, and affiliations and identity were attached to place. This continuity changes radically during the next 50 to 60 years, a transformation which, obviously, accentuates the lost stability and the loss of a familiar neighborhood in the narratives.

Lawyers and doctors and other professionals from a higher social class also followed the family traditions to a large extent but were more likely to move to a different locality. The exception to this traditional continuity is the poor. Those who did not have the means to make a living in the place where they grew up left in order to find more prosperous fields in other regions, or they emigrated in order to look for work elsewhere. The experiences of scarcity and hard work from an extremely early age take up a very significant part of these narratives, as they do in those of many small farmers, craftsmen, and women. Many claim to remember the exact (paltry) amount of money they were paid for work they carried out as children. The narratives contain accounts of daily life, tasks, working methods, food, and even personal hygiene – described as matters of social distinction – as well as stories of special events and feasts.

The regional, or even local, affiliation is striking. Only narrators from the region close to the border between Denmark and Germany mention a national collective identity, but even there this is regarded mainly as a regional characteristic feature. Cultural narratives of religious affiliations have several variants. A dominating religious or political movement could in some areas prompt a pragmatic adjustment, such as removing the "improper" deck of cards if one of the missionaries entered, or result in more open fights about local souls and local values. The upcoming social movement also confronted the religious beliefs and the general, positive connotation of modesty and frugality in the way of thinking prevalent in the countryside in the first half of the twentieth century.

> He drove an asphalt drum and worked in the draining trenches in the winters. Then he had to enter the union. That was a sin to the evangelical family so they asked him if he had become a Red milch cow.
>
> (Man born 1923) (my translation)

However, in spite of there being common cultural narratives of the past, we do not find a unified interpretation of existence at work in the narratives of the old people. Indeed, there are a number of examples of clashes of values around different religious, political and social affiliations. There are several ways of life and several interpretations of existence in the homes of poor farm workers or fishermen, on the farms, in the bourgeois circles in the cities, and among working-class people respectively. The closeness of neighborhood and interpersonal interdependence correspond to the perceived social differences between those who were prosperous, and could offer help, and those who were poor and had to receive help with due humility. While values and attitudes emerge primarily from the conditions and circumstances of the different social groups in various local contexts, we do find a few examples of different values within one family. Social differences had a great impact on learning opportunities.[4] Narrators who grew up in poor families tell about how they had to leave home in order to work from an early age. The learning outcome from some of the village schools was rather poor, and only a very few had the opportunity to continue to secondary education. In particular, women complain of having been denied the opportunities for more education.

A certain resignation towards life's conditions characterizes the cultural narratives of many women. Traditional society depends on the family. We hear of young women having to defend their chastity and, once pregnant outside marriage, they are an easy prey. There are different moral rules and obligations for men and for women, less access to education for women, and unmarried female relatives are expected to assist the family when needed.

The attitude of resignation in the face of conditions and circumstances according to sex and social class results in an interpretation of existence that divides the responsibility for success or failure among a collective group; and so a part of the burden of insufficient achievement is lifted from individual shoulders. Many of the older narrators say, as they retrospectively evaluate their lives and achievements: "Well, that's how farm workers lived back then!" or, "These were the conditions!" "Women could not do that." A narrative of trying to cope in very difficult circumstances is actually supportive to the individual, since personal success, or failure, is not just a question of personal achievement. The typical configuration of a life story from this generation would be: we coped; we managed and, perhaps, even prospered, in spite of hard and difficult conditions, due to hard work, an attitude of thrift and frugality, and a strong sense of community.

Another interesting consequence of the interpretation of traditional life concerns the relationship between children and parents. Apart from the hour of twilight, which meant a break for play, storytelling, dance, or just quietly being together, for most of the time many children had duties; they had to work and help the adults. Looking back on this childhood, the only narrators who express feelings of being unwanted are those who did not grow up with their parents. The majority felt they were needed, and many speak in a very positive way of the feeling of participation and of being in a community.

The significance of community is prevalent in the narratives of the past. Concomitantly, socialists and liberals celebrate the communities of the past and express concern over increasing egotism and isolation in the modern welfare society. There are many expressions of ambivalence towards "project modernity," including fear of a globalized and strange world. This is particularly the case in areas where the past world was very narrow. There is fear of isolation as everyone seems to be so busy and change takes place so fast. Nevertheless, several narrators who experienced poverty praise the material improvement and the progress, better educational possibilities, not least for women.

> We always ploughed with horses. All this mechanization killed the Danish farmer. In the old days people were happy when we finish a task. We said: "Thank God, now we managed that." Today, they never finish. They are busy all the time because they have all those mechanic aids, and that's expensive. There is more routine work today. People have more land, but no one to help them. And they don't exploit it that well. When you plough you cannot get all the way into the corners. I always dug the corners with a spade by hand. But you don't do that anymore. In the old days, everything was used, and we were more grateful.
>
> (Man born 1906, interviewed when
> he was 84) (my translation)

Departure and emancipation

Departure and emancipation was the heading of the second chapter about the narrators born in the 1940s and the 1950s signifying a generation who opened the doors from the narrow traditional life-world into a world of new possibilities. Contradicting the title of the chapter of the previous generation, an interviewee born in 1944 exclaimed: "It was fantastic! We could do just what we wanted!" This new generation grew up in nuclear families in a traditional society about to move into post-war modern conditions in the beginning of the welfare society; they were the young generation in the 1960s and 1970s ready to celebrate change, progress, or even revolutions.

> In 1956 my parents bought a car. Then we made a trip every Sunday after church. My grandmother had paid half of the car so, naturally, she came along. Normally we brought coffee, so we unfolded a table and folding-chairs, but only my dad's chair had a back.
>
> (Woman born 1946) (my translation)

The old family patterns, with the father's preferential position and well-behaved children who did what they were asked to do were dissolving. A rebellion against authorities lay waiting round the corner.

The narrator from above continues:

> During secondary school I went into opposition to my mother. All my life I had been attending Sunday school and going to church with her, but now, I didn't bother anymore. I also stopped going with them on holidays, I was a nuisance to her and told her continuously how stupid she was. And then my hated math teacher would not recommend me to join upper secondary school, so to the horror of my mother I said I wanted to work as a drayman. I was so mad and found everything so idiotic. It all ended up with me finishing upper secondary school at a course in two years and getting an education as a teacher.
>
> (Woman born 1946) (my translation)

There is no longer just one track to follow. Different routes are tested concerning ways of living, collective beliefs, and attitudes. The narrators explain and argue for the routes they have chosen. This is contrary to the older generation, who did not need to defend why they took a certain path since their direction was determined in advance by tradition. The old told about their fate emotionally, it was either good or bad, you were lucky or you were not. Now, the way of living is a matter of choice as possibilities grow; and, looking back, the narrators construct explanations. Many young people throw themselves into experiments, fearless and full of curiosity. The wide open doors to freedom invite experiments, and no one really knows how or where to set the limits. Strangely enough, the rebellions and opposition to the parents are not thematized by the parents in their stories, and are only mentioned by the rebels themselves. Perhaps, the silence is due to shyness among the older generation, or indicates a wish to underscore positive family values. Most of the narratives of the rebels show, however, as does the one quoted above, that they become closer to the parents again later in life. At the time when the life stories are told, decades after the rebellion took place, the attitudes, values, and ideological standpoints of the mature narrators often approach elements of the original context in which they grew up. In spite of the extensive societal and cultural transformation in this generation, we find several narratives with the well known plot "home – out – home."

Grand narratives in the form of ideologies flourish in this generation, and several conflicting ideological affiliations converge in the individual narratives and point in all directions. Pivotal issues are a belief in freedom, emancipation, and possibilities. All of a sudden, it seems possible to change the world.

New concepts turn up in the narratives: "boyfriends" and "girlfriends," and a variety of marital relations are tried out. Divorces become much more frequent, and living together without getting married is normal. But love life is not easy. Women join other women in feminist organizations and discuss female roles. Broken relationships often create conflicts around the children. Stories tell of fights about custody and access. How the stories of love life are told depends on the later developments. Narrative causations and turning points are constructed. In some cases, the experiments with different forms of life could lead to serious problems, drug abuse being one of them. Resources from a secure childhood, a sure support base, seems central in determining the chance of overcoming the risks of the experiments of emancipation. Isolation or emotional dependency permeates vulnerable voices in some narratives due to the lack of a support base.

Obviously, the extent of radicalism in the departures and emancipation from the traditional ways of life in narratives varies a great deal. In some narratives the youth rebellion is only mentioned as a picture of the period, or, perhaps, omitted entirely, because neither ideological positions nor affiliations to subcultures are part of the story. But, even there, in the stories of those who did not challenge family traditions by transgressing the norms we are likely to find a life trajectory disembedded from place, continuity, and tradition.

This generation talks about immense societal change. The vast majority of women start working, and soon the life of most families depends on income from two jobs. Accordingly, material progress is a big issue and influences people's lives. People move from the country to the cities, and in the cities they often move to better flats or to houses with little gardens in the growing suburbs. Change of employment causes movement to other cities and regions. The choice of new partners also causes movements to new places. Children go to preschool and to school and move to new schools along with the relocations of their parents. The period of childhood is extended by several years. The old generation in general left their family to earn their living, or at least support the family income, by the age of 14, with a very few lucky enough to continue their education, and some poor children even had to leave their homes at a very young age – nine, ten, eleven. Now, upper secondary school and continuing education is no longer exclusively a privilege of the upper class. Education has become a matter of choice.

In contrast to the old generation of a traditional society in which farming was the major occupation, this generation has grown up in the industrial era in Denmark. This affects the interpretations of existence because everyday life now is conceived as divided into several independent spheres: working life, family life, leisure life. In traditional society this division did not really exist, at least not on the farms or on the small enterprises. People worked continuously whenever they could. An old man tells about how he was, all of a sudden, granted four holidays and consequently went to work in the fields picking peas during those four days so as not to waste the time. Now, people go on holidays. During the 1950s people began to travel during holidays, go abroad and visit new places.

Some narrators fall between the two generations. They seem to accept the given conditions in their youth, such as a choice of education being according to the wish of their fathers or no education at all. Many of them, however, seem later to catch up by participation in adult education or to change track in other aspects in later life. An outstanding metaphor of the interpretation of existence in this generation is the significance of "being able to form your own life." Some of those who did not feel they had done this were keen to support their children to do better. Not everyone, however, cares for or values educational achievements.

The individualization and cultural emancipation implies a possible departure from a form of life determined by inherited circumstances. But when we enter the wide new world to test its possibilities we leave for ever the "natural" context, and from now on we need to show and prove our positions, and we need explicit affirmation of our individual right to be and take up a position and a space in this world. This need for affirmation, which many sociologists and psychologists – incorrectly – labeled as narcissism, is a result of the emancipation and departure from a traditional society into a world of choice and individual responsibility for the course of life.

You are valuable if the community needs you – and your working capacity. Individual value – being appreciated as the special person you are – is far more affirmative, but it is equally painful if this appreciation is denied.

The rebellious generation carries with them memories of the world from which they departed, hidden in photo-albums or in the narratives of the past. Their mothers were mostly housewives, and there were fewer siblings than in the previous generations. Many children had more attention, which influenced their self-confidence. This stability and security bolstered their courage to break out and try out what post-war life had to offer.

Acknowledging our increasing ability to shape a life does not mean, however, that circumstance and conditions no longer have any influence; they certainly do, whether they are caused by coincidence or fate. The narratives tell of life trajectories full of drawbacks: illnesses, accidents, separations, unemployment upset plans and turn lives upside down. A feeling of personal responsibility for the course of life increases as we approach the younger generations. The very existence of possibilities produces a feeling that so much depends on individual choice. The younger the narrators, the more reflexivity and personal responsibility comes to the fore. Choice creates doubt – is this right or could you have done something else? A burden is placed on the shoulders of the single individual who no longer can refer to general conditions, traditions, or habits, to what is natural or normal but must take individual responsible for the chosen life project.

> Today, we have to reflect and make decisions ourselves all the time. As a woman you have to make up your mind about things you didn't have to decide on before. We must provide for ourselves, take part in politics, be engaged in the labor marked, be committed parents – preferably be in the governing body in the kindergarten, etc. I tend to get involved in a lot of things, and I like to be where things are happening.
>
> (Woman born 1961) (my translation)

Finding yourself

It is striking that everyone from the previous two generations spontaneously mentions the profession of the fathers (the majority of women were housewives). Social reference seemed absolutely natural. The young people, on the contrary, do not mention anything about the jobs or social status of their parents unless the profession of one of their parents becomes an issue in connection with a different theme. The collective narrative of class does not seem to be adequate for this generation. There are different matters at stake. The emancipation and departure from the traditional society radically altered childhood for the next generation. Increasing mobility and economic growth along with other transformations and experiments caused relocations which the children experience as disrupting continuity. Many children had to face new homes and new surroundings, new regions, different dialects, new schools with different children and ways of teaching, and new codes of behavior. These ruptures are referred to as cultural chocks in the narratives of the next generation. A clash of cultures due to the parents' divorce, relocations, and change of schools create problems of coherence. And the clash of cultures seems to continue in adolescence.

> Two years later, my boyfriend went to Iceland to stay. We were still together, but this made things worse; how could I find a solution to this split between environments, my home in Western Jutland, Iceland, and the university. All three environments were incompatible, and I couldn't get them to merge.[5]
>
> (Woman born 1970) (my translation)

The simultaneous and serial participation in different – and sometimes almost incompatible – cultural contexts is a profound challenge in contemporary society and quite distinct in the narratives. Life has become an individual project, preferably to become successful, and the individual human being feels a personal responsibility for the outcome. Reflexive identity work plays a significant role in the narratives. "Finding yourself" is the heading of the third chapter in the book. It is now a demanding existential project to figure out who you are and where you fit in. "Now, when I started most of my fears have been disproved. I was afraid I wouldn't fit in. Right now, I am sort of OK as a person, but it takes time to find yourself" (Man born 1966) (my translation).

A lot of energy is taken up with doubt. Is this the right choice? Or should I have chosen differently? The metaphors of the narrative are striking. "Right now I am floating," he says. Many talk of the problems of fitting in, or settling down, or finding the right vocation. But how to act so one can find some coherence and fit in, and yet, be allowed to be one's self without pretending? The discourses of self in the life story narratives change. The search has turned inwards; it is not about leaving home for the big world to find the answers out there like in the fairytales. The unknown is oneself or one's self. Arguably, young people do travel around the world, but in order to get to know themselves rather than to discover the world.

Some of the metaphors applied to the discourses of the self identify the concept of an authentic nuclear self – "the real me" – which is opposed to playing out or adopting more or less distorted roles. A discovery of such a nuclear self would – according to the narrators – enable more authentic decisions to be taken in order to achieve success in the life projects.

The discourses of the self are rooted both in a Kantian and in an expressive romantic conception of the subject. One of the narrators, an artist, initiates his artistic project – in perfect harmony with his ancestors from Romanticism – to find the authentic nuclear self by transgressing the limits of the self, because he, as well as many others, felt he had to perform. Eventually, he fails: "It remains an empty form, and I discover that it is impossible to find the truth about the person. There is no nuclear self you can point to and say: 'This is me!'" (Man born 1967) (my translation).

The endeavor to achieve autonomy was an essential part of the "project modernity." If people could be released from all the prejudices emanating from superstition and routine they could liberate the immanent rationality, the distinguished mark of the human being, and a new happy world would arise, created by sovereign, rational subjects. A subject–object dichotomy has been displayed in different philosophical and epistemological variations, which separates the individual subject from his environment and from the other subjects who are positioned outside. A theory of consciousness of this type leads to an essentialist idea of autonomy, a belief in the independent will and the notion of a nuclear self.

The notion of personal development is an obvious model for the construction of identity permeated by modernist discourses, although, the notion of personal development has a dynamic aspect as new encounters with the world shape and change our "selves." The dynamic aspect – containing the possibility of transformation – is often connected to an idea of an authentic nucleus like a germ that may unfold and flourish under the right circumstances. This way of thinking gives rise to a project which precisely demands that you have to get to know yourself and find out if you are in a "right" or a "wrong" kind of development, so that you can quickly withdraw from something which is not really you. The cultural narratives of the self represented in these stories are, furthermore, influenced by psychological discourses.

The notion of personal development is in some of the narratives encumbered by a figure of thought – perhaps originating in Eastern spiritual philosophy – which encourages the idea that you have to work with yourself and learn to love yourself before you are able to deal with the world outside. Several young people who suffer from low self-esteem speak of attending courses in personal development.

> For two years I was teaching sexuality and self-development, "learn to love yourself" as a theme. This has been an extremely optimistic thing, to be able to give to other girls the tools I was given and feel how they could push back the boundaries of the individual.
>
> (Woman born 1976) (my translation)

The privilege of the teacher and the therapist is to give something to others. In spite of the discourse of the self as the final focus, the participation in different courses – including courses about personal development – may provide an opportunity for interpersonal relationships. When someone is listening and attentive the participant may also feel better. The problem of this discourse of self is, however, that the participant, in opposition to the teacher, must work out when she is capable of loving herself enough in order to be able to attend to others.

Some of the narrators tell of the pain they have experienced in this inward self examination. Abuse of alcohol or drugs provides a means of forgetting. A homeless drug addict tells:

> I must admit, it isn't really the drugs – I like being on drugs – so I don't have any problems, so I can be everywhere and feel OK – but it's all that it carries with it –jail, and that I hurt my family every time.
>
> (Man born 1970) (my translation)

To have a space, a relationship, an environment where you can be, where you feel OK, is a basic, existential need. It is extremely difficult to fight a way out of an abusive habit if the flight into drugs or alcohol is the only context in which you can "be everywhere."

Some of the narratives indicate that personal abuse from a close relative leaves the abused with a feeling of having deserved it, of not being worth any better. Human value seems to depend on the function assigned by related others. However, participation in new communities creates the possibilities of forming new and better relationships. Repeated positive or negative experiences of interaction in the different communities of practice reinforce an open, confident self-image or a vulnerable, fragile self-image respectively. The latter tend to cut themselves off from the diversity of the world.

Another striking feature of the narrative identities constructed by this generation is the need to be in control – perhaps, another element of defense against a seemingly chaotic world.

> All my life is built on what I choose to do. I don't just do things. I like to think that everything I do is deliberate. A consequence of a choice I make. Nothing is unpremeditated – that's how I want to see myself, and that's how I want others to see me. I aim at this, aim at an ideal.

> (Man born 1975) (my translation)

The narrator wants to be a good person. He says it is wrong to be egoistic, and defends his independent and reflexively controlled self-image.

From time to time, the body becomes the instrument of self-control. Narrators suffering from eating disorders, dancers, or extreme sportsmen tell stories constructed around routines of body control and discipline. Through the modeled body a "self" is constructed. It is peculiar to see how an attempt at autonomous and rational control of existence can lead to the opposite as the life of the individual becomes completely guided and controlled by self-inflicted challenges.

The surplus of energy required to engage in a wider world and interact with the different environments and cultures emanates from other stories. Fortunately, several narrators express an ability to feel at home in a bigger world, mastering the increasing demands for reflexive identity work, for a continuous construction of coherence and interpersonal commitments in new contexts. The sample of young people's life story narratives clearly contradicts the claims of "narcissism" and "egoism" frequently used to label the young by the older generation. Again and again, we hear of the need to mean something to others, to make a difference, to be of significance in other people's lives.

Narrative collective identity

Different interpretive frameworks accentuate the quest for meaning and narrative articulation, according to Charles Taylor:

> But the invocation of meaning also comes from our awareness of how much the search involves articulation. We find the sense of life through articulating it. And moderns have been acutely aware of how much sense being there for us depends on our powers of expression. Discovering here depends, is interwoven with, inventing. Finding a sense to life depends on framing meaningful expressions which are adequate. There is thus something particularly appropriate to our condition in the polysemy of the word "meaning": lives

can have or lack a point; while it also applies to language and other forms of expression. More and more, we moderns attain meaning in the first sense, when we do, through creating it in the second sense.

(1989: 18)

The dissolution of a common interpretation of existence may imply that "the meaning of life" seems fragile as a threat of meaninglessness lurks beneath the surface. On the other hand, this provides new possibilities for negotiations and co-existent interpretations. Cultural canonical narratives are rarely open for discussion in an authoritarian society. Taylor's demonstration of accordance between the linguistic and existential sense of meaning points to a need for narrative competence, but also to the need for a cultural space for negotiation. The possibility actively to question and to negotiate cultural narratives and different interpretations of existence depends on social conditions as well as culturally acquired means of expression. The implicit, "natural" character of many of the cultural narratives that make up part of our narrative identity underscores the importance of the ability to discuss their legitimacy and implications. In his article "Life as narrative" (1987) Bruner suggests that narratives not only imitate life, as indicated by the concept of "*mimesis*" but our lives also imitate cultural narratives. We live our lives according to the interpretive frameworks of self and existence. The cultural narrative of individuality and reflexive modernity (Giddens, 1990) seems to make up an interpretive framework for an entire generation.

The important issue of personal identity will be taken up in the next chapter. From my point of view, there is more to identity than narrative constructions, although the narrative constructions of personal identity are absolutely crucial. Cultural, collective narratives constitute a significant part of our identity in different ways. Apart from framing interpretations of self and existence, as demonstrated above, they form shared fates, imagined communities, construct different variations of "we" and construct "the other" who, in his distinctive difference, mirrors ourselves.

Some of the cultural narratives are closely connected to shared forms of practice, common rituals and other kinds of interpersonal interactions. From interpersonal interactions and narratives "we" are constructed in families, in organizations, in nations. The tendency towards hegemony, repression, and projection in group identities may prove to be fatal in many cases depending on the construction of the other (Sarup, 1996). Cultural narratives are neither neutral nor free of power, and we are not equally legitimate or capable participants in the constructions and communications of cultural narratives.

Narratives about communities in which "we" are the good, chosen, just, clean, healthy, normal, right, valuable collective subject, contrary to "them," "the others" may support the identity of a group and the self-confidence of the individual within the group, as long as the stories are retold and their credibility not significantly contested.

The relationship to the other also depends on how comprehensive the collective subject "we" is. Some cultural narratives claim universality and articulate the natural being of things in the world. Some groups construct narratives about themselves which claim universality and, as a result, the other is denied the status of a real human being. The narrative of the human being as an autonomous, rational individual has positioned large groups of the human race in a dubious relation to their humanity for a long period of time. How about women, children, the uneducated? This cultural narrative influenced the view of nature and fueled another hegemonic and immensely influential narrative, the story of development, progress, and growth.

Globalization and migration challenge cultural narratives. Life story narratives with immigrants show how different cultural narratives are negotiated. Sometimes, they clash, and sometimes narrators tell about how they have to navigate between different contexts, affected by different cultural narratives. The life stories of minorities reveal the overwhelming impact of cultural narratives told by the majority. Cultural narrative identity is affected not only by the cultural narratives we tell about ourselves and about the other, but how we are being told by the others has an enormous influence on our own identity construction. A defensive side-effect may be – as one narrator phrases it – the construction of a nostalgic ethnic identity.

Collective identity may be challenged by new experience and by increasing mobility. As we encounter new people – if we approach them and engage in dialogue – our interpretive frameworks may be negotiated. In the encounter, our framework expands if you – to use Gadamer's expression (1965: 288) are able "to lift your own and the other's particularity." As we move, our horizon moves. If we understand the impact of cultural narratives on collective identity our narratives about ourselves may appear less evident. Perhaps, instead of constructing a collective "we" contrary to "the other," who is considered to be different (and inferior), mobility between different cultural contexts could assist a growing intercultural competence, which would make it possible to conceive the other as someone who might be a future member of a potential "we." Participation in new communities of practice enables new affiliations and interpersonal relations across cultural demarcations. Then, perhaps, instead of claiming the hegemony of our cultural narratives and cultural identity we may employ the BA: principle (Taylor, 1989) meaning: this is the Best Account so far.

Movement and mobility are crucial elements of societal and cultural change. The transformation from the traditional society into the contemporary society which the old people in the sample of life story narratives tell about is distinctively represented by an image of mobility. If we compare a map of a small part of the country as it looked at the beginning of the twentieth century to a similar map of today, some changes are evident: there are more people today; in particular the cities are much larger. If we imagine that all the people living in the area are represented as dots on the two maps and, accordingly, we picture and compare the movements of those people now and 100 years ago, the differences really stand out. In the beginning of the twentieth century many people stayed in the local community most of the time; the majority would stay within the small map. Today people would move into or outside the map much more frequently; they would be here and there, now and then, and the speed of the movements has increased enormously. This is why many old people would say: "Well, we did not talk much about it." No; all the neighbors around had experienced the same things, so what they did talk about was the secrets, the gossip, and the rare news about newcomers and travelers. Today we are together with different people in different contexts most of the time. But who has time to listen?

Chapter 11

Personal identity

The self after postmodernity

The significance of being appreciated as an individual person stands out as a prominent feature in the numerous life story narratives I have collected. Across all the differences, it is a lifelong human need to be recognized in a cultural space in a mutual world. To be allowed to be, without having to reject, or cut out the experiences or the narratives we feel are part of our identity, seems crucial. Denial or repression of the past, especially if enforced by others, is, as Charles Taylor argues, quite problematic:

> We want our lives to have meaning, or weight, or substance, or to grow towards some fullness, or however the concern is formulated that we have been discussing in this section. But this means our *whole* lives. If necessary, we want the future to "redeem" the past, to make it part of a life story which has sense or purpose, to take it up in a meaningful unity ... To repudiate my childhood as unredeemable in this sense is to accept a kind of mutilation as a person; it is to fail to meet the full challenge involved in making sense of my life.
>
> (1989: 50)

I find it important to emphasize the social nature of sense making. We can easily become entangled with figments of the imagination when we are left to make sense of confusing experiences alone. But a restless adaptation to or assimilation of the expectations of our surroundings can involve a pruning which does not promote growth. But what does it actually mean to be the person you are? How are we to understand the issue of personal identity?

A narrative personal identity is constructed through the life stories. We can tell about our lives and our experiences at different times, in different situations, and to different interlocutors and thus construct different versions of our personal identity. Contrary to the writing of dairies and journals, orally narrated life stories are in most cases told at the request of somebody else. Someone asks for the life story narrative; the narrative construction of personal identity emerges as a response to another person's request. The issue of "self" involves co-construction of narratives in an interpersonal communicative space; but as we are embodied creatures there is more to it than co-construction of stories.

I have argued that the cultural space in which a life story narrative is told is very significant; and in the following I shall explore the issue of personal identity with a focus on the interaction in the cultural space, inspired by some of our excellent philosophers.

In *Sources of the self*, Taylor discusses the significance of the other as the original source of our lives and identities and the importance of being called. He says:

> The close connection between identity and interlocution also emerges in the place of *names* in human life. My name is what I am "called." A human being *has* to have a name, because he or she has to be *called*, i.e. addressed. Being called into conversation is a precondition of developing human identity, and so my name is (usually) given me by my earliest interlocutors.
>
> (1989: 525)

A name is a mark of personal identity given by others. But if no one is calling out for you, there is no need for a name.

Schrag argues in his fascinating book, *The self after postmodernity* (1997) for a self in interactional contexts: discursive contexts, contexts of action, ritual contexts, and transcendental contexts. He wants to shift the focus on self from the question of *what* to the question of *who*. First, he talks about the who of discourse manifest in the narratives of the individual.

> The who of discourse is an achievement, an accomplishment, a performance, whose presence to itself is admittedly fragile, a performance, subject to forgetfulness and semantic ambiguities. But in all this there is still a unity and a species of self-identity, secured not by an abiding substratum but rather by an achieved self-identity, secured through a transversal extending over and lying across the multiple forms of speech and language games without coincidence with any of them. This transversal dynamics, effecting a convergence without coincidence, defines the unity, presence, and identity of the self. And they are a unity, presence, and identity that are concretely manifest in narration, in the telling of the story by the who of discourse, emplotting the multiple and changing episodes of her or his endeavors.
>
> (1997: 33)

A narrative definition of the self does not entail a free and autonomous self-creation. Language, cultural codes, and narrative structures exist before the individual person enters the stage. The narrative is dialogic. Meaning exists in narratives already told as well as in the narratives produced throughout life by the who of discourse. To Schrag, the self is, however, more than the who of discourse. He talks of an embodied self situated in between action and suffering.

The situating of speakers, authors, and actors within an intentionality of embodiment functioning at the interstices of activity and passivity, doing and suffering, vitalizes and enriches the self as a source of empowerment. This recognition of dynamics of bio-power in the life of the self announces a more robust sense of self-identity into the domain of embodied action. It is in this wider perspective that self-identity appears in the guise of *self-consistency* and *existential continuity*.

(1997: 62)

In Schrag's conceptual framework you do not *have* a body, you *are* embodied. He opposes dualism and a subject–object dichotomy; the body is not an object but a living body.

We encounter the world, engage in forms of practice, actively and passively, and form a narrative self though lived experience. Schrag does not understand narrative as a representation of something but in an ontological sense. An ontological conception of narrative implies that we experience in a narrative form. Schrag shares Carr's view on the ontological claim of narrative and refers to his comment that "narrative form is not a dress which covers something else but the *structure inherent in human experience and action*" (1997: 43).[1]

According to Schrag, our actions and our narratives respond to other actions and narratives; they are creative in relation to what already exists. Discourses and actions are intimately connected when we make promises and keep our word. Self-identity involves a certain degree of coherence over time in our discourses and actions. This means that the question of who we are is inseparable from the question of how we are in relation to others. Schrag rephrases Descartes (1997: 78): "We interact, therefore we are." But who is the other I meet when I interact with the environment, and am I ready to confront the otherness of the other? Schrag refers to Levinas (1996) and explains:

The otherness of the other needs be granted its intrinsic integrity, so that in seeing the face of the other and hearing the voice of the other I am *responding* to an exterior gaze and an exterior voice rather than carrying on a conversation with my alter ego.

(1997: 84)[2]

The fitting response is not a question of simple accommodation, and he underscores the difference between being context-conditioned and context-determined. In his view, we are neither context-determined nor contextless. He opposes both relativism and an ahistoric universalism.

Language is a semiotic system which transcends the individual speech act, and the self in action moves beyond the present state of affairs. But Schrag also discusses transcendence in a more radical sense, echoing Levinas' discussion of "radical exteriority." We need, he claims, transcendence "in its guise of radical alterity, as a critical principle" in order to relativize "the culture-spheres and install a vigilance over their claims and presuppositions, curtailing any temptations to achieve a God's-eye view of the panorama of human history" (1997: 124). Transcendence in this radical aspect and its function as a critical principle helps us to avoid ideological hegemonies in any sphere. He argues in favor of a dynamic transversality in opposition to both relativism and unity, and introduces, following Kierkegaard and Levinas one further aspect of transcendence: "an ethic of the fitting response" beyond reciprocity and reimbursement, and concludes:

> Transcendence in its threefold function as a principle of protest against cultural hegemony, as a condition for a transversal unification that effects a convergence without coincidence, and a power of giving without expectation of return stands outside the economies of science, morality, art, and religion as culture-spheres.
>
> (1977: 148)

Schrag provides us with "a revised narrative on self-understanding ... that sets forth a who of discourse, engaged in action, communally situated, and tempered by transcendence" (p. 148). Besides Kierkegaard and Levinas, another significant source of inspiration for his book is Paul Ricoeur who, a few years before, had published his immensely inspiring book on identity: *Oneself as another* (1994/1990). There are many similarities in the approach and conclusions between the two almost contemporary books on identity, one American the other French, a difference which, however, inevitably influences the style of writing.

Oneself as another

The crucial significance of finding oneself called upon in the second person is the core issue of *Oneself as another*. Throughout ten studies Ricoeur explores the issue of self and identity. The starting point is again the question of "*who*": "Who is speaking? Who is acting? Who is recounting about himself or herself? Who is the moral subject of imputation?"[3] (1994: 16). The response to these questions: "It is me!" shows that the starting point of his analytical approach to an analysis of self and identity is not the first person "I," it is not the Cartesian Cogito, but the second person "me" who is called upon. At the same time, his studies on self and identity oppose the relativity of a constructivist approach. He criticizes the linguistic turn and the theories on language games of ethical neutrality. Theories which claim that "everything is language" cannot come close to what actually happens in the world (p. 301).

The first study is semantic and discusses the concept of "person" as the identifying reference. We are able to identify what we are talking about as we refer to an object or a person. We can refer to this particular individual object or to a class or category of objects, or to an individual person or a generalized group of human beings ("women"). Furthermore, we can identify the same (object or person) at different times and places, "the same" in this context, signifies the individual, recurrent referent.

In his second study Ricoeur applies a pragmatic approach in the discussion of utterances in situated interlocutions. A speech act may be locutionary, illocutionary, or perlocutionary. A speaker can refer to something or do something with his utterance, promise, pray, judge, threaten, etc. but Ricoeur argues that all utterances contain an element of action. He says in a footnote to Récanaty:

> Someone's utterance of this sentence [water boils at 1000° C], the fact that someone says this, is an event that occurs, as do all events, at a certain time and in a certain place: This spatiotemporally determined event is the saying, or the utterance. The fact of saying something is an event, like the fact of breaking one's leg, the fact of receiving a decoration, the fact of being born or dying. The expression "the fact of saying" underscores the eventlike character of utterance, insofar as it is a fact: a fact is above all something that "takes place," or that "is the case," to use an English expression.
>
> (1994: 50)

The fact that interlocutionary acts are situated in space and time is an important point. Speech acts presuppose a listener towards whom the utterance is directed. Ricoeur explains:

> In short, utterance equals interlocution. A theme begins to take shape this way, which will continue to take on greater dimensions in the studies that follow, namely that every advance made in the direction of the selfhood of the speaker or the agent has as its counterpart a comparable advance in the otherness of the partner. At the stage of our present study, this correlation does not yet take on the dramatic character which the polemical confrontation between two narrative programs will introduce at the heart of interlocution.
>
> (1994: 44)

After a description of how the deictic shifters, "I," "you," "here," "now," anchor the utterance in a given perspective of the world, he compares the two studies and the two aspects of the person: the speaker and the "person" identified by the reference.

The next studies take up theories of action: the issue of attribution of an action to an agent and the role of attestation. The attestation of the intention to do something is at the same time an attestation of the self. The analysis of actions involves more than the question of the who of action, also: what? why? how? and when? How the action is defined (how the limits of the action are defined) – as actions are responded to by new actions – determines how we can answer the question of ascription and responsibility. Who initiated the action? And who carried on? The agent has the power-to-do and is responsible.

The temporal dimension of the self enters the fifth study on identity and narrative. Ricoeur makes a distinction between the same (*idem*) and identity as self (*ipse*). The difference between the two concepts appears in relation to temporality. "The same" can be a numerical identity (*idem*), two or more occurrences of a thing or creature that we re-identify as the same; or "the same" may refer to a qualitative identity, a resemblance in spite of divergence (*ipse*). Across temporal distance recognition and identification may introduce a doubt: is it really the same across temporal transformations? We may ascribe permanence in time, an uninterrupted continuity in spite of numerical diversity to a living creature that grows and ages. The acorn becomes an oak; and although we change every cell in our body over the years, the genetic code remains the same. We recognize ourselves and each other, and remain ourselves, as we change. Ricoeur speaks of "character," dispositions, habits, etc. behind the stability that defines sameness. Here, the discordant concordance, characteristic of Ricoeur's description of narrative composition comes in as a synthesis of the heterogeneity. "The narrative constructs the identity of the character, what can be called his or her narrative identity, in constructing that of a story told. It is the identity of the story that makes the identity of the character" (p. 148).

At the same time, the body as one's own has a mediating function in the structure of being in the world, "the feature of selfhood belonging to corporeality is extended to that of the world as it is inhabited corporeally" (p. 150).

The starting point in narrative makes Ricoeur elaborate the concept of action. Actions are immersed in other actions, and interactions in other interactions. He discusses the interactive character of the concept of practice.[4] Although we may practice different skills, games, or professions on our own, a practice is an art learned from someone else (p. 156). Interactions may include activity and passivity, action and suffering, action and response, as well as omission or submission.

The chapters on narrative are central because the narrative configuration establishes a relationship with ethics and morality, which are studied in the following parts of the book. The hypothetical form of a narrative places it in between description and prescription. The ethical dimension of personal identity implies continuity, permanence across time in order to be a person others may count on. The accountability is ascribed to some permanence in time and character and, again, it is the other who is the starting point for the responsibility of the self. There is no self without the other who calls for a response and responsibility. The priority given to responsiveness delimits the notion of self both against lack of, and against a rigid form of, constancy.

Ricoeur defines the ethical intention as "aiming at the 'good life' with and for others, in just institutions" (p. 172). According to him, we live in a kind of hermeneutic circle of infinite interpretations of the choices we make in different fields of practice and in life as a whole. Self and other, active and passive, action and happening are reciprocal and interchangeable. We change roles like the shifters "I" and "you," but at the same time we are irreplaceable to the other. We may estimate others as ourselves and estimate ourselves as another; "becoming in this way fundamentally equivalent are the esteem of the *other as a oneself* and the esteem of *oneself as an other*" (p. 194). The foundation of justice is both equality and the irreplaceable uniqueness of the individual.

In chapter 9, Ricoeur discusses the ancient drama *Antigone* in order to illustrate the danger of one-sidedness in moral principles in a complex life. We are born into institutional environments which may have a totalitarian character. He stresses the point that you cannot determine "the good" either scientifically or dogmatically. Ricoeur advocates the fundamental indefinable character of democracy. He opposes Kantian universalism to Aristotle's concept phronesis, practical reason. The universalist claim may threaten the otherness of the other and thus endanger the respect for the unique individual in a particular situation. He employs examples of ethical conflicts concerning terminally ill old people and unborn babies in order to demonstrate how problematic a starting point in a universalist concept of autonomy can be. At the same time, he makes a plea for universality of the golden rule of reciprocity: do not do to others what you do not want them to do to you, but love the other as yourself. He writes in favor of a reflexive equilibrium between the universal and the historical and contextual.

In the final study, Ricoeur moves towards an ontology of the self drawing on the writings of Heidegger and Levinas. A self must transcend the accidental here and now of the present and the ontology is established by an analogical unity of action. Ricoeur introduces Heidegger's concept of care (Sorge): "The being of the self, presupposes the totality of a world that is the horizon of its thinking, acting, feeling – in short, of its *care*" (p. 310). Ricoeur discusses Levinas' radical distinction between the other who we imagine, and by representation assimilate to the same, denying the otherness of the other, and the other who calls on us by his voice:

> It is in me that the movement coming from the other completes its trajectory: the other constitutes me as responsible, that is, as capable of responding. In this way, the word of the other comes to be placed at the origin of my acts.[5]

> (p. 336)

He continues to say that my answer is my action, and the self who responds is me – in the accusative – who is relating to you. In his discussion on Levinas, Ricoeur emphasizes the reciprocity and he insists on holding the relationship between the other and the self to be dialectically complementary in order that the self does not become a hostage to the other. Accountability is important. How can I learn to be responsible and to keep my word if no one counts on me? We did not give birth to ourselves; right from the beginning we are entangled in a net of intersubjectivity. The otherness is primary; we are in the world on the terms of others before we are capable of recognizing ourselves; in a variety of ways we have been influenced by others. I am, by virtue of others, who, nevertheless, have a different perspective which I can only appropriate by analogy. The relationship to the other is marked by symmetry and dissymmetry, as the other is someone like me as well as an irreplaceable unique other. Called upon by others, I stand here and must respond and act according to practical reason and consciousness, listen to others and make a choice in the face of a conflict of obligations. The acting and suffering self elicited from Ricoeur's analyses, is sharply opposed to a judging self who creates a distance to "them," the others who are neither looked upon in their uniqueness, nor as an obligation. There is a due distance to identity constructions based on a prejudiced "us–them" dichotomy.

Throughout the book, attestation – testifying to our reliability – plays a central role. Identity, understood as the answer to the question of who is speaking, acting, narrating, and responsible – is testified to and confirmed. But Ricoeur points out that attestation is always accompanied by doubt. This duality between confirmation and doubt is inevitable.

The issue of the relationship with the other turns up again in his book, *Memory, history, forgetting* (2004):

> To be sure, we may find this surprising: is our identity so fragile that we are unable to endure the fact that others have different ways than our own of leading their lives, of understanding themselves, of inscribing their own identity in the web of living together? This is so. There are indeed humiliations, real or imagined attacks on self-esteem, under the blow of poorly tolerated otherness, that turns into rejection, into exclusion – this is the relation that the same maintains with the other.
>
> (2004: 82)

Memory and forgetting influence attestation and testimony. Memory and forgetting mediate time and narrative, so in order to understand history and life we have to take memory into account. Ricoeur's philosophical and phenomenological examination of memory takes the works of Plato and Aristotle as its starting point with the notion of the image (*eikon*) representing something absent.[6] Memory is connected to our capability for imagination. The image as a representation is not necessarily a true copy but, perhaps, just something similar. We may have a bad memory, make mistakes, or forget. Spontaneous or searched for memories about past happenings are distinguished from imaginations of the future. The metaphor of a trace or imprint is attached to the image. Ricoeur expresses the phenomenology of memory as an image of things past in the living presence. Further on, he confronts the individual phenomenological approach to the sociology of memory and to a philosophy of history. Testimonies are archived, and archives are critically examined, and history is written based on the former two processes. Interpretations take place in each link. Memories are expressed in language and follow a narrative path (2004: 129). We are selective when we tell about what happened, and no archives are complete. Furthermore, historical writings have a narrative structure. We produce "a sense of an ending" (p. 276) in historical writings, as there is not a final point in time from which we can determine the meaning of a course of time (p. 336). Ricoeur uses the term "re-presentation," which does not signify a correspondence but rather a "standing for." We talk about the past, "as" it happens, implying the distance within the term "as."

Too much can disappear into oblivion, but we can also have a surplus of memory. Ricoeur repeats Plato's metaphor *pharmacon*, originally used about the invention of writing. It is not clear if this remedy will heal or poison. History writing and cultural heritage may each be a pharmacon in this ambiguity, healing or poisonous. What do we chose to remember or to forget? And what is the impact of this on the future? Forgetting can also be enforced, and memories excluded from individual or collective consciousness. Ricoeur rephrases the Kantian expression from his article on enlightenment *Sapere aude* into "Dare to give an account yourself!" (p. 449).

Ricoeur ends by reminding us of another aspect of memory and forgetting: forgiveness, the letting go of old grudges and injustices. He ends his book with the following assertion:

> Under history, memory and forgetting.
> Under memory and forgetting, life.
> But writing a life is another story.
> Incompletion.
>
> (p. 605)

I find Schrag's and Ricoeur's contributions to a theory of identity more inspiring and convincing than any other presentations of this comprehensive subject I have met so far. Their positions, in between modernity and postmodernity, in between universalist claims and relativism, and their efforts to find a third path, provide a theoretical framework which sheds new light on the rich material embedded in the life stories. Identity-work is a lifelong endeavor depending on narrative performance in a cultural space. There is no immutable nuclear self. On the other hand, jumping from one role to another in various contexts, without any sense of narrative and existential continuity entails fragmentation.

Their visions of a good life "with and for others in just institutions," and the inclusion of the notion of charity, depend on the co-existent symmetry and dissymmetry in the relationship with the other. Experience shows, however, that in spite of the general wish to be recognized by others as the persons we are, as I noted at the beginning of this chapter, it is sometimes difficult to recognize the other in his alterity and to "grant the other his intrinsic integrity" (Schrag, 1997). Ricoeur (2004: 82) correctly connected this disability to a fragile sense of identity. I shall return to this issue in the following chapter. The starting point for an inquiry into personal identity in the other – which to me seems so evident and convincing – instead of in the first person I, is still a counter-narrative in scientific discourse. The achievements of these philosophers, together with recent studies in social neuro-psychology, may, hopefully, begin to change this picture.

Continuity and change

During the last years of my mother's life I began to fear the transformations in her appearance each time I went to see her. Due to age and illness she became increasingly fragile and immobile, her vitality diminished, and her appearance changed like a withering rose. I made a drawing of her so that I could really see her and integrate these transformations. A while after she died the situated image of her appearance from our last encounters dissolved. I began to remember her in a variety of images of appearances across the entire lifelong period I had known her. I thought of her on the beach when she was young and I was little, I saw her digging potatoes in the garden as an old woman, or I recalled an image of her dressing up for a party. This unlimited access to images other than the most resent situated memory was comforting in spite of the loss; perhaps, because the last transformations had been so painful.[7]

Normally, we remember people and places as we last saw them. Reunions across a temporal distance make changes very obvious. The child has grown bigger, the adults look older. Migrants who revisit their country of origin after a long time may be confused by the extensive changes. When we, as adults, return to the school we attended in our childhood, the classroom has shrunk. The paradox of identity, the continuity across change and transformation, is a fundamental experience that gives rise to many explanations.[8]

According to Damasio (2000), each encounter we have with the world encompasses, consciously or unconsciously, the sensation and feeling that this is happening to me; our perceptions and experiences are embodied. When I return to the landscape where I grew up I perceive and sense my present encounter with this landscape; simultaneously, I recall moments of interaction in the same environment, perhaps, 40 or 50 years ago. These embodied, autobiographical memories include the physical and emotional interaction of a child or a young person with the environment. I, in the present, remembering a former I ("me" as a child in interaction with an environment) acknowledge the difference as well as the identity. And the surroundings are recognized in the same duality, the present and the past of the hills and the woods, they are the same, in spite of the difference.

An explanation of the change and continuity paradox put forward by several authors (Damasio, 2000; McAdams, 1996)[9] stating that "I" is the ever-changing part of the self, existing in the transient present, while "me" is the resource of continuity and stability seems, from my point of view, too simple.

When we remember episodes in situated contexts and recall the mind and the body in interplay with the environment we are able to experience the difference as well as the continuity between the present situation, the present here and now remembering self and the remembered self in a different interaction in a different spatiotemporal context. The embodied memory of movement in time and space between contexts helps us – within limits[10] – to date events as we transfer physical movement to abstract time and experience the passing of time. Beyond the highly selective fragments of autobiographical episodic memory that may emerge in a given moment – and from which a version of a life story narrative can be constructed – is an implicit awareness of embodied continuity, an implicit awareness of the embodied trajectory, the journey of life in time and space. I have traveled this path in time and space in my body, in spite of all transformations.

At the same time, recalling an episode, thinking about it, telling about it in different situations may result in reconstructions of memory. "Me" is likely to change in accordance with the changes of the present I in interpersonal interactions. "Me" is not fixed but is likely to change due to the tellings and retellings of past and present happenings. Evidently, our experiences of time and space in relation to the self are influenced by the cultural context.

The sense of continuity derives, first of all, from autonoetic awareness; the feeling of embodied existence beyond the here and now, the feeling of an extended autobiographical self expanding the present in both directions as a continuity of the remembered past and as a possible extension into the imagined future. But it is the present situated I who is capable of experiencing continuity and change at the same time by a comparison of embodied interactions.

The emphasis on the future as well as the past in autonoesis is important. Personal identity is not only about the past but about becoming, about emerging selves in new encounters.[11]

Change does not catch your eye so much if you are close to people and see them almost all the time. The perception is so frequent, and the minor changes so gradual, that they pass unnoticed. We mainly experience the continuity. Our situated self-perception is continuous, but memories, movement to other environments, and others' reactions, prompt the sense of change and transformation. Radical change in everyday life may severely break the sense of continuity. Radical change in the world around us may be very hard to integrate.

Nevertheless, continuity and change are indissoluble; I notice the scars on my hands, some of them I can trace back to my childhood almost 50 years, but I see the hands of quite an old woman, and I know that all the cells have been replaced again and again. I know how it was to be 10, 20, 30, 40, I carry with me various experiences of interactions, but I am still in a state of becoming.

As mentioned earlier, narrative plays a significant part in the development of autobiographical memory and autonoetic awareness. And narrative plays an irrefutable role in the continuous construction of identity across the emerging selves in interpersonal interaction. The stories we are told by our families and other people around us are the first source of personal identity. We are part of the stories of others, and they are part of our stories. Some stories are retold repeatedly, may even come to serve as labels; other stories are soon forgotten. Establishing some narrative coherence across diverse experiences in different contexts is a dynamic lifelong project. Identity is a performance, but obviously more so in changing environments. Familiarity, sameness, and stability do not challenge the issue of identity, although the transformations resulting from age are universal.

The narrative construction of coherence implies that there is a cultural space for negotiation of meaning. It is a dialogic unfinished achievement. The other, and our relationship to the other, as argued by Schrag, Levinas, and Ricoeur, concerns the construction of personal identity in fundamental ways.

Not only are we narrated by others, immersed in cultural narratives, and reliant on others as partners of our dialogues for negotiation of meaning and for co-constructions of our narrative identity, but how we interact with, and respond to the others, has a decisive impact on our identity construction. No doubt, an experience of self-consistency in a moral sense, keeping one's word, acting in a responsible way, supports the autonoetic awareness of existential continuity in time. Ricoeur rightly argues that the focus on responsiveness delimits the notion of self, both against a rigid form of constancy and against relativity. Rigid identity constructions result in a decreased flexibility towards open negotiations in new contexts. The otherness of the other (say of the foreigner or the stranger) as well as rapid environmental change may arouse fears in some people, and rigid identity constructions are more likely to dissolve in chaos. On the other hand, a lack of responsibility may tempt some people to perform a variety of roles in different contexts without any quest for authenticity and coherence. Also assimilation and exaggerated adaptation may result in the feeling of meaninglessness.

The emphasis on the self as becoming, on identity as a continuous endeavor and performance supported by continuous co-construction of narratives throughout life, implies a view of the other not as a contrast, the opposite of who we are, but as a potential member of new contexts and communities in which we may participate in the future. Ambiguities continuously appear and require negotiations. Sense making is always provisional. Creation of coherence and integration of experience is a permanent challenge, along with our responsibility towards our ways of responding to the other. Continuity and change go hand in hand with the interdependency between communities and the interacting individuals. And, as Ricoeur reminds us, even the good cannot be determined scientifically or dogmatically.

In spite of the plurality of narratives, all of them based on the embodied journey through life, the endeavor to recognize the person we encounter as an individual other who walked a particular path in space and time of which she may tell a story means that we appreciate the other as unique and irreplaceable and equal. Very often, however, others in various contexts are met and responded to not as individuals but as generalized representatives of a group in this particular context. You meet pupils in the school, patients in the hospital, clients at the social security office, and immigrants in Western cities. Instead of generalizations, we will encounter unique individuals who may tell a unique story, perhaps, similar to other stories, but not exactly the same, as her journey through life in space and time from community to community is individual and personal. Unfortunately, life is too short to listen to all the wonderful stories that exist, but at least it helps to know that they do exist.

Chapter 12

Active citizenship and biographical learning

Education for citizenship

Besides the need to be appreciated as an individual person, another common and salient feature emerged from the entire sample of life story narratives, namely, the expression of a strong wish to be of use to others. Although not everyone felt they were at present in a position in which this was possible, positive experiences of having been useful at some point were mentioned across generations.

Consequently, the Danish research project on Identity, Learning and Democracy (Horsdal, 2000a: 198) concluded describing the vision of society as: "A society in which everybody is needed in her/his individual diversity, where everyone has a responsibility, and can feel it is possible to belong and to have a voice." This vision came close to the societal vision expressed in the introduction to *The memorandum on lifelong learning* (2000: 5): "Our shared aim is to build a Europe in which everyone has the opportunity to develop their potential to the full, to feel that they can contribute and that they belong."

The following year I was engaged in applied narrative research on a European level concerning the issue of active citizenship.[1] This research confirmed the significance of participation and affiliations, and of the need to be of use, and indicated that learning for active democratic citizenship could provide a pathway toward the European vision.

We interviewed active citizens in several European countries (using life stories as described in Chapter 8 followed by a qualitative narrative interview) in order to learn about the competencies and values they possessed and how they had been acquired. In particular we inquired into the role of non-formal adult education in learning for active citizenship.

The development of democracy as a form of governance has been closely connected with education throughout its history (Korsgaard, 2000, 2004). The early development, at least in a Danish context during the nineteenth century, was, in various combinations, strongly influenced by the German philosophers Hegel and Kant; the former for his ideas of "The spirit of the people" ("Volksgeist") which inspired the construction of national identities, the latter for the claim of universal reason which might be approached if the individual person, through education, could be liberated from subjugation. The first democratic constitutions in many countries which set out the rights and duties of the citizens did, however, only include a very small part of the population – in Denmark about 10 percent (1849): namely white, wealthy males above 30. Women, uneducated workers, and servants were, like the sick, considered irrational and unsuitable for political participation. Over the years more groups acquired political and civil rights, and, after the Second World War, also social rights (Marshall, 1950). This was a development which went hand in hand with educational initiatives, not least of which were in liberal adult education.

The aim of education ("enlightenment") inspired by Kant was, as mentioned earlier, to free the subjugated people from their superstitious beliefs and provide the educational means for a development of the courage to trust their own rationality ("sapere aude") as the rational autonomous individual was looked upon as an ideal, and as a precondition for democratic participation in the beginning of the democratic era.[2] The enlightenment was closely connected to the emancipation from traditional society and nation-building. Even today, the belief in individual autonomy and universal reason remains a strong inheritance from the end of the eighteenth century, in spite of the fact that democracy in contemporary society faces other, more urgent issues, at least in a European context.

Ricoeur, as we saw in the preceding chapter, maintained a critique of universalist ideas of individual autonomy, advocating the fundamentally indefinable character of democracy. I agree with his critique that points to the risk of reducing the significant relationship to the other, and I find it urgent that we face the new challenges in contemporary society regarding education for democratic citizenship. Following societal, national, and global changes we need now to reconsider the relationship between citizenship, education, and learning.

Individualization, and the attendant emancipation from stable identity-creating communities, have been in focus in several, mainly critical, discussions and analyses of contemporary society.[3] Emancipation from a traditional society did not, however, liberate the individual from any kind of dependency but changed the character of interconnectedness (cf. Chapter 10). Even self-determination and autonomous behavior are social acts. The solitary individual is a contradiction in terms, just as our individual future is inseparable from our mutual future. Globalization and individualization are intertwined and promote interconnectedness far beyond the local communities of a traditional society. Interdependencies grow across large distances, and many are impersonal and not transparent. Local or national independence becomes a nostalgic illusion. Local communities also change due to increased mobility and migration. Rapid change challenges solid knowledge, and earlier certainties are questioned or deemed outdated. Inclusion and exclusion become important issues which threaten social coherence. In a traditional society, where wealth is based on land or on some industrial means of production, the poor are needed to provide the workforce. In the knowledge society, there is little use for the uneducated, and they are at risk of exclusion. A decline in active participation, or a consumerist attitude towards democracy, may threaten the democratic development. Those challenges of the contemporary society call for educational initiatives which help people to cope with change, and enable people to face change, and to face the other without putting up too many defenses.

In 1986, Bruner argued:

> We are living through bewildering times where the conduct of education is concerned. There are deep problems that stem from many origins – principally from the changing society whose future shape we cannot foresee and for which it is difficult to prepare a new generation.
>
> (1986: 121)

Bruner emphasizes negotiation of meaning and the development of the cultural tools[4] necessary in order to live in a changing world, not as a passive or impotent victim but as an active participant in the constant process of recreating, reinterpreting, and renegotiating culture.

A Finnish unionist from the project on competencies for citizenship expressed his contemporary worries:

Unionist: Somehow I am afraid of how I will get along in this world that is changing all the time. It is so fast and challenging.

Interviewer: What are you afraid of in that?[5]

Unionist: I mean that, working at the union, what I have heard so far; I began my career there with this course, they are running there and back and competing over who has the most meetings agreed in his calendar. How can I manage with it and control it, when at the same time all kind of things are happening in the world ... I would like to concentrate on one thing at a time; I hate that, when I have to eat a bit of the cake there and the next bit in some other place and so on so that I can't enjoy the cakes anywhere ... How am I able to educate myself to cope with the many tasks there are in terms of the union work and in the changing world. And what kind of educational tools will I be asked to have in the future. Now I feel I have some kind of tool to work with, but are my tools too old after one week and do I desperately need new tools? These nerve-racking, uncertain times about what is needed and when, is this it, or are there going to be some easier times as well?

We cannot pretend that time stands still, we cannot manage and control everything, and we can rarely concentrate on one thing at a time, nor can we pretend once and for all to come of age as fully educated, skilled, and authoritative adults in no need of further learning.

The Council of Europe faced the educational challenges concerning democratic citizenship by launching the project "Education for democratic citizenship"

(EDC) from 1997 to 2000. In one of their reports[6] they state that "democracy is at the same time a *value* and a *method of governing*." Between democracy as a value, as a project under continuous construction, and social reality there is a constant tension.

> In other words, the democratic project is not maintained automatically, by itself, through simple social reproduction. *Citizenship learning* is the main instrument for this purpose ... Currently, the balance between project and method, between ideal and reality can be affected by two challenges: erosion of democratic virtue; establishing legitimacy through passive consent and acceptance.
>
> (Council of Europe, 2000: 12)

The EDC project investigating the new challenges for citizenship learning came out with two conclusive aspects: One was "that learning democratic citizenship involves a constant need for a *normative code* (represented by Human Rights), the other aspect concerned the importance of *learning to live together*."

The Budapest Declaration (Council of Europe, 1999) agreed on the following vision at a conference during the EDC project. It declared that education for democratic citizenship:

1   constitutes a lifelong experience and a participating process developed in various contexts;
2   equips men and women to play an active part in public life and to shape in a responsible way their own destiny and that of their society;
3   aims to instill a culture of human rights which will ensure full respect for those rights and understanding of the responsibility that flows from them;
4   prepares people to live in a multicultural society and to deal with difference knowledgably, sensibly, tolerantly, and morally;
5   strengthens social cohesion, mutual understanding, and solidarity;
6   must be inclusive of all age groups and sectors of society.

Unfortunately, it is all too easy to point to the gap between the vision of 1999 and present reality. Amongst a range of political and societal factors, it addresses the issue of learning. To quote Liam Carey from the same report:

> We do not adequately conceptually understand how this learning takes place. The emphasis in the past by pedagogy on *what* should be taught has resulted in the "how" issues being largely unaddressed. Learning has, in the main, been taken for granted.
>
> (Council of Europe, 2000: 31)

The inquiry into competencies for citizenship brings us a little closer to the "how" issue. Nevertheless, I believe that the vision encapsulated in the Budapest

Declaration is of central importance because we need a normative code in order to learn to live together.

Competencies for active citizenship

The research project focused on the following questions: What does active citizenship mean and imply? Which competencies are involved? Where and how do you learn to be an active citizen? Which attitudes and values do the narrators identify with? Which social communities do the narrators feel they belong to and identity with? A comparative analysis of the life stories from the four participating countries made it possible to consider citizenship in a European context, to note similarities and differences,[7] and to consider the different perspectives and local pre-understandings.

Despite the different context of the interviews, there were recurrent themes, attitudes and statements about the conditions and competencies required for active participation in a rapidly changing world. The significant competencies or "cultural tools" for active democratic participation are listed below.[8]

Self-expression

Unless you can express yourself, active participation is impossible. Without the competence for self-expression the individual is forced passively to accept the interpretations, meanings, and actions of others without objection, and is sometimes even forced into isolation and loneliness. A voice can be silenced for different reasons, external and internal. Mastering a common symbolic language, or several, the more the better, is a precondition for expression, and so is a cultural space for the voice to be heard and responded to. Many people have limited arenas for self-expression; they do not know how, dare not, or are not allowed to communicate just anywhere. Clearly, restricted contexts for self-expression limit possibilities for participation.

Belonging

We prefer to express ourselves in situations and contexts in which we feel secure and confident. Those comforting feelings grow out from a sense of belonging, acceptance, and affiliation. However, numerous communities are characterized by a particular set of canonical rules and codes. "The other thing is that people are afraid of being 'weighed in scales.' People are very much conscious of other people's judgement, of what other people think about them" (Hungarian man, born 1956). In such a community, self-expression may even be regarded as a violation of codes and threaten the sense of acceptance. The fear of exclusion can be devastating. All of us are longing to belong. Passive resignation, adaptation, or more or less self-inflicted subjugation may be preferable to exclusion and isolation. Social anchorage is important. Exclusion may promote private frustrations as well as destructive outlets.

Attentiveness and sensitivity towards different codes

The dynamics, flexibility, and mobility of contemporary society add new dimensions to the question of belonging. The pathways of our lives describe trajectories between many different communities with different cultural norms and codes and more or less canonical pre-understandings. In each context we enter a scene already in action. And we need attentiveness and sensitivity towards different codes in order to figure out what the play is about and how it is played, before we can take part in the action. Attentiveness and sensitivity towards different codes reduce the exposed position and vulnerability of a very constrained and dependent sphere of action and assist with the creation of new affiliations through participation. Furthermore, attentiveness modifies self-expression. Dominating and self-asserting individuals can deny the voices and responses of others in their own impatient self-expression if they lack attentiveness and the ability to listen.

Negotiation of meaning

One issue is the courage it takes to stand up in front of an assembly or audience, to express experiences, opinions, suggestions, or critique, another is the encouragement of others to do the same, and the ability to respond to, and to learn from, the voices of others. It also takes courage to admit that "OK, I was not the person who knew most about this matter, but now I know more" (Danish man, born 1972). The tentative quest for understanding as a never-ending process is part of the human condition and indispensable in a democracy. Without the ability to negotiate, people are either left to "repeat and perpetuate what they have been shown" (French woman, born 1968) or, perhaps, exposed to the risk of loss of meaning. Competencies for negotiation of meaning are crucial in relation to conflict-management and form an essential part of learning. Negotiation of meaning involves a plurality of voices: "for me, it is important to protect a certain plurality of voices; of voices that you can hear against a standardization of mind in a cultural as well as in a political context" (French woman, born 1966). And negotiation implies the acknowledgement of different perspectives. New understandings may emerge through a plurality of perspectives in respect of diversity.

Identity

In the process of sense making it is crucial to consider the trajectories within different contexts of contemporary life, as well as the renegotiation and reinterpretation of the past, the present, and the future. In critical life situations identity work is intensified. Without any sense of meaning and orientation the fragmented self loses foothold. We cannot know where to go if we do not know where we are. And we cannot know where we are if we do not know how we got here. A very short-term life perspective, or a fragmented sense of identity, is a severe impediment in the exertion of influence over the life course.

Therefore, the issue of identity must be on the agenda in educational contexts in order to help the individual student to answer the question: "How do I learn to be me?" Both individual and collective elements of identity are constructed through narratives and experience of practice. Some of the interviews show that, in order to identify with any kind of community in the broad sense of the word, the answer to the question: "Has this anything to do with me?" must be answered positively. The feeling of being of use to others, and the ability to act and do something, support a positive identification with the community. The narrative interviews demonstrate a wide range of cultural identities, ranging from the family to the family of man. The constraints of cultural identities are equally varied. Concerning the question of a European identity, there are different views in the material.

Externalization

Active participation must proceed from dialogue and negotiation to the sphere of action. "The beautiful ideas in our heads" must be confronted with the social world, contested by other voices, and "the beautiful discourses" in our communities must be put into practice. This transition plays a central role in active citizenship. Planning, organizing, and actually doing things are important competencies. Creativity plays a significant part. In the French sample, several interviewees also talk about the readiness to go right through with things, insistently, and not giving up or quitting halfway if difficulties or other fields of interest turn up. Persistent commitment can be a problem, both in the case of disappointment in the face of slow results and other impediments, and because of the lack of perseverance in the lives of young, impatient, and very mobile people. The experience of even a small-scale achievement is very important and fuels the feeling that the effort "does make a difference." Thus, the transformation from being a consumer in a society to an active participant is accomplished.

Knowledge

In many interviews the importance of knowledge is accentuated; first of all, political knowledge, but also social, societal, historical, and cultural knowledge. While many competencies for active citizenship are learned informally in different communities of practice, the responsibility of formal and non-formal educational institutions concerning the transmission and dissemination of the abovementioned types of knowledge should not be underestimated. It is important not to be ignorant of how democracy works. Knowledge about democratic institutions and about political and social history is not as highly prioritized as it ought to be. People who feel they do not know enough about those matters may abstain from participation, and politics will remain an alienated domain reserved for "experts." Knowledge is also an indispensable ingredient in developing a broad and spacious horizon. Cultural ignorance affects the relationship to the other in a negative way. Ignorance sustains the dominant positions of both political authorities and the authorities of the media.

Empowerment

Development of the competencies listed above powerfully facilitates democratic participation and brings about experiences of success in deliberate attempts to make a positive difference. It was clear from the interviews how this creates empowerment. If we try to imagine an individual who cannot express himself, who feels expelled from the communities around him, who is without anchorage, not attentive towards others, who does not understand the different codes, who cannot negotiate and often find things meaningless, who is closed and narrow-minded and with a fragile sense of identity, this person is utterly powerless – except perhaps in the domain of violence and destruction. A disempowered person is very susceptible to social exclusion, and, as part of a growing number, can pose a serious threat to societal coherence. We all carry along with us numerous experiences of defeat, disappointment, and failure, experiences which, nevertheless, do not have to determine the rest of our lives if actual achievements are made, supported, and recognized. Empowerment through successful participation is a vital feature of active citizenship.

"First of all, I have learned how to help. This has motivated me in my studies. It has motivated me to succeed in other respects of life. To be more strong" (French man, born 1979).

> I also think that you cannot live in a town without interfering with the social, cultural, and economic life, if you do not, you live selfishly, and I do not want to do that. It is a bit of therapy in itself to turn towards the others, to be in front of the others, our own problems disappear confronting the difficulties of the families, violence, aggression, the children that are the only persons in the families to rise through education as their parents who do not work finally surrender to the injustice of the situation ... I have learned everything thanks to my benevolent engagement, I could grow and develop along with my children and therefore understand them better. I think, the two most important things are that my engagement in voluntary work allowed me to gain the confidence of others and finally to get confidence in myself, and this is significant especially thinking of my childhood in Madagascar and considering the path I followed.
>
> (French woman, born 1956)

Values and attitudes

Most of the interviewees fluctuate between pessimism and optimism. Optimism gains weight along with positive experiences of being useful and seeing the effect of efforts and contributions. Active participation is rewarding "much more than money." "It gave me everything," one of the narrators said. To be a co-creator of something which supports or improves human existence in some way or other gives a meaning to life. To be useful, supportive, and creative makes sense in people's lives. The environmental issue plays a significant role. Responsibility toward our future from a global perspective is expressed in different ways in many interviews. Materialism and the power of money are criticized in some interviews, and so is the standardization of a commercial culture. Diversity is highlighted as a positive value.

The visions of a good life point towards a coherent authenticity in, and across, the different spheres of interaction, and to the possibility of functioning as an entire human being – preferably in all domains and contexts of everyday life. Accomplishments in vocational life are not enough, and lifelong learning is not identical to vocational training. Human resources should preferably be used in the whole life-situation, in family life, in voluntary work locally or in more comprehensive contexts, as well as in working life. Continuous learning and involvement in further education should have as its aim the personal development of the entire human being in order to support future commitments and contributions. People in the research material want to be seen as whole individuals and they resent being regarded only as consumers, customers, clients, employees, or to be reduced to any other restricting category.

Life-wide learning takes place no matter what you choose to do with your life, but the outcome of learning differs enormously. Learning in favor of democratic co-existence and in favor of active participation in future life-projects encompasses the entire human being and promotes the development of competencies for meaningful interaction.

Learning democratic citizenship

The research project also addressed the question of where and how people learn to become active citizens. The interviews confirmed the first statement in the Budapest Declaration: "Education for democratic citizenship constitutes a lifelong learning experience and a participating process developed in various contexts" (Council of Europe, 1999). The variety of contexts included formal, non-formal, and informal contexts. Many of the competencies are learned through practice by active participation itself. But very often the starting point for participation derives from problems or challenges connected to the immediate life-world. The situation here and now calls for some action. Young people become parents and get involved in improving children's conditions. Also, a need to make new connections in a new place may initiate activities. Feelings of injustice or the need to pay back help received in a previous period may motivate commitment. But, very often, active participation is "inherited" from older family members or brought about by the influence of significant others such as partners, friends, teachers, or personal supporters. People are much more likely to get involved if they grew up or live in an environment in which active participation is natural; in contrast to extended passivity, which is a severe obstacle for democratic participation. Coincidence, however, plays a role. What the individual happens to encounter on his pathway through life may very well have a substantial impact on future decisions.

Many of the interviewees have learned to be on a stage, performing drama, music, dance, narration, etc. Being able to stand up in front of an audience and perform in front of others, apart from the fun of creative engagement, has helped to develop important personal and social courage. The ability to plan, organize, and carry out different activities is another skill which is mentioned in relation to leisure activities and non-formal education. It is beyond any doubt that non-formal education can play a vital role in the development of competencies for active citizenship. In Denmark, the folk high schools have played this role ever since the first democratic constitution, although the challenges for democratic participation have naturally changed over the years, and the educational needs have changed accordingly.

After this research project had finished, a Danish folk high school, together with partners from five different European countries, took up the challenge and created the TEACh – Teaching European Active Citizenship Courses designed according to the findings of the previous research project. The courses developed over the years, inspired by the professional experience of the tutors. The In-Service Training Course is now included in the Comenius/ Grundtvig Catalogue of The European Commission and is offered to teachers/ trainers from all over Europe at various locations. So far, 15 courses have been held, the latest in Milan February 2010. The aim of the program as set out in the Course Pack folder (2004) and on the website is as follows:

> The general aim of the TEACh Courses is to improve the training of persons involved in non-formal education in the area of teaching active citizenship. The teachers/trainers participating in the courses will acquire first-hand knowledge about the competencies related to active citizenship and methods for teaching these competencies. Thus equipped, they will improve the quality of education in their home institutions, will raise the awareness of citizens and increase participation in democracy.

The course is structured in the following modules:

1 Self-expression
2 Intercultural dialogue, negotiation
3 Belonging, inclusion
4 Attentiveness and sensitivity
5 Openness, externalization
6 Empowerment
7 Knowledge
8 Values and attitudes.

The competencies and values addressed show the affinity between the previous research and the training. Furthermore, we can see a marked similarity between the above competencies and some of the listed competencies of active citizenship and some of the elements of narrative competence described in Chapter 7. I will now consider the reasons for this coincidence.

In the research, we discovered the competencies from an analysis of the interviews, and we also learned something about how they were acquired. Most of the competencies grew out of practice. In spite of inevitable frustrations, active participation together with others engaged in a positive development of the immediate future created new affiliations, local anchorage, meaningfulness, coherence, at the same time that the skills and knowledge of the participants improved. But non-formal education was also significant, not least as a context which gave the opportunity to meet new people and do things together. These findings confirmed previous biographical research in the significance of a rich and poly-contextual formation. The quality and scope of biographical learning[9] seems to be crucial for the development of competencies and aptitudes such as those listed above.

The interviews clearly highlighted two distinct pitfalls. On the one hand, rapid transformations and movements between many different contexts, without the necessary tools for the integration of experience, may cause stress, insecurity, fear of fragmentation and of loss of one's footing. On the other hand, a secluded life, without commitment and only a narrow perspective, is a great danger too.

> The danger, of course, is that you go to the other extreme and search yourself more than necessary, and then that you turn around and say that you shall only concern yourself with the Danish, or you shall only concern yourself with your family, or you shall only concern yourself with your job, and that is it. This is a danger in these current times, and some people are caught.
>
> (Danish man, born 1972)

> [P]eople easily become narrow-minded, soon it is only their own tip of the nose, their own little house, their own little apartment building, because that is enough for them, but I think it is important to get out into the surroundings.
>
> (Danish man, born 1979)

In the face of this double challenge for contemporary society, the important affinity between narrative competence development and active democratic participation becomes clearer. Narratives give us vicarious access to others and to different life courses. Narratives can convey understanding and affiliations, and narrative competence helps us to make sense, to integrate experience, to negotiate meaning and create some kind of coherence in a diversified world, still maintaining a critical and reflexive stance against dominant and excluding stories. Yet, we need to underscore the significance of the narrative environment for the performance of narrative practices (cf. Chapter 3).

> I feel good with people who have a rather open and tolerant spirit ... Well. People who have been traveling, who have been moving, seen different things, having a certain maturity, a certain open spirit, a certain tolerance in the face difference. In fact, what makes problems in this world is difference; that is, ignorance of the other who is different ... It is necessary to reflect, analyze, criticize, take, and reject. But many people are not capable of doing this. Because they are living in a rather narrow world, they do not want to open. And then. They repeat and perpetuate what they have been shown.
>
> (French woman, born 1968)

A crucial question, both regarding the individual and the society, is: How much can you hold? How broad and spacious can you be without losing coherence? The coherence of a society depends on active citizens. Education for active citizenship is thus very much a question of broadening the life-world of the individuals and strengthening their capacity for negotiation of meaning. Narrative competence plays a significant role, not least concerning the question of difference emphasized in the quotation above. The vision of the Budapest Declaration that citizenship education "prepares people to live in a multi-cultural society and to deal with difference knowledgeably, sensibly, tolerantly and morally" seems now remote compared to the statement in the interview: "In fact, what makes problems in this world that is difference, that is ignorance of the other who is different," a problem which Ricoeur also noted.

There is a certain sad irony in the apparent contradiction between, on the one hand, the need to be appreciated as an individual human being, which emerged from the analysis of the numerous life story narratives, and, on the other hand, the reluctance to grant foreign others the same right.

The fact, that our ability to distinguish between very small differences and variations grows with familiarity and thorough knowledge of the particular object, is a well-known phenomenon. Looking at a field, I may observe that grain grows there. If I know more, I may notice the particular kind of grain, perhaps barley. With even more knowledge I am able to say if it is spring or winter barley and how well it is growing. We easily notice the differences between people who look like ourselves compared to people from a different part of the world. Ignorance may result in the inclination to regard the foreigner without considering her unique individuality. But if we listen to the life story narratives of foreign others we can learn a lot; the stories can be a way of combating ignorance of the other and enriching us with some knowledge and familiarity which facilitates an appreciation of diversity. Listening to the narratives of other people could be possible on a much larger scale, in comparison with the lucky few who get the chance to participate in transnational and intercultural citizenship education.

One of the results of the research on active citizenship was the emphasis on knowledge: political, cultural, societal, and historical knowledge. Therefore, there is a great need for citizenship education on various levels, including in formal education, in order to approach the achievement of the visions embedded in "The memorandum on lifelong learning" and the Budapest Declaration. If too many passive citizens for some reason abstain from active participation, societal coherence is in danger. A further implication is that too many citizens are excluded from the opportunity to feel that they contribute to society as co-creators of the individual, as well as our mutual future, and from the feeling that they belong; not to mention the people who are excluded from citizens' rights in some nations.

Chapter 13

Educational perspectives and concluding remarks

"We feel, therefore we learn" is the title of an article by Immordino-Yang and Damasio on "The relevance of affective and social neuroscience to education" (2007). The authors note:

> Modern biology reveals humans to be fundamentally emotional and social creatures. And yet those of us in the field of education often fail to consider that the high-level cognitive skills taught in schools, including reasoning, decision making, and processes related to language, reading, and mathematics, do not function as rational, disembodied systems, somehow influenced by but detached from emotion and the body.... In brief, learning, in the complex sense in which it happens in schools or the real world, is not a rational or disembodied process; neither is it a lonely one.
>
> (2007: 3–4)

The authors suggest that the culture in which we are embedded provides emotional, social, and moral feedback on our actions which helps us to cope and respond to the environment in an appropriate way. Our experiences of pain and pleasure, influenced by the rules that govern social and moral behavior, help us to survive in an ambivalent world. Emotional and social functioning is extremely important in order to be able to respond in a nuanced manner in complex situations.[1] The authors argue that several aspects of cognition, which play a significant role in education, "learning, attention, memory, decision making, motivation, and social functioning, are both profoundly affected by emotion and in fact subsumed within the processes of emotion" (p. 7). They conclude by pointing to the potential for innovations in the science of learning and the practice of teaching based on this neurobiological evidence regarding the fundamental role of emotion; and they make a call for further research on the educational implications.

The acknowledgement of the cultural impact on emotional and social feedback does, however, in contemporary society, give rise to an additional problem. As many people experience a clash of cultures[2] they also receive conflicting feedback in the different communities of practice throughout their lives. This presents a further challenge for education. Some students may react with absolute surprise and astonishment to the feedback they receive in new learning environments if the feedback is very different from what they knew before. Some students may feel bewildered, or anxious, or at least ambiguous, in relation to the difference between the expected and the experienced reactions and responses. The strong impact of early and, perhaps, implicit learning may aggravate the problem. Many students, as well as people in general, are faced with the challenge of moral and cultural negotiations alongside strong experiences of pain or pleasure.

The whole idea behind formal education is a future re-contextualization of what has been learned. We should be able to use our knowledge and skills in different contexts. This does not only apply to formal education, but the learning outcomes from non-formal and informal learning contexts should, hopefully, also be transferred to new appropriate situations. But how to deal with the associated emotions from the, perhaps, conflicting or contradictory cultural feedback? A countermeasure against transferred negative or anxiety-provoking elements could be to sharply separate the different communities of practice: this you can do only here, and not there, and vice versa. This reaction could, on the other hand, reduce the possible learning transfer.

We need further research to describe and understand the impact of conflicting emotional and moral feedback due to a clash of cultures, and we need to research how this problem may be addressed in educational settings in order not to inhibit learning. Attentiveness and sensibility toward different codes, mentioned in the last chapter as one of the features of competence for democratic citizenship, are, presumably, of interest in relation to this problem.

No doubt, neurobiology and neuropsychology will influence education as we come to understand how social interactions influence our brains and how and what we learn. The pleasure we feel when performing particular activities, and the dislike of other occupations, show traces of the emotional, social, and moral feedback we have experienced in various communities of practice, perhaps long ago or long forgotten, in our history of biographical learning. I have noticed several striking incidents in the life stories. The narrators communicate memories of positive interactions in their childhood, situations in which they were engaged in a particular activity together with a person they really appreciated, and, later on, their choice of profession or a significant hobby reveals a connection to this childhood experience. The experience of negative interactions in learning contexts may also seriously impact future engagement in learning.

A volume of *New directions for adult and continuing education*, edited by Sandra Johnson and Kathleen Taylor (2006) is dealing with *The neuroscience of adult learning*. In this volume, Perry, in a chapter on fear and learning, points to our human drive to explore new things. He says:

> Optimal learning depends on this process – a cycle of curiosity, exploration, discovery, practice, and mastery – which leads to pleasure, satisfaction, and the confidence to once again set out and explore. With each success comes

more willingness to explore, discover, and learn. The more the learner experiences this cycle of discovery, the more he or she can create a lifelong excitement for, and love of, learning.

(2006: 26)

He continues to explain how fear and anxiety kill curiosity and inhibit learning. Negative experiences are deeply engrained and limit human exploration. The focus on the learning environments is one important aspect of the social and emotional influences on learning and cognitive development. In another chapter, Cozolino and Sprokay (2006), in the context of adult learning, discuss how best to tailor an enriched learning environment that enhances brain development. They emphasize the close connection between what is being learned, and the interpersonal relationships in the learning situation. Many adult learners have negative memories from school, memories of failure or of negative relationships in the classroom. The authors point out that negative school memories may become a self-fulfilling prophecy in that they increase stress, which affects the plasticity of the brain. The experience of the learning site as a safe place is, without doubt, immensely important when we set out in unknown territory, perhaps anxious, because of previous negative experiences in educational contexts. Cozolino and Sprokay point to the role of the teacher and its significance in the creation of an emotionally supportive learning environment. Memories of anxiety in relation to the teacher or the learning situation can obviously create a general fear of learning and an inability to learn (see also Taylor, 2006; Caine & Caine, 2006).

A good learning environment is characterized not only by what is said. The non-verbal communication and the "phatic" dimension and its vitality play a significant role. However, the relationship with the other pupils and students in educational settings is, in some cases, equally important in determining the experience of the learning environments. Stories of bullying and harassment in school or in other formal or non-formal learning contexts take up considerable space in some narrative interviews, and the impact of such experiences on the future is significant. An optimal learning environment depends on good teachers having good relations with the students, as well as the students' mutual relationships. Furthermore, the experience of making progress and achieving results, of actually learning something, is indispensable. A good learning environment results in the experience of having profited from participation. The significance of the learning outcome concerns more than the possibility of garnering praise and appreciation, and thus enhancing self-confidence. The acquisition of new competencies creates a potential for participation in new communities of practice. The ability to ride a bicycle is a precondition for racing around with other children, just as mastering a foreign language enables us to communicate with foreigners who do not know our mother-tongue. It is important to keep in mind that one of the major motivations for learning is to acquire the ability to master and perform a particular activity, mostly in a social context, and that the acquisition of knowledge and competence is decisive in this respect.

In the same volume, Zull discusses how the brain changes physically as we learn (2006). He lists four pillars of learning: gathering data, reflection, creating, and testing. And he deplores that gathering information sometimes seems to be the only goal in schools, although this is not enough to reach understanding and mastery. He emphasizes that educators "cannot give their ideas to adult learners as birthday presents. What we can give is new experiences" (p. 8). I agree with Zull that gathering information is not in itself sufficient for learning, we also need to categorize and analyze the information, and to use, symbolize, and in other ways experiment with, the gathered information.

The gathering of information through the senses is enriched by emotional responses. Sense impressions may be associated with a wide variety of aesthetic and emotional experiences, implicitly or explicitly, and this may also influence learning. It matters whether particular sense impressions evoke enthusiasm, disgust, or indifference. Furthermore, I suggest, that a development of our senses, and of our ways of categorizing and articulating sense impressions is a somewhat neglected part of education. This is about asking the students to try to answer the question of *how* in relation to the senses in order to enhance new associations and articulateness, for example by using metaphor. How is this item red? Like raspberry, or like salmon, or like blushing? How is that movement? Like a pheasant, like a toddler? How is the sound of that laughter? Together with the articulation of emotions, these nuances improve and refine our sense impressions and enable us to participate in a richer form of storytelling.

And storytelling does play an important role in how our brains develop as we learn. Cozolino and Sprokay write:

> Throughout the life span, we all need others who show interest in us, help us feel safe, and encourage our understanding of the world around us. Brains grow best in this context of interactive discovery and through cocreation of stories that shape and support memories of what is being learned.
>
> (2006: 11)

The authors continue:

> In times of fear and anxiety, the verbal centers of the left hemisphere tend to shut down, impairing the semantic and narrative aspects of learning that are central to academic success. Decreasing stress as a part of teaching balances hemispheric functioning and activates semantic and narrative processes.
>
> (p. 15)

They suggest two important roles of narrative in adult education: one is the learner's narrative, what I refer to as biographical learning, and its impact on future engagement in new learning; the other concerns the fact, that narratives, because of their broad neural base, are "a more resilient matrix for memory." It is easier to remember a story than a list. It is easier to learn something that makes sense and is meaningful. Also, Kathleen Taylor emphasizes meaningful learning, particularly learning that involves self-reflection and creation of meaning, and encourages increased cognitive complexity (2006: 72).[3]

Taylor argues in favor of including narratives, journals, autobiography, writing-to-learn as possible experience-based learning strategies in adult education. I fully agree with her about the significance of making the experience and prior knowledge of the adult learner the starting point for new learning in adult education, as we continuously build onto existing networks. Her emphasis on the goal of involving self-reflection and creation of meaning is very important, and the consequent development of experience-based learning strategies which support different kinds of storytelling is crucial. Nevertheless, I have reservations concerning the use of some autobiographical methods in educational settings. I believe that therapists, rather than educators, should work with reconfigurations of autobiographical stories in order to replace a life story, full of failure and shame, with a more self-confident narrative co-construction of identity.[4] And I object to the practice of simply asking adult learners to tell their life stories in the class. I am familiar with examples of the practice of letting a year group of students in professional education (pre-school teacher training in some colleges in Denmark) begin by telling their life story narratives to one another.

As I mentioned before, the privilege of listening to another person's life story narrative is a gift we receive. Whether we are offered this gift and privilege in an educational setting, or in a research context, we should always be acutely aware that a gift is freely offered, and that any kind of pressure should be avoided. Students should not feel under pressure to tell their life story, and neither should interrogations or rhetorical justifications take place in an educational context (cf. Chapter 7 above). However, there are other learning strategies that can support experience-based reflection and narrative constructions.

One of the reasons why I published samples of life story narratives was to provide material that could be used in adult education. We know how memories, experiences, and stories are triggered by similarities and analogies in stories that we read or listen to. Reflective discussions and processes of sense making can easily be initiated through inspiration from other people's narratives. Using as a starting point life stories told, and published, with the consent and acceptance of the narrators, prevents pressure to produce a life story in a context where you do not feel like doing so; but, on the other hand, the discussion of the life story narratives of other people may invite spontaneous narrations limited to the subjects and issues which the adult learner chooses to share.[5] Spontaneous narrations, on the other hand, should be given ample space in education – not least in adult education. It is the educator's responsibility to create a potential (or transitional) space for safe emergence in the case of personal storytelling, and to display openness in relation to narrative practices, instead of exerting control so that "the right story" will be told "in the right way." We put our vulnerable selves at stake in the stories we tell, as discussed in Chapter 2.

Another way of approaching this type of reflection is to encourage adult learners to carry out narrative interviews with other people (outside the educational context) and teach them how to do it. Afterwards, I have asked the adult students to read aloud in the class the stories they have produced in co-construction with the narrator (cf. Chapter 8); and the impact of those orally communicated life story narratives on the group of learners, including their teacher, is fantastic.

Naturally, narratives encompass much more than life stories. I have often used an exchange of narratives, however confined to a particular theme, in an educational setting. For example, stories of particular experiences of learning may give rise to many interesting discussions. Significant stories of learning from whatever context, formal or informal, negative or positive, but resulting in a substantial new recognition or realization or a move forward can be exchanged.

The learning of highly theoretical subjects, such as epistemology, may also be supported by using narratives. I have organized courses for graduate students with professional, vocational experience, in which they start with a narration from their previous workplace that illustrates conflicting actions, objectives, ideas, goals, or ideologies in the professional practice. Then they take this story as a point of departure for the theoretical exploration in order to eventually be able to throw more light on the conflict in accordance with the knowledge acquired. The close affinity between experience, practice, theory, and analysis encourages theoretical studies and make them more meaningful.

Although I believe that collaboration in the re-editing of the life story narrative in order to construct a more optimistic biography is not primarily the task of an adult educator, it is quite clear that, at one point, adult educators do get involved in reconfigurations. In a rapidly changing society, lifelong learning not only implies a continuous accumulation of knowledge and skills; frequently we have to unlearn old practices and familiar habits, revise firm beliefs or basic assumptions. In the cases of unlearning and relearning we face a necessary reconfiguration of the narratives that explain and make sense of the world. This may include a reconfiguration and reinterpretation of self and existence.

The fruitful space between rigidity and chaos in which new meanings emerge (cf. Siegel, 1999) may be a dangerous space to some people. Rossiter (1999) suggests that, if people are scared of the future because changes threaten their narrative construction of identity, they may counteract the risk of a transformed, or destroyed, identity by rigidly maintaining the prior self in the encounter with changing circumstances and thus try to prevent change and resist learning. The reflexive identity work in the tension between continuity and change, with its focus on becoming in new encounters, is a serious challenge for some people, as we saw in relation to the Finnish man in the previous chapter who could not find a place to enjoy his cake. There is, in some cases, an element of destruction and chaos in the act of refiguration.[6] The learner's experiences, not least concerning the emotional and cultural impact, have a crucial impact on her readiness to learn or her resistance toward learning and transformations. Implicit memory, old habits, and implicit models of the world (cf. Chapter 5) make the process of unlearning and re-learning more difficult. In order to negotiate sense making in a re-editing of our understanding we need to make tacit and implicit knowledge explicit. Storytelling is the best cultural tool we possess in this respect.

Some of the learning strategies mentioned above that enhance narrative competence may be of use in order to support the activity of sense making and overcome the fear of chaos and change. In addition, it may be possible to find a starting point in an experience of meaningful learning and transformation in the student's history of biographical learning. No matter how miserable our memories of school and other learning arenas have been, normally, there have been moments of success in people's lives. The life story narratives provide numerous examples. And many people, who were afraid of joining new educational settings, have changed their minds after a successful experience. If a person became involved in a good learning environment, often informal or non-formal, directed towards something which, at the same time, made good sense in the present life situation of the learner, caught her spontaneous interest, and held a possibility for achieving mastery, this experience of success quite often opened the way for further engagement in learning. Now, the learning experience allowed her to re-edit her conception of herself as being stupid and a failure and thus find the courage to face new challenges.

These findings from the biographical research point, however, to a further issue apart from the question of the learning environment, namely the question of access. If a person with a less successful history of biographical learning should transcend this problem and dare to become engaged in lifelong learning, a broad and wide scope of non-formal learning opportunities should be available. Perry's description of optimal learning quoted above as a circle of curiosity, exploration, practice, and mastery which leads to pleasure, satisfaction, and confidence may take place in any field. The wider the access and range of educational opportunities, the more possibilities exist so that many people can find and experience a context of optimal learning and thus may recreate an excitement for, and love of learning. When tailoring a good learning environment, we should also keep in mind that enthusiasm, curiosity, playfulness, and commitment are likely to be contagious.

However, in many countries the versatility of educational offers is limited. If we try to imagine a society in which only the appropriate knowledge acquisition in order to perform the job, secure the reproductive tasks, and be passively entertained by the media, is highlighted and supported, we face a very gloomy vision. In such a nightmare society there would be a limited use of narratives and no means to counter the stories with which one was fed.

An entirely different vision is the image of a society that offers life-wide, life-long learning in a variety of educational environments which appreciate generosity, diversity, versatility, and creativity, and in which children and adults learn to tell rich stories full of poetry and compassion.

The developing brain is described in terms of increased neural integration aiming at higher levels of plasticity and complexity. The developing mind can be described in a similar way, in terms of increased integration of experience aiming at higher levels of flexibility and complexity, plus the expansion of the horizon, as the mind has no physical limit, through new encounters of experience and new narratives of experience. The acquisition of narrative competence in different cultural spaces open to negotiation may enhance this development and help us to understand that we are intertwined and interdependent and, at the same time, equal and irreplaceable. Perhaps even help us to improve a little the ways in which we respond to and behave toward other human beings and other living creatures in our mutual world.

I shall end this journey by telling a story. Ten years ago, at an international conference, I was responsible for a workshop on narrative affiliations and identity. An African woman provided one of the concluding statements from the workshop. Her statement echoes Ricoeur's rephrasing of the Kantian dictum "Sapere aude": "Dare to give an account yourself." She said:

Narratives may be a way for all people to have voice, so that one day even our leaders will regard us as human beings.

Notes

I Time and plot

1   Now a whole is that which has a beginning, a middle, and an end. A beginning is that which does not necessarily come after something else, although something else exists or comes after it. An end, on the contrary, is that which naturally follows something else either as a necessary or as a usual consequence, and is not itself followed by anything. A middle is that which follows something else, and is itself followed by something.

(On the Art of Poetry) (1967: 41)

2   See, for example, Winograd, Fivush, and Hirst (1999).
3   Chronology comes from Chronos who, according to Greek mythology, ate his own children.
4   Also, Connelly and Clandinin (1999) speak about "being in the midst."
5   For example, the longer the distance you have travelled from the starting point, the closer you are to the destination.
6   Ricoeur, however, does not discuss this connection between time, space and movement.
7   The fact that we are able to remember the way we went is important in order to find our way back. One curious example of the significance of the movements of the body in contexts in connection with memory is when we go somewhere in order to fetch something, or to do something and, all of a sudden, arriving at the destination we have forgotten what we went there to do. Walking back to where we came from may sometimes help us to re-establish our intention.
8   Polkinghorne, who is deeply inspired by Ricoeur, has a similar description:

To be temporal, an event must be more than a singular occurrence; it must be located in relation to other events that have preceded it or will come after it. The first level of connection is a mere listing of events one after the other, as in a chronicle. This listing reflects the ordinary representation of time as one moment following the other in a linear fashion. By gathering these events together into the unity of a story, the plot makes them stand out from the plane of linear time by giving them significance in relation to other events. Plot combines two dimensions – one chronological, the other nonchronological. The chronological dimension characterizes the story and shows that it is made up of events along the line of time. The nonchronological dimension lifts the events into a configuration so that, scattered though they may be, they form a significant whole. Ricoeur uses Louis Mink's notion of "grasping together" as a description of the configurational act.

(1988: 131)

The issue of the temporality of a single occurrence will be taken up later.

9 As we shall see later (Chapter 3) the listener to a story has a more active role in the act of negotiation of meaning than the reader of fiction, although the reader also has some work to do in this respect.

10 Bruner is here somewhat in line with László (2008) who writes:

The omnipresence of human choice in narrative is the factor that questions the applicability of scientific causality in the human world. Intentional stances do not cause things. Nobody can be held morally responsible for something that was caused by some other things. Responsibility implies choice. In narrative we seek intentional stances that underlie action; they are *motives* or *reasons*, not *causes*.

(pp. 15–16)

11 Lakoff and Johnson talk of prototypical causation as an application of force resulting in motion or other physical change: "At the heart of causation is its most fundamental case: the manipulation of objects by force, the volitional use of bodily force to change something physically by direct contact in one's immediate environment" (1999: 177).

12 I agree with Somers and Gibson (1994: 59) in the following statement: "Above all, narratives are *constellations of relationships (connected parts) embedded in time and space*, constituted by *causal emplotment*."

13 See Polkinghorne (1988: 9). Ochs and Capps (2001) note how students in a laboratory in their scientific work use narratives in their construction of hypotheses. See also Orr (1990).

14 Although certain episodes in life may be narrated in different ways – the narrator may shift tense from past to present and use the device of "showing" instead of "telling" as if the episodes were relived in the narrative performance, or an episode is told in a fixed form created a while ago though numerous retellings – the configuration of the life story is always constructed from the perspective of the here and now of the telling.

2 Vicarious experience

1 There is some disagreement among the researchers concerning the question of the ability to learn through imitation; is it, exclusively, a human faculty, or is it shared by some of the monkeys? (see Tomasello, Kruger, & Ratner, 1993; Tomasello, 2000). We may be on safe ground applying the old formulation by Aristotle, quoted above: "he [man] is the most imitative of creatures."

2 See, for example, Gallese (2007), "Mirror neurons and the social nature of language: The neural exploitation hypothesis." At page 322 he argues that "[t]he meaning of 'table' stems from its use, from what we can do with it, that is from the multiple and interrelated possibilities for action it evokes." This argument is somewhat in line with Tomasello (2002) in his article: "Things are what they do: Katherine Nelson's functional approach to language and cognition."

3 Sarbin (2004) investigates the role of imagination in narrative construction by employing psychological parameters of imagining. He links the act of imagining to imitative "as if" constructions and talks about an "as if" skill that enables construction of hypothetical worlds. The theory of mirror-neurons may support his ideas.

4 Synapse is from the Greek and means "connection."

5 This is understood in a sense that goes beyond Bakhtin's concept of polysemi (Bakhtin, 1981).

6 Or in drama.

7 Bruner also relates the concept of vicarious experience to the ability to negotiate meaning (1990: 54).

3 Telling stories

1 In line with Bruner, Hayden White, in his article "The value of narrativity," maintains that we are not able to narrativize a discourse without moralizing (Mitchell, 1980: 13). White is opposed by Mink who is doubtful about a necessary connection between a narrativizing and a moralizing discourse. He suggests that any narrative can have a moral interpretation attributed to it, but not all narratives claim a moral interpretation (p. 237). White continues his argument by saying that we learn to be moral creatures through narratives (p. 253). Sarbin (2004: 6) also includes the moral element, stating that the essential criteria for telling a story are: "duration – a beginning, a middle, and an ending – and, importantly, the presence of a moral issue." Insofar as no narratives are emotionally neutral or independent of cultural prejudices in a hermeneutic sense, there is bound to be an element of morality in a broad sense in stories, although Mink is right in stating that all narratives are not necessarily directly moralizing forms of discourse.

2 Cf. Bruner (1990) who describes stories as especially viable instruments for social negotiation because of their "subjunctivity" and perspective.

3 See also Ochs and Capps (1996), Ochs and Capps (1997) and Ochs (1998).

4 As mentioned in Chapter 1, a linear temporal organization, in my point of view, is in itself not sufficient to capture the temporal organization of narrative. The act of emplotment, the configuration of the story that transforms mere chronology into a meaningful whole, is required in order to distinguish a narrative from a list, a simple sequence of incidents.

5 I owe this fine concept to Nils Wahlin, Umeå University Sweden.

6 See Michaels in McCabe and Peterson (1991) and Daiute (2004) in Daiute and Lightfoot (2004).

7 Hydén (2010) talks of disciplination, Freeman (2000) about "fore-closure" of narratives. See also Holstein and Gubrium (2000), McEwan (2004), Gergen (2004), Daiute and Lightfoot (2004).

8 Ochs and Capps (1997) quote Labov (1982) saying that a story worth telling is, almost by definition, unusual, and so less credible than usual events. This means that the more tellable a narrative is, the less credible it is; and yet credibility is as important for the success of a story as its tellability.

9 Like Aristotle, who talked of verisimilitude and necessity (1965).

10 Not all narrative genres manifest coherence to the same extent. Generally, stories encompassing a large time span, such as life story narratives, show a less coherent

configuration than stories about a single event. As mentioned in Chapter 2, narratives of personal experience can be incoherent due to disintegrated material or a position in the middle of a crisis. Hyvärinen Hydén, Saarenheimo, and Tamboukou, (2010) claim a shift of paradigm away from the demand of coherence in a well-formed narrative in their book, *Beyond narrative coherence*. In the last chapter of the book, Mark Freeman, however, adopts a more nuanced point of view.

11 According to Peterson and Langellier (2006) narrative as performance is "embodied in communication practices, constrained by situational and material conditions and embedded in fields of discourse" (2006: 173).

12 "The dispense of disbelief" is a concept we know from the reception of works of fiction. It has a weak parallel in the conventional fake response to narratives about unusual happenings: "Really! Come on! Are you serious?"

13 Nair (2001) uses the metaphor "the Indian rope trick" about narrative. A rope is cut into pieces then thrown up into the air and, finally, miraculously turns whole again.

14 The research context and the interaction between the interviewer and interviewee will be elaborated in Chapter 8.

4 The body, the brain, and experience

1 Or elements of the environment known by comparison and analogy.

2 Westbury and Dennet quote Reid (1815) in connection with the storage metaphors:

> The analogy between memory and a repository, and between remembering and retaining, is obvious and is to be found in all languages; it being natural to express the operations of the mind by images taken from things material. But in philosophy we ought to draw aside the veil of imagery, and to view them naked.
>
> (2000: 11)

3 Damasio researched the impact of brain damage and found that lesions affecting the emotions strongly inhibit rational functioning.

4 I find that Damasio takes the concept of narrative too far in his description of transient happenings. The temporal dimension is lacking, and single interactions are not strictly demarcated and happen, mostly, as simultaneous processes, where some of them will reach consciousness, and others will not.

5 Damasio does not refer to Wheeler et al., nor does he use the term "autonoetic consciousness."

6 Glaser writes:

> We are well accustomed to observe and study "mind" functions which include emotion, cognition, perception, and behavior. There are equivalent neurological processes accompanying these mind functions. It is increasingly possible to study brain structures, localization of function and precise timing of brain activity, and neurochemical changes in the brain, simultaneously with observed behavior and other "mind" functions, by the use of neurophysiological measures and brain imaging techniques.
>
> (2003: 118)

There are conflicting views regarding the relationship between mind and brain (see, for example, LeDoux, 2002 and Siegel, 2007).

7 Siegel (2007: 29–30) expresses the relationship thus: "nature needs nurture."

8 Siegel (2007: 23) refers to a research meeting in which the following dialogue emerged: "When I asked: 'Who here knows how the brain works?' one of my panel partners, the renowned researcher of affective neuroscience, Richard Davidson, replied 'None of us!' We all laughed and realized how correct he was."

9 Compare the well-known metaphor: "use it or lose it" (LeDoux, 2002: 75).

10 Nutrition also has a significant impact on brain development.

11 Bretherton (1993) mentions that Stern's RIGs are context dependent (pp. 248–9). They are not recalled in a new situation with a different context.

12   The script construct developed by Schank and Abelson applied to both social (intermental) and individual (intramental) knowledge. In Nelson (1986), my colleagues and I differentiated among these levels, proposing general event representations (GERs) as a more cognitive term not necessarily implying all the structural characteristics of scripts. To make this differentiation more apparent, both specific and general mental representations of events are designated "MERs" in this work.

(Nelson, 1996: 16)

In a footnote, the concept is compared to "Scenario." Nelson is well aware of the significance of the body in cognitive development. She says:

many other theorists recently have proposed alternatives to standard cognitive theories, with their emphasis on the disembodied autonomous mind. In reaction they have stressed that the mind must be situated in the body, and the body must be situated in the world (e.g., Varela, Thomson, & Rosch, 1991); and when the body is a human body, it becomes important that the world is both social and cultural.

(1996: 84)

She is also referring to Lakoff and Johnson.

13 I agree with Nelson in this differentiation between a happening in Damasio's sense and an event.

14 In a special edition of the *Journal of Cognition and Development* published at Katherine Nelson's retirement from the Graduate School of the City University of New York, Fivush et al. write:

Challenging the then-current Piagetian metaphor of a single mind learning about an objective world through actions on objects, Nelson focused our attention on how the social and cultural context in which the child is embedded facilitates the development of skills and strategies for creating meaning in the world.

(Fivush et al., 2002: 2)

15 Nelson uses the expressions "syntagmatic" and "paradigmatic," but with reference to Saussure.

16 See also Gallese (2007) for a similar viewpoint.

17 Schore quotes Winson (1990) for the following description of the unconscious: "Rather than being a cauldron of untamed passions and destructive wishes, I propose that the unconscious is a cohesive, continually active mental structure that

takes note of life's experiences and reacts according to its scheme of interpretation" (1990: 96).

18 Attachment theories (see Bowlby, 1969; Ainsworth, 1969; Bretherton, 1993; Siegel, 1999; Schore, 1994, 2003 and others) suggest a long-term effect of non-verbal and verbal interactions between infant and caregiver.

19 Researched by Tevarthen, Schore, and Meltzoff among others (see Tomasello, 1993).

20 Autistic children have problems with joint attention and with the use of "shifters" like "I" and "you" (see Loveland and Hobson in Neisser, 1993a).

5 Memory

1 See also, for example, Beike, Kleinknecht, and Behrend (2004a), Winograd et al. (1999), Schacter and Scarry (2001), Conway et al. (1992), Gazzaniga and Heatherton (2006), Neisser and Fivush (1994), Nelson (1993).

2 Within this framework we meet another example of the fascinating relationship between the interpersonal and the individual. The development of the individual brain depends on the individual's experiential history of interactions, on the individual's physical journey through life from community to community, from one interpersonal interaction to the other.

3 Squire, Knowlton, and Musen (1993) make a distinction between "skill learning" and "habit learning," both independent of explicit, declarative memory systems, although the acquisition of certain skills may be supported by explicit learning strategies. Ricoeur (2004) who discusses memory from a philosophical and phenomenological perspective, refers to Bergson's distinction between "habit learning" (described as part of procedural memory) and declarative memory, the explicit recollection in the present of something of the past. Many writers do not accept the theory of two memory systems (see Reed in Neisser and Fivush, 1994: 283). Brewer writes of explicit memory:

> The strong bias of philosophers towards conscious recollection can be seen in terms used to describe this form of memory – Henri Bergson referred to it as "memory par excellence" (Bergson, 1911) and Bertrand Russell referred to it as "true memory" (Russell, 1921).
>
> (Brewer, 1992: 33)

4 Bauer, Hertsgaard, and Wewerka, 1995; Bauer, Wenner, and Kroupina, 2002; Bauer and Wewerka, 1995; Bauer and Dow, 1994.

5 Not all researchers agree on Tulving's proposal of two explicit memory systems (see, for example, Baddeley in Neisser and Fivush, 1994).

6 The context of an episodic recollection may, however, fade and vanish into oblivion; we forget the source in time and space of our knowledge; it just becomes part of "something we know."

7 The authors describe how those components may deteriorate due to some kinds of mental disease.

8 Tessler (1986, 1991) studied the influence of mother–child conversations in joint encoding on the development of autobiographical memory.

9 We often simultaneously use embodied, tacit knowledge and conscious thought when we are learning and remembering new codes and passwords; the remembering is both in our minds and in our fingers.

10 For a discussion of embodied knowledge and learning, see Freiler (2008).
11 Middleton and Brown (2005: 14) quote Misztal:

> Although it is the individual who is seen as the agent of remembering, the nature of what is remembered is profoundly shaped by "what has been shared with others" such that what is remembered is always a "memory of an intersubjective past, of past time lived in relation to other people.
>
> (2003: 6)

On collective memory see also Middleton and Edwards (1990), Middleton and Hewitt (1999), Brockmeier (2002).
12 Several articles in Neisser and Fivush (1994) and Conway et al. (1992) deal with the reliability of memory (see, for example, Wagenaar (1994), Bell (1992), Auriat (1992), Hirst (1994); see also Hyman (1999)).
13 "Time-slice errors" are relatively frequent. Quite often we remember only the "gist" of an episode and not any details. Furthermore, experiments show that it is possible to plant false memories which people later truly believe are genuine (Hyman, 1999).
14 Horsdal (2007a).
15 Compare the notion of "grasping together" which Ricoeur borrows from Mink (1966) (see Chapter 1).

6 Early interactions

1 In the Danish book, *Livets Fortællinger* (Horsdal, 1999), I argued that meaning was simultaneously created and found. Freeman (2002: 24) proposes a similar idea (see also Freeman, 2010).
2 Bauer et al. studied memory and learning of young children, they state that verbalization enhances children's recall of specific sequences end events (see Bauer et al., 1995; Bauer et al., 2002; Bauer and Wewerka, 1995; Bauer and Dow, 1994).
3 Using Snow's expression: the children's autobiographies develop from their biographies (Snow, 1990).
4 Daiute (2004: 111) discusses the, simultaneously, "adaptive and subversive process" of children's narrating practices. Narrating encompasses both "issues of power and creativity."
5 In families with single, isolated, or very busy parents, stories around and about the children may be less frequent.
Cultural differences in the narrative environment are also discussed by Ochs and Capps (2001).
6 To use Lave and Wenger's expression (Lave and Wenger, 1991).
7 This article, "The emergence of autobiographical memory: A social cultural developmental theory" provides an excellent overview of American research on autobiographical memory. The authors underscore the significance of narrative and interpersonal interaction.
8 Not to mention the massive production of narratives in other media (television, film, etc.).
9 See Oppenheim, Nir, Warren, and Emde (1997) on regulation of emotion as a function of narrative.

7 Narrative competence

1 See, for example, Beattie (2009), Connelly and Clandinin (1994), Trahar (2006).
2 Bruner (1986, 1990, 1996), Siegel (1999).
3 However, the problem of tellability of a story in a specific context, as discussed in Chapter 3, remains in spite of the narrator's articulateness.
4 Identity is a very comprehensive issue, and some of the aspects – individual and collective identity, self as *ipse* and *idem*, and self in relation to the Other – will be unfolded in Chapters 10 and 11 in relation to the discussion of the findings from my research on life story narratives.
5 The theory of mirror-neurons discussed in Chapter 2 is interesting in this respect.
6 The term Bruner applies (1990).
7 Several studies deal with use of narratives among teachers for the purpose of professional development (see Huttunen, Heikkinen, and Syrjälä, 2002; Mørch, 2004; Connelly & Clandinin, 1999).
8 On ambiguous narrative practices, see also Brockmeier and Harré (1997) and Ochs and Capps (2001).
9 See also Lee, Rosenfeld, Mendenhall, Rivers, and Tynes (2004) and Daiute (2004).
10 The teachers, well-acquainted with the tradition of "appreciative inquiry," spontaneously transferred the appreciative mode to the traditional interview that adults use with children when they want them to tell something about what has happened.
11 Cf. The Madeleine cake in Proust's novel (1954).
12 Ochs and Capps (2001: 259) say: "Indeed, generating a coherent narrative may be more central to healing than reviewing every aspect of a traumatic event in search of what really happened." Also, Pennebaker has written extensively on the healing effects of narrative activity (see, for example, Pennebaker, 1993).

8 The narrative interview

1 In Denmark, education is part of the humanistic faculty and not, as in some other countries, a part of social science. The narrative approach to educational research was partly influenced by a background in literature and by previous employments at the Department of Literature and at the Department of Cultural Studies.
2 Horsdal, 1991.
3 See, for example, Horsdal (1998, 1999[2011], 2000a).
4 Horsdal (2001b).
5 Valorisation Report European Commission (Horsdal, 2003a).
6 Horsdal (2002a).
7 Horsdal (2004, 2008b).
8 Besides some articles and papers, I published a Danish monograph in 2008, At Lære, At Huske, *At Være. Gensyn Med Fortællingen* (To learn, to remember, to be – narrative revisited) (Horsdal, 2008a).
9 See, for example, West, Alheit, Siig Andersen, and Merrill (2007), Clandinin and Connelly (2000), Alheit, Bron-Wojciechowska, Brugger, and Dominicé (1995), Chamberlayne, Bornat, and Wengraf (2000).
10 See Chapter 2, Vicarious experience.

11 See Schäfer, in Mitchell, 1981. Some researchers are, of course, psychologists, and some narrative inquiries have goals other than researching biographical learning or analyzing interpretations of experience, of self and identity. See, for example, László (2008).

12 The narrator, on the other hand, may herself interrupt the telling, if she wants a break, wants to serve coffee or lunch, etc.

13 A wonderful example – almost a caricature – of the co-constructed plots (and futures) can be found in Holstein and Gubrium (2000).

14 Some of my students write the stories on a laptop, a method I find perfectly acceptable.

15 A concept I borrow from Siegel (1999).

16 See Hof and Fischer in Horsdal (2010).

17 In this case, it is often a great relief to focus on the entire life course instead of just the one problematic period or theme. See Ramian and Gústafsson, *Liv I Fokus* (Life in focus) (1998) and Gústafsson & Ramian, *Livshistorien – en vej til det menneskelige* (*The life history – A road to the human*) (2003).

18 "When Narrative inquirers are in the field, they are never there as disembodied recorders of someone else's experience. They too are having an experience, the experience of the inquiry that entails the experience they set out to explore" (Clandinin and Connelly, 2000: 81).

9 Interpretation and analysis of life story narratives

1 Gadamer (1965[1975]).

2 I am, of course, well aware that methodological approaches to interpretation and analysis are strongly contested among different "schools" of biographical research. For a recent European overview of biographical research in education see West et al. (2007).

3 I owe this distinction to Mey (2000) *When voices clash.*

4 For example, Propp (1968) and Greimas (1966).

5 Or "discourse" and "story" (Chatman, 1978: 62). In German, "Erzählzeit" and "erzählte Zeit." Eagleton (1983: 105) describes Genette's distinction: "*récit*, by which he [Genette] means the actual order of events in the text; histoire, which is the sequence in which those events 'actually' occurred, as we can infer this from the text."

6 Wenger (1999) later on developed the theory including a discussion of trajectories between different communities of practice. See also: *Learning for a small planet* (2005).

7 The evaluation may change over time:

> I remember thinking that I felt like a servant and what on earth was I doing there? I remember writing to my boyfriend that I felt that everything was quite horrible. I remember vividly that walk – was I going to have a good cry or just laugh? Now it is great fun to look back, because there were all these small obstacles to cope with.
>
> (Woman born 1979)

Many narrators assess early impediments as having a learning impact later in life.

8 Anderson (1983).

9   Twice, I put my fingers into a machine. They say – as a joke – that I did it
     in order to see if the machine I made was working. The first time, I cut
     halfway through my wrist. It grew together, but some nerves were stuck,
     so I lost many cups of coffee on this account, and later it caused the loss
     of two fingers as I got the other hand caught in a sawmill. This is serious
     stuff. I used to say, it won't hit me, but it did, and now I am 10 percent
     handicapped, and I have a reduced working power of 15 percent, but I did
     manage to finish the machines.

                                        (Man born 1947) (my translation)

10 Antikainen, Houtsonen, Huotelin, and Kauppila (1996: 95) describe three types
    of applications of "we," differing according to depth and intensity in the feeling
    of commonality: mass, community, and communion.
11 Who, by the way, finished her story with the following remark: "If my parents had
    not dissociated everything that I did to such an extent, perhaps, I wouldn't need
    to prove that I was right – even when I wasn't."
12 Interviewed when she was 23 years old.
13 This was an interview one of my students made with her mother-in-law in order
    to try out the methodology with a relative or friend.
14 An interview with a man born in the 1930s. This is important as a childhood in
    a time of severe financial crisis is more likely to create an emphasis on the material
    aspects of life.
15 Cf. Chapter 1, the section on Narrative causality.
16 The problem of translation between different sociocultural environments is
    discussed by Cortazzi and Jin, 2006.
17 After all, doing narrative research is, as Clandinin and Connelly (2000) empha-
    size, a way to oppose reductionism in favor of a more complex understanding of
    lived experience.
18 See West (1996, 2001, 2002).

10 Cultural identity

1 Taylor's concept "common space" equals my use of "cultural space." Other terms
   with similar denotations are "potential space" or "transitional space" (Winnicott,
   1971) and "common ground" (Shotter, 1993).
2 As interviewees receive the fair copy of the biographical interview they are offered
   the opportunity to become: "conscious of the narratives that we already live with
   and in" and how "they significantly contribute to the material from which our
   own narratives are derived." Thus, the method of constructing narrative interviews described in Chapter 8 may support reflexivity as a consequence of narrating and revisiting the narration.
3 Kim Etherington, discussing reflexivity in narrative research, argues:

     The narrative "turn" is away from reification of grand narratives or dominant
     discourses and towards the valuing of local stories; away from the idea that
     there is a single "right" way to approach social research and towards a plural-
     ist tradition and multiple ways of understanding and conducting narrative
     research and reflexivity.

                                                              (2006: 79)

The focus on local stories in academia which, of course, is basic to biographical narrative research, and the recognition of increasing reflexivity among people in the Western world in general concerning the interpretations of existence does not, however, imply a diminished significance of "grand" cultural narratives in life story narratives.

4 In this respect, this result of this research is very much in line with Antikainen et al. (1996).

5 Analysis of a large number of life story narratives from different parts of Denmark has led me to the notion of "extreme localism," signifying a rather typical aspect of Danish cultural identity. Small differences obviously seem to have a great impact. Extreme localism puzzles foreigners and does not facilitate integration.

11 Personal identity

1 The discussion on a representational vs. an ontological conception of narrative in favor of the latter is taken up by, for example, Somers and Gibson:

> One aspect of many new works in narrative studies, however, is especially relevant to our understanding of how identities are constituted, namely the shift from a focus on *representational* to ontological narrativity. Philosophers of history, for example, have previously argued that narrative modes of representing knowledge (telling historical stories) were representational *forms* imposed by historians on the chaos of lived experience (Mink, 1966; Hayden White, 1984). More recently, however, scholars ... are postulating something much more substantive about narrative: namely, that social life is itself storied and that narrative is an *ontological condition of social life*. Their research is showing us that stories guide action; that people construct identities (however multiple and changing) by locating themselves or being located within a repertoire of emplotted stories; that "experience" is constituted through narratives; that people make sense of what has happened and is happening to them by attempting to assemble or in some way to integrate these happenings within one or more narratives; and that people are guided to act in certain ways, and not others, on the basis of the projections, expectations, and memories derived from a multiplicity but ultimately limited repertoire of available social, public, and cultural narratives.
>
> (Calhoun, 1994: 38)

Also, Freeman argues, "that human life is itself narratively structured" (2004: 63). In consequence of the previous chapters I am inclined to argue in favor of an ontological position. I agree with the statement that people make sense of what happens through narratives, although I do not claim that all experience is constituted through narratives. The understanding of autobiographical, episodic memory put forward in this book and the idea of narrative cognition, designating our conception and experience of a bounded space of time as well as the theory of vicarious experience based on neuropsychological findings supports an ontological notion of narrative. Nevertheless, oral and written narratives are symbolic, esthetic constructions more or less creatively applying available cultural forms of discourse, some of them pieced together from representations of experience, some of which did not originally have a narrative form.

2 As embodied, contextually situated creatures we do not posses any God's-eye view of the panorama of human history. Both historical writings and the more humble life story narratives are told from a certain perspective but, ironically enough, in fictional narratives it is possible to create an omniscient narrator.

3 In another great work: *Memory, history, forgetting* (2004) Ricoeur adds the question: Who is remembering? (faire mémoire).

4 In his discussion of practice, Ricoeur refers to Aristotle's concept phronesis, often translated as practical reasoning. Phronesis involves ethics as it is practice in order to do what is good.

5 In a continuation of Levinas, Ricoeur explains that the voice of the other tells me: "Thou shall not kill." He writes:

> To find oneself called upon in the second person at the very core of the optative of living well, then of the prohibition to kill, then of the search for the choice appropriate to the situation, is to recognize oneself as being enjoined to *live well with and for others in just institutions and to esteem oneself as the bearer of this wish.*
>
> (1994: 352)

Thus, he only involves the relationship to other human beings in the world. If we expand the ethical obligation to a responsibility toward our entire environment, to nature and to other living creatures, the demand: "thou shall not kill!" becomes inadequate or impossible, since all living organisms survive by devouring other living organisms. This matter of fact, however, does not free us from responsibility concerning our responses and actions to other living creatures besides our fellow human beings. Accordingly, I suggest a transformation of the demand that will cover the expanded sphere of interrelations and responsibilities: the voice which says: "What are you doing to me?"

6 The point of departure from phenomenology may explain Ricoeur's lack of interest in what happens in the brain. He writes:

> For the philosopher there is no parallel between the two sentences: "I grasp with my hands," "I understand with my brain." The phenomenological philosopher senses the touch by grasping, but has no similar embodied sensation of the functioning of the brain. This remains outside phenomenology, yet acknowledged as a kind of "causa sine qua non."
>
> (pp. 420–1)

Unfortunately, his opposition to neuropsychology makes him criticize a taxonomy of memory (with a reference to Schacter, p. 591) although, there are interesting analogies between Ricoeur's distinctions and those of Tulving (2002). In spite of his application of the term "re-presentation" he fails to notice that each repetition or recall implies a new representation; on the contrary, he argues in favor of latent memory traces (a backup) in a positive sense as a not activated memory. The seeking of a memory if successful is described as a matter of recognition, "it is really her," or as "a happy memory" (p. 427ff.). In my experience, reading neuropsychological literature has caused an increasing number of instances of attention to brain functioning in the experience of everyday life, mostly in connection with mistakes and malfunctioning due to tiny temporal displacements between thoughts, intentions, and embodied actions. Actually, some neuroscientists behind the theory of the mirror-neuron system refer to phenomenologist writers such as Husserl (see Gallese, 2005).

7 Later in life, in connection with the loss of other beloved persons, I have learned that the more radical the transformations, as in some cases of cancer, the more difficult is the integration, and the longer time it takes to recall the person beyond the last period of illness and death.

8 Beike, Kleinknecht, and Wirth-Beaumont write: "This change/stability paradox is one of the thorniest dilemmas in the study of self, and a number of different solutions have been offered" (2004: 147).

9 There are variations in the distinctions between the I and me self among different authors. See Beike, Kleinknecht and Wirth-Beaumont (2004).

10 Skowronski, Walker, and Betz (2004) discuss "The timekeeping self in autobiographical memory" and our problems with accuracy of this function.

11 Cf. Lightfoot (2004: 36) who quotes Bakhtin and Winnicott in saying that "we experience ourselves within a liminal space between what is and what could be."

12 Active citizenship and biographical learning

1 Active citizenship is a concept closely linked to lifelong learning. *The memorandum on lifelong learning* states that lifelong learning should promote employability, active citizenship, personal development, and social coherence.

2 In Habermas' writings on communication and democracy (1984) you still find echoes of the idea of universal reason.

3 See Bauman (1991, 2003), Lash and Urry (1993), Sennet (1998) etc.

4 A concept inspired by Vygotsky.

5 The question reveals that the Finnish interviewer in this case became involved in a discussion with the interviewee at the end of the interview, contrary to the instructions.

6 "Education for democratic citizenship: a lifelong learning perspective," Council of Europe (2000).

7 The national differences were quite interesting, but they are not an issue in this publication. See Horsdal (2002a).

8 The coincidence between several of the competencies listed and the previously listed features of narrative competence (Chapter 7) is by no means accidental. As I explained earlier, the listed features of narrative competence were inspired partly by applied biographical research, and this research project was particularly influential in regard to the aforementioned suggestions.

9 Cf. Chapter 9 , the term "biographical learning" refers to the narrated experience of learning in the various communities of practice in which the individual participated throughout life.

13 Educational perspectives and concluding remarks

1 They discuss patients with brain damage who are insensitive to others' responses to their actions. These patients lack "the emotional rudder" and lose the commensurate decision-making abilities in contrast to people with no such brain damage. Probably, the pleasant and unpleasant generalized patterns of experience discussed in Chapter 4 – Katherine Nelson's MER (mental event representation) – are significantly influenced by cultural feedback.

2 Cf. Chapter 10, Finding yourself.
3 Clark and Rossiter also discuss the connection between experiential and narrative learning in the article "Narrative learning in adulthood" (2008).
4 Although a practice of working with different versions and different perspectives, and different genres of particular stories can be a fantastic exercise (see Horsdal, 2003b).
5 At the same time, this material is excellent for discussing cultural differences, different perspectives, and life strategies.
6 This is why Gregory Bateson warned against the danger of "learning 3" (Bateson, 1973).

Bibliography

Ainsworth, M. (1969). "Object relations, dependency and attachment: A theoretical review of the infant–mother relationship." *Child Development, 40,* 969–1025.

Ainsworth, M., Blehar, M. C., Waters, E. & Wall, S. (1978). *Patterns of attachment: A psychological study of the strange situation.* Hillsdale, NJ: Lawrence Erlbaum Associates.

Albright, D. (1994). "Literary and psychological models of the self." In Neisser, U. & Fivush, R. (Eds.), *The remembering self: Construction and accuracy in the self-narrative.* Cambridge: Cambridge University Press.

Alheit, P., Bron-Wojciechowska, A., Brugger, E. & Dominicé, P. (Eds.) (1995). *The biographical approach in European adult education.* Wien: Verband Wiener Volksbildung.

Anderson, B. (1983). *Imagined communities: Reflections on the origins and spread of nationalism.* London: Verso.

Antikainen, A., Houtsonen, J., Huotelin, H. & Kauppila, J. (1996). *Living in a learning society: Life-histories, identities and education.* London: Falmer Press.

Aristotle (1965). *On the Art of Poetry.* Baltimore, MD: Penguin Books.

Aukrust, V. (1995). *Fortellinger fra stellerummet. To-åringer I barnehage; en studie av språkbruk – innhold og struktur.* Universitetet i Oslo: Pedagogisk forskningsinstitutt, rapport nr. 4/95.

Auriat, N. (1992). "Autobiographical memory and survey methodology: Furthering the bridge between two disciplines." In Conway, M., Rubin, D., Spinnler, H. & Wagenaar, W. (Eds.), *Theoretical perspectives on autobiographical memory.* Dordrecht: Kluwer.

Baddeley, A. (1988). "But what the hell is it for?" In Gruneberg, M., Morris, P. & Sykes, R. (Eds.), *Practical aspects of memory: Current research and issues, Volume 1.* New York: John Wiley.

Baddeley, A. (1994). "The remembered self and the enacted self." In Neisser, U. & Fivush, R. (Eds.), *The remembering self: Construction and accuracy in the self-narrative.* Cambridge: Cambridge University Press.

Bakhtin, M. (1981). *The dialogic imagination: Four essays.* Austin: University of Texas Press.

Bamberg, M. (2004). "Positioning with Davie Hogan: Stories, tellings, and identitites." In Daiute, C. & Lightfoot, C. (Eds.), *Narrative analysis: Studying the development of individuals in society.* Thousand Oaks, CA: Sage.

Bartlett, F. (1932). *Remembering: A study in experimental and social psychology.* Cambridge: Cambridge University Press.

Bateson, G. (1973). *Steps to an ecology of mind.* London: Granada.

Bateson, M. C. (1975). "Mother–infant exchanges: The epigenesis of conversational interaction." In Aronson, D. & Rieber, R. W. (Eds.), *Developmental psycholinguistics and communication disorders. Annals of the New York Academy of Sciences* (Vol. 263). New York: New York Academy of Sciences.

Bateson, M. C. (1994). *Peripheral visions*. New York: HarperCollins.

Bauer, P. (1993). "Identifying subsystems of autobiographical memory: Commentary on Nelson." In Nelson, C. (Ed.), *Memory and affect in development*. Hillsdale, NJ: Lawrence Erlbaum Associates.

Bauer, P. & Dow, G. (1994). "Episodic memory in 16- and 20-month-old children: Specifics are generalized but not forgotten." *Developmental Psychology, 30,* 403–417.

Bauer, P., Hertsgaard, L. & Wewerka, S. (1995). "Effects of experience and reminding on long-term recall in infancy: Remembering not to forget." *Journal of Experimental Child Psychology, 59,* 260–298.

Bauer, P., Wenner, J. & Kroupina, M. (2002). "Making the past present: Later verbal accessibility of early memories." *Journal of Cognition and Development, 3(1),* 21–47.

Bauer, P. & Wewerka, S. (1995). "One- to two-year-olds' recall of events: The more expressed, the more impressed." *Journal of Experimental Child Psychology, 59(3),* 474–496.

Bauman, Z. (1991). *Modernity and ambivalence*. Oxford: Blackwell.

Bauman, Z. (2003). "Education's challenges in the liquid modern era." In Bron, A. & Schemmann, M. (Eds.), *Knowledge society, information society and adult education*. Münster: LIT Verlag.

Baumer, S., Ferholt, B. & Lecusay, R. (2005). "Promoting narrative competence through adult–child joint pretence: Lessons from the Scandinavian educational practice of playworld." *Cognitive Development, 20,* 576–590.

Beattie, M. (2009). *The quest for meaning: Narratives of teaching, learning and the arts*. Rotterdam: Sense Publishers.

Beck, U., Giddens, A. & Lash, S. (1994). *Reflexive modernization*. Cambridge: Polity Press.

Beike, D., Kleinknecht, E. & Wirth-Beaumont, E. (2004). "How emotional and nonemotional memories define the self." In Beike, D., Lampinen, J. & Behrend, D. (Eds.), *The self and memory*. New York: Psychology Press.

Beike, D., Lampinen, J. & Behrend, D. (2004a). "Evolving conceptions of the self and memory". In Beike, D., Lampinen, J. & Behrend, D. (Eds.), *The self and memory*. New York: Psychology Press.

Beike, D., Lampinen, J. & Behrend, D. (Eds.) (2004b). *The self and memory*. New York: Psychology Press.

Bell, C. (1992). "Memory for an early school report." In Conway, M., Rubin, D., Spinnler, H. & Wagenaar, W. (Eds.), *Theoretical perspectives on autobiographical memory*. Dordrecht: Kluwer.

Bergson, H. (1911). *Matter and memory*. London: Allen & Unwin.

Bergson, H. (1999 [1922]). *Duration and simultaneity*. Manchester: Clinamen.

Bowlby, J. (1969). *Attachment and loss, Volume 1: Attachment*. New York: Basic Books.

Bretherton, I. (1993). "From dialogue to internal working models: The co-construction of self in relationships." In Nelson, C. (Ed.), *Memory and affect in development*. Hillsdale, NJ: Lawrence Erlbaum Associates.

Brewer, W. (1992). "Phenomenal experience in laboratory and autobiographical memory tasks." In Conway, M., Rubin, D., Spinnler, H. & Wagenaar, W. (Eds.), *Theoretical perspectives on autobiographical memory*. Dordrecht: Kluwer.

Brockmeier, J. (2002). "Remembering and forgetting: Narrative as cultural memory." *Culture and Psychology, 8(1)*, 45–64.

Brockmeier, J. & Carbaugh, D. (Eds.) (2001). *Narrative and identity: Studies in autobiography, self and culture*. Amsterdam: John Benjamins.

Brockmeier, J. & Harré, T. (1997). "Narrative: Problems and promises of an alternative paradigm." *Research on Language and Social Interaction, 30(4)*, 263–283.

Bron, A. (2000). "Floating as an analytical category in the narratives of Polish immigrants to Sweden." In Szwejkowska-Olsson, E. & Bron, M. (Eds.), *Allvarlig debatt och rolig leg. En festskrift tilägnad A,N, Uggla*. Uppsala: Centrum för multietnisk forskning.

Bron, A. & Schemmann, M. (Eds.) (2003). *Knowledge society, information society and adult education*. Münster: LIT Verlag.

Brooks, P. (1984). *Reading for the plot: Design and intention in narrative*. Cambridge, MA: Harvard University Press.

Bruner, E. (1986). "Experience and its expressions." In Turner, V. & Bruner, E. M. (Eds.), *The anthropology of experience*. University of Illinois Press.

Bruner, J. (1986). *Actual minds, possible worlds*. Cambridge, MA: Harvard University Press.

Bruner, J. (1987). "Life as narrative." *Social Research, 54(1)*, 11–32.

Bruner, J. (1990). *Acts of meaning*. Cambridge, MA: Harvard University Press.

Bruner, J. (1996). *The culture of education*. Cambridge, MA: Harvard University Press.

Caine, G. & Caine, R. (2006). "Meaningful learning and the executive functions of the brain." In Johnson, S. & Taylor, K. (Eds.), *The neuroscience of adult learning: New directions for adult and continuing education*. San Francisco, CA: Jossey-Bass.

Calhoun, C. (1994). *Social theory and the politics of identity*. Oxford: Blackwell.

Cameron, J., Wilson, A. & Ross, M. (2004). "Autobiographical memory and self-assessment." In Beike, D., Lampinen, J. & Behrend, D. (Eds.), *The self and memory*. New York: Psychology Press.

Carr, D. (1986). *Time, narrative, and history*. Bloomington: Indiana University Press.

Carr, L., Iacobini, M., Dubeau, M., Mazziotta, J. & Lenzi, G. (2003). "Neural mechanisms of empathy in humans: A relay from neural systems for imitation to limbic areas." *Proceedings of the National Academy of Sciences, 100(9)*, 5497–5502.

Carrol, R. (2003). "At the border between chaos and order: What psychotherapy and neuroscience have in common." In Corrigall, J. & Wilkinson, H. (Eds.), *Revolutionary connections. Psychotherapy and neuroscience*. London: Karnac.

Carroll, L. (1982 [1865]). *Alice's adventures in Wonderland*. London: Chancellor Press.

Chamberlayne, P., Bornat, J. & Wengraf, T. (Eds.) (2000). *The turn to biographical methods in social science*. London: Routledge.

Chatman, C. (1978). *Story and discourse*. Ithaca, NY: Cornell University Press.

Cicchetti, D. & Beeghly, M. (Eds.) (1990). *The self in transition: Infancy to childhood*. Chicago: The University of Chicago Press.

Clandinin, D. J. & Connelly, F. M. (2000). *Narrative inquiry*. San Francisco, CA: Jossey-Bass Publishers.

Clark, M. C. & Rossiter, M. (2008) "Narrative learning in adulthood." In *New Directions for Adult and Continuing Education*. Wiley Periodicals, Inc. Wiley Interscience (www.interscience.wiley.com).

Connelly, F. M. & Clandinin, D. J. (1994). "Telling teaching stories." *Teacher Education Quarterly, 21(1)*, 145–158.

Connelly, F. M. & Clandinin D. J. (1999). *Shaping a professional identity: Stories of educational practice.* New York: Teachers College Press.

Conway, M., Rubin, D., Spinnler, H. & Wagenaar, W. (Eds.) (1992). *Theoretical perspectives on autobiographical memory.* Dordrecht: Kluwer.

Conway, M. & Pleydell-Pearce, C. (2002). "The construction of autobiographical memories in the self-memory system." *Psychological Review, 107(2)*, 261–288.

Corrigall, J. & Wilkinson, H. (Eds.) (2003). *Revolutionary connections: Psychotherapy and neuroscience.* London: Karnac.

Cortazzi, M. & Jin, L. (2006). "Asking questions, sharing stories and identity construction: Sociocultural issues in narrative research." In Trahar, S. (Ed.), *Narrative research on learning: Comparative and international perspectives.* Oxford: Symposium Books.

Council of Europe (1999). "The Budapest Declaration."

Council of Europe (2000). "Education for Democratic Citizenship." DECS/EDU/CIT.

Cozolino, L. (2002). *The neuroscience of psychotherapy: Building and rebuilding the human brain.* New York: Norton.

Cozolino, L. (2006). *The neuroscience of human relationships.* New York: W.W. Norton.

Cozolino, L. & Sprokay, S. (2006). "Neuroscience and adult learning." In Johnson, S. & Taylor, K. (Eds.), *The neuroscience of adult learning: New directions for adult and continuing education.* San Francisco, CA: Jossey-Bass.

Czarniawska-Joerges, B. (1995). "Narration or science? Collapsing the division in organization studies". *Organization, 2(1)*, 11–33.

Daiute, C. (2004). "Creative uses of cultural genres." In *Narrative analysis: Studying the development of individuals in society.* Thousand Oaks, CA: Sage.

Daiute, C. & Lightfoot, C. (Eds.) (2004). *Narrative analysis: Studying the development of individuals in society.* Thousand Oaks, CA: Sage.

Damasio, A. (2000). *The feeling of what happens: Body, emotion and the making of consciousness.* London: Vintage.

Damasio, A. (2001). "Thinking about belief: Concluding remarks." In Schacter, D. & Scarry, E. (Eds.), *Memory, brain, and belief.* Cambridge, MA: Harvard University Press.

DeHart, G. (1993). "Placing affect and narrative in developmental and cultural context: Comments on Miller et al." In Nelson, C. (Ed.), *Memory and affect in development.* Hillsdale, NJ: Lawrence Erlbaum Associates.

Denzin, N. (1989). *Interpretive biography.* Newbury Park, CA: Sage.

Eagleton, T. (1983). *Literary theory.* Oxford: Blackwell.

Ekman, K. G. (1996). *Gör mig levande igen (Make me alive again).* Stockholm: Bonnier.

Engel, S. (1986). *Learning to reminisce: A developmental study of how young children talk about the past.* PhD thesis. City University of New York.

Etherington, K. (2006). "Reflexivity: Using our 'selves' in narrative research." In Trahar, S. (Ed.) *Narrative research on learning: Comparative and international perspectives.* Oxford: Symposium Books.

European Commission. (2000). "A memorandum on lifelong learning." Commission staff working paper.

Farrant, K. & Reese, E. (2000). "Maternal style and children's participation in remi-
    niscing: Stepping stones in children's autobigraphical memory development."
    Journal of Cognition and Development, 1(2), 193–225.
Faulkner, W. (1929/1989). *The sound and the fury*. London: Picador Classics.
Feldman, R., Greenbaum, C., & Yirmiya, N. (1999). "Mother–infant affect syn-
    chrony as an antecedent of the emergence of self-control." *Developmental
    Psychology, 53*, 151–160.
Fivush, R. (1993). "Emotional content of parent–child conversations about the
    past." In Nelson, C. (Ed.), *Memory and affect in development*. Hillsdale, NJ:
    Lawrence Erlbaum Associates.
Fivush, R. (1994). "Constructing narrative, emotion, and self in parent–child conver-
    sations about the past." In Neisser, U. & Fivush, R. (Eds.), *The remembering self:
    Construction and accuracy in the self-narrative*. Cambridge: Cambridge University
    Press.
Fivush, R. (2004). "The silenced self: Constructing self from memories spoken and
    unspoken." In Beike, D., Lampinen, J. & Behrend, D. (Eds.), *The self and memory*.
    New York: Psychology Press.
Fivush, R., Hudson, J. & Lucariello, J. (2002). "Katherine Nelson's theoretical vision."
    Journal of Cognition and Development, 3(1), 1–4.
Fivush, R. & Reese, E. (1992). "The social construction of autobiographical memory."
    In Conway, M., Rubin, D., Spinnler, H. & Wagenaar, W. (Eds.), *Theoretical perspec-
    tives on autobiographical memory*. Dordrecht: Kluwer.
Fivush, R. & Vasudeva, A. (2002). "Remembering to relate: Socioemotional correlates
    of mother–child reminiscing." *Journal of Cognition and Development, 3(1)*, 73–90.
Freeman, M. (2000). "When the story's over: Narrative foreclosure and the possibil-
    ity of self-renewal." In Andrews, M., Sclater, S., Squire, C. & Treacher, A. (Eds.),
    Lines of narrative: Psychosocial perspectives. London: Routledge.
Freeman, M. (2002)."The burden of truth: Psychoanalytic *poesis* and narrative under-
    standing." In Patterson, W. (Ed.), *Strategic narrative: New perspectives on the
    power of personal and cultural stories*. Lanham, MD: Lexington Books.
Freeman, M. (2004). "Data are everywhere: Narrative criticism in the literature of
    experience." In Daiute, C. & Lightfoot, C. (Eds.), *Narrative analysis: Studying
    the development of individuals in society*. Thousand Oaks, CA: Sage.
Freeman, M. (2010). "Afterword: 'Even amidst' – Rethinking narrative coher-
    ence." In Hyvärinen, M., Hydén, L-C., Saarenheimo, M. & Tamboukou, M.
    (Eds.), *Beyond narrative coherence*. Amsterdam: John Benjamins.
Freiler, T. J. (2008). "Learning through the body." In *New directions for adult and
    continuing education*. Wiley Periodicals, Inc. Wiley Interscience (www.interscience.
    wiley.com).
Freud, S. (1920/1983). "Jenseits des Lustprincipts." In *Studienausgabe 13*. Frankfurt:
    Fischer Verlag.
Gadamer, H. G. (1965). *Wahrheit und Methode*. Tübingen: J.C.B. Mohr.
Gallese, V. (2005). "Embodied simulation: From neurons to phenomenal experi-
    ence." In *Phenomenology and the cognitive sciences*. Berlin: Springer.
Gallese, V. (2007). "Mirror neurons and the social nature of language: The neural
    exploitation hypothesis." In *Social neuroscience*. London: Psychology Press.
Gallese, V., Fadiga, L., Fogasse, L., & Rizzolatti, G. (1996). "Action recognition in
    the premotor cortex." *Brain, 119(2)*, 593–609.

Gallese, V. & Lakoff, G. (2005). The brain's concepts: The role of the sensory-motor system in reason and language. *Cognitive Neuropsychology*, 22, 455–479.

Gazzaniga, M. & Heatherton, T. (2006). *Psychological science*. New York: W.W. Norton.

Genette, G. (1972/1980). *Narrative discourse*. New York: Cornell University Press.

Gergen, M. (2004). "Once upon a time: A narratologist's tale". In Daiute, C. & Lightfoot, C. (Eds.), *Narrative analysis: Studying the development of individuals in society*. Thousand Oaks, CA: Sage.

Giddens, A. (1990). *The consequences of modernity*. Cambridge: Polity.

Glaser, D. (2003). "Early experience, attachment and the brain." In Corrigall, J. & Wilkinson, H. (Eds.), *Revolutionary connections: Psychotherapy and neuroscience*. London: Karnac.

Greimas, A. (1966). *Sémantique structural*. Paris: Larousse.

Gústafsson, J. & Ramian, K. (2003) (Eds.), *Livshistorien – en vej til det menneskelige*. Århus: Systime Academic.

Habermas, J. (1984). *The theory of communicative action, Vol. 1*. London: Heinemann.

Hebb, D. (1949). *The organization of behaviour: A neuropsychological theory*. New York: Wiley.

Hirst, W. (1994). "The remembered self in amnesics." In Neisser, U. & Fivush, R. (Eds.), *The remembering self: Construction and accuracy in the self-narrative*. Cambridge: Cambridge University Press.

Hobson, R. (1993) "Through feeling and sight to self and symbol." In Neisser, U. (Ed.), *The perceived self: Ecological and interpersonal sources of self-knowledge*. Cambridge: Cambridge University Press.

Hof, C. & Fischer, M. (2010). "Lifelong learning as continuity and transformation. A qualitative longitudinal study about adults' biographies of learning and teaching." In Horsdal, M. (Ed.), *Communication, collaboration and creativity: Researching adult learning*. Odense: University Press of Southern Denmark.

Hoffmann, E. (1989). *Lost in translation*. Harmondsworth: Penguin.

Holstein, J. & Gubrium, J. (2000). *Constructing the life course*. New York: General Hall.

Horsdal, M. (1982). *Den lyserøde/lyserøde skæbne*. Odense: Odense Universitetsforlag.

Horsdal, M. (1991). *Danmark mit Fædreland*. København: Borgen.

Horsdal, M. (1998). *Halvfemserfortællinger*. København: Borgen.

Horsdal, M. (1999 [2011]). *Livets fortællinger*. København: Borgen.

Horsdal, M. (2000a). *Vilje og Vilkår – Identitet, læring og demokrati*. København: Borgen.

Horsdal, M. (2000b). "The life-story in adult education." In *Nordisk* Årbok, *Adult Education Research in Nordic Countries*. Trondheim.

Horsdal, M. (2001a). "Identity, learning and democracy." *Journal of World Education, 32(1)*, 27–33.

Horsdal, M. (2001b). "Democratic citizenship and the meeting of cultures." In Schemmann, M. & Bron Jr., M. (Eds.), *Adult education and democratic citizenship IV*, Krakow.

Horsdal, M. (2002a). *Active citizenship and non-formal education: Description of competences*. København: Højskolerne, FFD.

Horsdal, M. (2002b). "Affiliation and participation – narrative identity." In Korsgaard, O., Walters, S. & Andersen, R. (Eds.), *Learning for democratic citizenship*. København: The Danish University of Education.

Horsdal, M. (2003a). "Valorisation of Reflect." In *Valorisation of the Leonardo da Vinci products, Final Report*. Toscana.

Horsdal, M. (2003b). "Vold som blind passager. Et forsøg med erfaringslæring ved hjælp af fortællinger." In Gleerup, J. & Wiedemann, F. (Eds.), *Pædagogisk forskning og udvikling*. Odense: Syddansk Universitetsforlag, Odense.

Horsdal, M. (2004). "Democratic citizenship and biographical learning." *Journal of Adult and Continuing Education, 7*.

Horsdal, M. (2005). "Professional identities and development in partnership learning." In Bron, A., Kurantowitcz, E., Olesen, H. S. & West, L. (Eds.), *'Old' and 'new' worlds of adult learning*. Wroclaw: Wydawnictwo Naukowe.

Horsdal, M. (2007a). "The discourses of lifelong learning in a knowledge economy." In Rinne, R., Heikkinen, A. & Salo, P. (Eds.), *Adult education – liberty, fraternity, equality? Nordic views on lifelong learning*. Finnish Educational Research Association.

Horsdal, M. (2007b). "Therapy and narratives of self." In West, L., Alheit, P., Andersen, A. S. & Merril, B. (Eds.), *Using biographical and life history approaches in the study of adult and lifelong learning: European perspectives*. Frankfurt: Peter Lang.

Horsdal, M. (2008a). *At Lære, At Huske, At Være. Gensyn med fortællingen*. København: Billesø & Baltzer.

Horsdal, M. (2008b). "Professionsudvikling og partnerskabslæring." In Schwartz, I., Gleerup, J., Soelmark, E., Andersen, E. & Kruse, B. (Eds.), *Børneperspektiver på Døgninstitutioner*. Odense: Syddansk Universitetsforlag.

Horsdal, M. (Ed.) (2010). *Communication, collaboration and creativity: Researching adult learning*. Odense: University Press of Southern Denmark.

Hudson, J. (2002). "'Do you know what we're going to do this summer?': Mothers talk to preschool children about future events." *Journal of Cognition and Development, 3(1)*, 49–71.

Huttunen, R., Heikkinen, H. & Syrjälä, L. (Eds.) (2002). *Narrative research: Voices of teachers and philosophers*. Jyväskylän Yliopisto.

Hydén, L.-C. (2010). "Identity, self, narrative." In Hyvärinen, M., Hydén, L-C., Saarenheimo, M. & Tamboukou, M. (Eds.), *Beyond narrative coherence*. Amsterdam: John Benjamins.

Hyman, I. (1999). "Creating false autobiographical memories: Why people believe their memory errors." In Winograd, E., Fivush, R. & Hirst, W. (Eds), *Ecological approaches to cognition*. Hillsdale, NJ: Lawrence Erlbaum Associates.

Hyvärinen, M., Hydén, L-C., Saarenheimo, M. & Tamboukou, M. (Eds.) (2010). *Beyond narrative coherence*. Amsterdam: John Benjamins.

Iacobini, M., Molnar-Szakacs, I., Gallese, V., Mazziotta, J. & Rizzolatti, G. (2005). "Grasping the intention of others with one's own mirror neuron system." *PLoS Biology, 3(3)*, 79.

Immordino-Yang, M. & Damasio, A. (2007). "We feel, therefore we learn: The relevance of affective and social neuroscience to education." *Mind, Brain, and Education, 1(1)*, 3–10.

Jakobson, R. (1960). "Closing statement: Linguistics and poetics." In Sebeok, T. (Ed.), *Style in language*. Cambridge: MIT Press.

Jefferson, A. & Blagov, P. (2004). "The integrative function of narrative processing: Autobiographical memory, self-defining memories, and the life story of identity." In Beike, D., Lampinen, J. & Behrend, D. (Eds.), *The self and memory*. New York: Psychology Press.

Johnson, M. (1987). *The body in the mind: The bodily basis of meaning, imagination, and reason*. Chicago: Chicago University Press.

Johnson, M., Griffin, R., Csibra, G., Halit, H., Farroni, T., De Haan, M., et al. (2005). "The emergence of the social brain network: Evidence from typical and atypical development." *Development and Psychopathology, 17(3)*, 599–619.

Johnson, S. & Taylor, K. (Eds.) (2006). *The neuroscience of adult learning: New directions for adult and continuing education*. San Francisco, CA: Jossey-Bass.

Jopling, D. (1993). "Cognitive science, other minds, and the philosophy." In Neisser, U. (Ed.), *The perceived self: Ecological and interpersonal sources of self-knowledge*. Cambridge: Cambridge University Press.

Jopling, D. (1999). "Five kinds of self-ignorance." In Winograd, E., Fivush, R. & Hirst, W. (Eds.), *Ecological approaches to cognition*. Hillsdale, NJ: Lawrence Erlbaum Associates.

Kafka, J. (1925/1935). *Der Prozess*. Frankfurt: Fischer Taschenbuch Verlag.

Kerby, A. (1991). *Narrative and the self*. Indiana: Indiana University Press.

Kermode, F. (1966). *The sense of an ending*. Oxford: Oxford University Press.

Klein, S., German, T., Cosmides, L. & Gabriel, R. (2004). "A theory of autobiographical memory: Necessary components and disorders resulting from their loss." *Social Cognitions, 22(5)*, 460–490.

Kolk, B. van der (2003). "EMDR and the lessons from neuroscience research." Paper from EMDR conference.

Korsgaard, O. (2000). "Learning and the changing concept of enlightenment: Danish adult education over five centuries." *International Review of Education*. Dordrecht: Kluwer.

Korsgaard, O. (2004). *Kampen om folket*. København: Gyldendal.

Korsgaard, O., Walter, S. & Andersen, R. (Eds.) (2002). *Learning for democratic citizenship*. København: The Danish University of Education.

Kruger, A. & Tomasello, M. (1996). "Cultural context of human development and education." In Olsen, D. (Ed.), *The handbook of education and human development*. London: Sage.

Labov, W. (1966). *The social stratification of English in New York City*. Washington: Center for Applied Linguistics.

Labov, W. (1972). *Language in the inner city*. Philadelphia: University of Pennsylvania Press.

Labov, W. (1982). "Speech actions and reactions in personal narrative." In Tannen, D. (Ed.), *Georgetown University round table on language and linguistics 1981: Analyzing discourse: Text and talk*. Washington, DC: Georgetown University Press.

Lakoff, G. & Johnson, M. (1980). *Metaphors we live by*. Chicago: University of Chicago Press.

Lakoff, G. & Johnson, M. (1999). *Philosophy in the flesh*. New York: Basic Books.

Lampinen, J., Beike, D. & Behrend, D. (2004). "The self and memory: It's about time." In Beike, D., Lampinen, J. & Behrend, D. (Eds.), *The self and memory*. New York: Psychology Press.

Lampinen, J., Odegard, T. & Leding, J. (2004). "Diachronic disunity." In Beike, D., Lampinen, J. & Behrend, D. (Eds.), *The self and memory*. New York: Psychology Press.

Lash, S. & Urry, J. (1993). *Economies of signs and space*. London: Sage.

László, J. (2008) *The science of stories*. London: Routledge.

Lave, J. & Wenger, E. (1991). *Situated learning: Situated peripheral participation*. Cambridge: Cambridge University Press.

LeDoux, J. (2002). *Synaptic self: How our brains become who we are*. New York: Penguin.

Lee, C. D., Rosenfeld, E., Mendenhall, R., Rivers, A. & Tynes, B. (2004). "Cultural modeling as a frame for narrative analysis". In Daiute, C. & Lightfoot, C. (Eds.), *Narrative analysis: Studying the development of individuals in society*. Thousand Oaks, CA: Sage.

Lessing, D. (1972). *Children of violence*. London: Granada.

Levinas, E. (1969/1996). *Totality and infinity*. Pittsburgh: Duquesne University Press.

Lieberman, M. (2000). "Intuition: A social neuroscience approach." *Psychological Bulleting, 126*, 109–137.

Lightfoot, C. (2004). "Fantastic self: A study of adolescents' fictional narratives, and aesthetic activity as identity work". In Daiute, C. & Lightfoot, C. (Eds.), *Narrative analysis: Studying the development of individuals in society*. Thousand Oaks, CA: Sage.

Lohmann, H. & Tomasello, M. (2003). "Language and social understanding: Commentary on Nelson et al." *Human Development, 46*, 45–50.

Loveland, K. (1993). "Autism, affordances, and the self." In Neisser, U. (Ed.), *The perceived self: Ecological and interpersonal sources of self-knowledge*. Cambridge: Cambridge University Press.

Lyotard, J.-F. (1979) *La Condition post-moderne*. Paris: Minuit.

McAdams, D. P. (1985). *Power, intimacy, and the life story: Personological inquiries into identity*. New York: Guilford Press.

McAdams, D. P. (1996). "Personality, modernity, and the storied self: A contemporary framework for studying persons." *Psychological Inquiry, 7*, 295–321.

McCabe, A. & Peterson, C. (1991). *Developing narrative structure*. Hillsdale, NJ: Lawrence Erlbaum Associates.

McEwan, H. (2004). "Fortællingens funktioner og pædagogisk forskning." In Buur Hansen, N. & Gleerup, J. (Eds.), *Videnteori, Professionsuddannelse og Professionsforskning*. Odense: Syddansk Universitetsforlag.

Manturana, H. & Varela, F. (1992). *The tree of knowledge: Biological roots of human understanding*. Boston: Shambhala.

Marshall, T. (1994 [1950])."Citizenship and social class." In Turner, B. & Hamilton, P. (Eds.), *Citizenship: Critical concepts*. London: Routledge.

Mey, J. (2000). *When voices clash*. Berlin: Mouton de Gruyter.

Michaels, S. (1991). "The dismantling of narrative." In McCabe, A. & Peterson, C. *Developing narrative structure*. Hillsdale, NJ: Lawrence Erlbaum Associates.

Middleton, D. & Edwards, D. (Eds.) (1990). *Collective remembering*. London: Sage.

Middleton, D. & Brown, S. (2005). *The social psychology of experience*. London: Sage.

Middleton, E. & Hewitt, H. (1999). "Remembering as social practice: Identity and life story work in transitions and care for people with profound learning disabilities." *Narrative Inquiry, 9(I)*, 97–122.

Miller, P. (1994). "Narrative practices: Their role in socialization and self-construction." In Neisser, U. & Fivush, R. (Eds.), *The remembering self: Construction and accuracy in the self-narrative*. Cambridge: Cambridge University Press.

Miller, P., Hoogstra, L., Mintz, J., Fung, H. & Williams, K. (1993). "Troubles in the garden and how they get resolved: A young child's transformation of his favorite story." In Nelson, C. (Ed.), *Memory and affect in development*. Hillsdale, NJ: Lawrence Erlbaum Associates.

Miller, P., Potts, R., Fung, H., Hoogstra, L. & Mintz, J. (1990). "Narrative practices and the social construction of self in childhood." *American Ethnologist, 17(2)*, 292–311.

Milner, B., Squire, L. & Kandel, E. (1998). "Cognitive neuroscience and the study of memory." *Neuron, 20*, 445–468.

Mink, L. (1966). "The autonomy of historical understanding." *History and Theory, 5(1)*, 24–47.

Misztal, B. (2003). *Theories of social remembering*. Buckingham, UK: Open University Press.

Mitchell, W. (Ed.) (1980). *On narrative*. Chicago: University of Chicago Press.

Mouritsen, F. (1996). *Legekultur*. Odense: Odense Universitetsforlag.

Mørch, S. (Ed.) (2004). *Pædagogiske Praksisfortællinger*. Århus: Systime Academic.

Nair, R. (2001). *Narrative gravity*. New Delhi: Oxford University Press.

Neimeyer, G. & Metzler, A. (1994). "Personal identity and autobiographical recall." In Neisser, U. & Fivush, R. (Eds.), *The remembering self: Construction and accuracy in the self-narrative*. Cambridge: Cambridge University Press.

Neisser, U. (Ed.) (1993a). *The perceived self: Ecological and interpersonal sources of self-knowledge*. Cambridge: Cambridge University Press.

Neisser, U. (1993b). "The self perceived." In Neisser, U. (Ed.), *The perceived self: Ecological and interpersonal sources of self-knowledge*. Cambridge: Cambridge University Press.

Neisser, U. (1994). "Self-narratives: True and false." In Neisser, U. & Fivush, R. (Eds.), *The remembering self: Construction and accuracy in the self-narrative*. Cambridge: Cambridge University Press.

Neisser, U. & Fivush, R. (Eds.) (1994). *The remembering self: Construction and accuracy in the self-narrative*. Cambridge: Cambridge University Press.

Nelson, C. (Ed.) (1993). *Memory and affect in development*. Hillsdale, NJ: Lawrence Erlbaum Associates.

Nelson, K. (Ed.) (1989). *Narratives from the crib*. Cambridge, MA: Harvard University Press.

Nelson, K. (1991). "Remembering and telling: A developmental story." *Journal of Narrative and Life History, 1(2–3)*, 109–127.

Nelson, K. (1993). "Events, narratives, memory: What develops?" In Nelson, C. (Ed.), *Memory and affect in development*. Hillsdale, NJ: Lawrence Erlbaum Associates.

Nelson, K. (1996). *Language in cognitive development: The emergence of the mediated mind*. Cambridge: Cambridge University Press.

Nelson, K. (2001). "Memory and belief in development." In Schacter, D. & Scarry, E. (Eds.), *Memory, brain, and belief*. Cambridge, MA: Harvard University Press.

Nelson, K. (2002). "Developing dual-representation processes." *Behavioral and Brain Sciences, 25(6)*, 693–694.

Nelson, K. (2005a). "Language pathways into the community of minds." In Astington, J. & Baird, J. (Eds.), *Why language matters to theory of mind*. Cambridge: Cambridge University Press.

Nelson, K. (2005b). "Emerging levels of consciousness in early human development." In Terrace, H. & Metcalfe, J. (Eds.), *The missing link in cognition: Origins of self-reflective consciousness*. Oxford: Oxford University Press.

Nelson, K. & Fivush, R. (2004). "The emergence of autobiographical memory: A social cultural developmental theory." *Psychological Review, 111(2)*, 486–511.

Nietzsche, F. (1983 [1874]). "On the uses and disadvantages of history for life." *Untimely meditations*. Cambridge: Cambridge University Press.

Ochs, E. (1998). "Narrative." In Van Dijk, T. (Ed.), *Discourse as structure and process*. London: Sage.

Ochs, E. & Capps, L. (1996). "Narrating the self." *Annual Review of Anthropology, 25*, 19–43.

Ochs, E. & Capps, L. (1997). "Narrative authenticity." *Journal of Narrative and Life History, 7 (1–4)*, 83–89.

Ochs, E. & Capps, L. (2001). *Living narrative: Creating lives in everyday storytelling*. Cambridge, MA: Harvard University Press.

Oppenheim, D., Nir, A., Warren, S. & Emde, R. (1997). "Emotion regulation in mother–child narrative co-construction: Associations with children's narratives and adaptation." *Developmental Psychology, 33(2)*, 284–294.

Orr, J. (1990). "Sharing knowledge, celebrating identity: Community memory in a service culture." In Middleton, D. & Edwards, D. (Eds.), *Collective remembering*. London: Sage.

Papousek, H. & Papousek, M. (1995). "Intuitive parenting." In Bornstein, M. (Ed.), *Handbook of parenting. Volume II: Ecology and biology of parenting*. Hillsdale, NJ: Lawrence Erlbaum Associates.

Pennebaker, J. (1993). "Putting stress into words: Health, linguistic and therapeutic implications." *Behavior Research and Therapy, 31(6)*, 539–548.

Perry, B. (2006). "Fear and learning: Trauma-related factors in the adult education process". In Johnson, S. & Taylor, K. (Eds.), *The neuroscience of adult learning*. San Francisco, CA: Jossey-Bass.

Peterson, C. & McCabe, A. (Eds.) (1991). *Developing narrative structure*. Hillsdale, NJ: Lawrence Erlbaum Associates.

Peterson, E. & Langellier, K. (2006). "The performance turn in narrative studies." In Bamberg, M. (Ed.), *Narrative – State of the art*. Amsterdam: John Benjamins.

Pillemer, D. & White, S. (1989). "Childhood events recalled by children and adults." In Reese, H. (Ed.), *Advances in child development and behaviour* (Vol. 21). New York: Academic.

Polkinghorne, D. (1988). *Narrative knowing and the human sciences*. The University of New York Press.

Propp, V. (1968). *The morphology of the folktale*. Austin: University of Texas Press.

Proust, M. (1954) *A la recherche du temps perdu*. La Pléiade: Gallimard.

Ramachandran, V. (2001). "Memory and the brain: New lessons from old syndromes." In Schacter, D. & Scarry, E. (Eds.), *Memory, brain, and belief*. Cambridge, MA: Harvard University Press.

Ramian, K. & Gústafsson, J. (1998). *Liv i Fokus*. Århus: Systime Academic.

Reed, E. (1994). "Perception is to self as memory is to selves." In Neisser, U. & Fivush, R. (Eds.), *The remembering self: Construction and accuracy in the self-narrative.* Cambridge: Cambridge University Press.

Reese, E. & Fivush, R. (1993). "Parental styles of talking about the past." *Developmental Psychology, 29(3),* 596–606.

Ricoeur, P. (1984 [1983]). *Time and narrative.* Chicago: University of Chicago Press.

Ricoeur, P. (1994 [1990]). *Oneself as Another.* Chicago: University of Chicago Press.

Ricoeur, P. (2004). *Memory, history, forgetting.* Chicago: University of Chicago Press.

Rizzolatti, G. & Craighero, L. (2004) "The mirror-neuron system." *Annual Review Neuroscience, 27,* 169–192.

Rizzolatti, G., Fadiga, L., Gallese V., & Fogassi, L. (1996). "Premotor cortex and the recognition of motor actions". *Cognitive Brain Research, 3,* 131–141.

Rizolatti, G., Fogassi, L. & Gallese, V. (2001). "Neurophysiological mechanisms underlying the understanding and imitation of action." *Nature Reviews Neuroscience, 2(9),* 661–670.

Rogoff, B. (1990). *Apprenticeship in thinking: Cognitive development in social context.* New York: Oxford University Press.

Ross, M. & Buehler, R. (1994). "Creative remembering." In Neisser, U. & Fivush, R. (Eds.), *The remembering self: Construction and accuracy in the self-narrative.* Cambridge: Cambridge University Press.

Ross, M. & Holmberg, D. (1990). "Recounting the past: Gender differences in the recall of events in the history of a close relationship." In Zanna, M. & Olson, J. (Eds.), *The Ontario symposium: Vol. 6. Self-inference processes.* Hillsdale, NJ: Lawrence Erlbaum Associates.

Ross, M. & Wilson, A. (2001). "Constructing and appraising past selves." In Schacter, D. & Scarry, E. (Eds.), *Memory, brain, and belief.* Cambridge, MA: Harvard University Press.

Rossiter, M. (1999). "A narrative approach to development: Implications for adult education." *Adult Education Quarterly, 50(1),* 56–71.

Ryan, T. & Walker, R. (2009). *Life story work.* London: BAAF.

Sarbin, T. (1986). *Narrative psychology.* New York: Praeger Science.

Sarbin, T. (2004). "The role of imagination in narrative construction." In Daiute, C. & Lightfoot, C. (Eds.), *Narrative analysis: Studying the development of individuals in society.* Thousand Oaks, CA: Sage.

Sartre, J. P. (1938). *La nausée.* Paris: Gallimard.

Sarup, M. (1996). *Identity, culture and the postmodern world.* Edinburgh: Edinburgh University Press.

Schacter, D. & Scarry, E. (Eds.) (2001). *Memory, brain, and belief.* Cambridge, MA: Harvard University Press.

Schafer, R. (1981). "Narration in the psychoanalytic dialogue." In Mitchell, W. (Ed.), *On narrative.* Chicago: University of Chicago Press.

Schall, J. (2001). "Neural basis of deciding, choosing and acting." *Nature Reviews Neuroscience, 2,* 33–42.

Schemmann, M. & Bron Jr., M. (Eds.) (2001). *Adult education and democratic citizenship IV.* Krakow: Impuls Publishers.

Schore, A. (1994). *Affect regulation and the origin of the self: The neurobiology of emotional development.* Hillsdale, NJ: Lawrence Erlbaum Associates.

Schore, A. (2003). "The seventh annual John Bowlby Memorial Lecture." In Corrigall, J. & Wilkinson, H. (Eds.), *Revolutionary connections: Psychotherapy and neuroscience*. London: Karnac.

Schank, R. & Abelson, R. (1977). *Scripts, plans, goals, and understanding*. Hillsdale, NJ: Lawrence Erlbaum Associates.

Schrag, C. O. (1997). *The self after postmodernity*. New Haven, CT: Yale University Press.

Schwartz, I. (Eds.) (2003). *Fortællinger fra praksis – om livshistorier og pædagogik*. København: Reitzels Forlag.

Sennet, R. (1998). *The corrosion of character*. New York: Norton.

Shotter, J. (1993). *Cultural politics of everyday life: Social constructivism, rhetoric and knowledge of the world*. Buckingham, UK: Open University Press.

Siegel, D. (1999). *The developing mind: Toward a neurobiology of interpersonal experience*. New York: Guilford.

Siegel, D. (2001a). "Toward an interpersonal neurobiology of the developing mind: Attachment relationships, 'mindsight,' and neural integration." *Infant Mental Health Journal, 22 (1–2)*, 67–94.

Siegel, D. (2001b). "Memory: An overview, with emphasis on developmental, interpersonal, and neurobiological aspects." *Journal of American Child Adolescence Psychiatry, 40(9)*, 997–1011.

Siegel, D. (2007). *The mindful brain*. New York: Norton.

Skowronski, J., Walker, W. & Betz, A. (2004). "Who was I when that happened? The timekeeping self in autobiographical memory." In Beike, D., Lampinen, J. & Behrend, D. (Eds.), *The self and memory*. New York: Psychology Press.

Snow, C. (1990). "Building memories: The ontogeny of autobiography." In Cicchetti, D. & Beeghly, M. (Eds.), *The self in transition: Infancy to childhood*. Chicago: University of Chicago Press.

Somers, M. R. & Gibson, G. D. (1994) "Reclaiming the epistemological 'other': Narrative and the social construction of identity". In Calhoun, C. (Ed.), *Social theory and the politics of identity*. Oxford: Blackwell.

Squire, L., Knowlton, B. & Musen, G. (1993). "The structure and organization of memory." *Annual Review of Psychology, 44*, 453–495.

Stern, D. (1985). *The interpersonal world of the infant*. New York: Basic Books.

Taylor, C. (1989). *Sources of the self: The making of modern identity*. Cambridge: Cambridge University Press.

Taylor, K. (2006). "Brain function and adult learning: Implications for practice." In Johnson, S. & Taylor, K. (Eds.), *The neuroscience of adult learning*. San Francisco, CA: Jossey-Bass.

Taylor, K. & Lamoreaux, A. (2008). "Teaching with the brain in mind." In *New Directions for Adult and Continuing Education*. Wiley Periodicals, Inc. Wiley Interscience (www.interscience.wiley.com).

Tessler, M. (1986). *Mother–child talk in a museum: The socialization of memory*. Unpublished manuscript. City University of New York Graduate Center.

Tessler, M. (1991). *Making memories together: The influence of mother–child joint encoding on the development of autobiographical memory style*. Unpublished Ph.D. Dissertation, City University of New York Graduate Center.

Thompson, R., Flood, M. & Lundquist, L. (1995). "Emotional regulation: Its relations to attachment and developmental psychopathology." In *Emotion, Cognition, and Representation*. New York: University of Rochester Press.

Tomasello, M. (1993). "On the interpersonal origins of self-concept." Neisser, U. (Ed.), *The perceived self: Ecological and interpersonal sources of self-knowledge.* Cambridge University Press.

Tomasello, M. (1999). "The cultural ecology of young children's interactions with objects and artefacts." In Winograd, E., Fivush, R. & Hirst, W. (Eds.), *Ecological approaches to cognition.* Hillsdale, NJ: Lawrence Erlbaum Associates.

Tomasello, M. (2000). "Culture and cognitive development." *Current Directions in Psychological Science, 9,* 37–40.

Tomasello, M. (2002). "Things are what they do: Katherine Nelson's functional approach to language and cognition." *Journal of Cognition and Development, 3(1),* 5–19.

Tomasello, M., Kruger, A. & Ratner, H. (1993). "Cultural learning." *Behavioural and Brain Sciences, 16,* 495–552.

Trahar, S. (Ed.) (2006). *Narrative research on learning: Comparative and international perspectives.* Oxford: Symposium Books.

Trevarthen, C. (1993). "The self born in intersubjectivity: The psychology of an infant communicating." In Neisser, U. (Ed.), *The perceived self: Ecological and interpersonal sources of self-knowledge.* Cambridge: Cambridge University Press.

Trevarthen, C. (2003). "Neuroscience and intrinsic psychodynamics: Current knowledge and potential for therapy." In Corrigall, J. & Wilkinson, H. (Eds.), *Revolutionary connections: Psychotherapy and neuroscience.* London: Karnac.

Tulving, E. (1972). "Episodic and semantic memory." In Tulving, E. & Donaldson, W. (Eds.), *Organization of memory.* New York: Academic.

Tulving, E. (1983). *Elements of episodic memory.* New York: Oxford University Press.

Tulving, E. (1985). "How many memory systems are there?" American Psychologist, *40(4),* 385–398.

Tulving, E. (2002). "Episodic memory: From mind to brain." *Annual Review of Psychology, 53,* 1–25.

Tulving, E. & Lepage, M. (2001). "Where in the brain is the awareness of one's past?" In Schacter, D. & Scarry, E. (Eds.), *Memory, brain, and belief.* Cambridge, MA: Harvard University Press.

Turnbull, O. (2003). "Emotion, false beliefs, and the neurobiology of intuition." In Corrigall, J. & Wilkinson, H. (Eds.), *Revolutionary connections: Psychotherapy and neuroscience.* London: Karnac.

Turner, M. (1996). *The literary mind.* Oxford: Oxford University Press.

Turner, V. & Bruner, E. M. (1986). *The anthropology of experience.* University of Illinois Press.

Tøsse, S. (Ed.) (2000). *Reforms and policy: Adult education research in Nordic countries.* Trondheim: Tapir Academic Press.

Van Maanen, J. (1988). *Tales of the field: On writing ethnography.* Chicago: Chicago University Press.

Varela, F., Thompson, E. & Rosch, E. (1991). *The embodied mind.* Cambridge: MIT Press.

Wagenaar, W. (1994). "Is memory self-serving?" In Neisser, U. & Fivush, R. (Eds.), *The remembering self: Construction and accuracy in the self-narrative.* Cambridge: Cambridge University Press.

Walter, A., Stauber, B. et al. (Eds.) (2002). *Misleading trajectories: Integration politics for young adults in Europe.* Opladen: EGRIS.

Watt, D. (2003). "Psychotherapy in an age of neuroscience: Bridges to affective neuroscience." In Corrigall, J. & Wilkinson, H. (Eds.), *Revolutionary connections: Psychotherapy and neuroscience*. London: Karnac.

Wenger, E. (1999). *Communities of practice: Learning, meaning, and identity*. Cambridge: Cambridge University Press.

Wenger, E. (2005). *Learning for a small planet* (www.ewenger.com/research).

West, L. (1996). *Beyond fragments: Adults, motivation and higher education*. London: Taylor & Francis.

West, L. (2001). *Doctors on the edge: General practitioners, health and learning in the inner-city*. London: Free Association Books.

West, L. (2002) *Glimpses across the divide: The community arts and disaffected young people*. London: London Arts and UEL.

West, L., Alheit, P., Siig Andersen, A. & Merrill, B. (Eds.) (2007). *Using biographical and life history approaches in the study of adult and lifelong learning: European perspectives*. Frankfurt: Peter Lang.

Westbury, C. & Dennett, D. (2001). "Miming the past to construct the future: Memory and belief as forms of knowledge." In Schacter, D. & Scarry, E. (Eds.), *Memory, brain, and belief*. Cambridge, MA: Harvard University Press.

Wheeler, M., Stuss, D. & Tulving, E. (1997). "Toward a theory of episodic memory: The frontal lobes and autonoetic consciousness." *Psychological Bulletin, 121(3)*, 331–354.

White, H. (1980). "The value of narrativity in the representation of reality." In Mitchell, W. (Ed.), *On narrative*. Chicago: University of Chicago Press.

White, H. (1984). "The question of narrative in contemporary historical theory." *History and Theory, 23(1)*, 1–33.

Winnicott, D. (1958). "The capacity to be alone." In *Maturational processes and the facilitating environment*. New York: International Universities Press.

Winnicott, D. (1971). *Playing and reality*. London: Routledge.

Winograd, E., Fivush, R. & Hirst, W. (Eds.) (1999). *Ecological approaches to cognition*. Hillsdale, NJ: Lawrence Erlbaum Associates.

Winson, J. (1990). "The meaning of dreams." *Scientific American, 263(5)*, 86–96.

Wolf, D. (1990). "Being of several minds: Voices and versions of the self in early childhood." In Cicchetti, D. & Beeghly, M. (Eds.), *The self in transition: Infancy to childhood*. Chicago: The University of Chicago Press.

Zull, J. (2006). "Key aspects of how the brain learns." In Johnson, S. & Taylor, K. (Eds.), *The neuroscience of adult learning*. San Francisco, CA: Jossey-Bass.